Contemporary Issues in Education

Contemporary Issues in Education

A Perspective

Editors
Mohammad Parvez
Mohd Shakir

SHIPRA

(First Published in India in 2017)

Rs.1450; US$ 48

ISBN: 978-93-86262-29-5

2022 Impression

Contemporary Issues in Education: A Perspective

Published by:

SHIPRA PUBLICATIONS
LG 18-19, Pankaj Central Market,
I.P. Ext., Patparganj, Delhi 110092, India
Ph.: 011- 47322068, 9650028065
Email: info@shiprapublication.com
www.shiprapublication.com

Preface

It is well known fact that the quality of education plays a very important role in the development of the country. Education is under the Ministry of Human Resource Development because it is an important source to develop human as an effective source for the development. If our youths are well equipped with knowledge and skill, then they can make India a global power. A highly over regulated system of education with most ideal values of life produces an ideal citizen which can keep the corruption and malpractices away from the society.

Therefore we must establish such education system, which brings transparency and accountability. The standard of the Indian universities has to be so high that they can compete with foreign universities. This target cannot be achieved without improving the funding mechanism and managing our education system effectively and efficiently within the available resources. We can improve employability skills among youth.

In present context, value based education is also important to develop a socially responsible society. Nowadays, there is deterioration of values in our society. Our youths are deviating from the traditional values under the umbrella of modernization. The gap between old and new values of the society can only be filled up by the education and a more equitable and just society can be established.

Indian universities suffer from quality and relevance gap in comparison to developed countries. Our universities should attract more scholars in teaching and research to improve our standard. Even universities should invite foreign scholars who may inspire their Indian counterparts.

The editors have pooled together such ideas through selected articles on contemporary issues in education. The contributors have done their sincere effort to place before the readers their scholarly articles, we are thankful to all of them. We hope this volume will be useful to researchers, educationists, academicians, Policy makers and opinion shapers.

We would like to thank our publisher Shipra Publications for publishing this in the shortest possible time. We look forward to suggestions, comments for the improvement of this book.

3 April 2017
Aligarh

Prof. Mohammad Parvez
Dr. Mohd Shakir

Contents

1

Role of Teacher Education Institutions in a Knowledge Society

Sajid Jamal

The changes, demands and new realities related to the knowledge society lead the gaze inexorably towards the teachers as they are "*potentially the most important asset in the notion of a learning society*" (Day, 2001). If this holds true, there is need for giving specific attention to teachers, their initial training, the period of their professional induction, their professional development and life-long learning. A change is required in the way the profession of teaching is viewed. There are professionals who do not spend their entire life working in just one educational system or even in a single country. Like students, the teachers must also be prepared to work in a changing and unpredictable environment, wherein knowledge is constructed from different sources and viewpoints.

Among all the professional jobs, only teaching is expected to create the human skills and capacities which would enable individuals and organizations to survive and succeed in today's knowledge society. Teachers, more than anyone, are expected to build learning communities, create knowledge society, and develop the capacities for innovation, flexibility and commitment to change that are essential to economic prosperity. At the same time, teachers are also expected to mitigate and counteract many of the immense problems that knowledge societies create, such as excessive consumerism, loss of community, and widening gaps between the rich and poor. What is important is that teachers must try to achieve these seemingly contradictory goals at the same time (Hargreaves, 2003).

The teaching profession is a key mediating agency for society as it endeavours to cope with social change and upheaval. For this, the teaching profession must be adequately trained and equipped in order to cope with the changes and challenges which lie ahead.

If the teaching profession is to retain the confidence of society, it must adapt a great deal so that it can act in a constructive manner within a fast-changing society (Coolahan, 2002). For this to be possible, certain changes must be made. If schools are to educate virtually all students for "knowledge work" and to prepare them for complex roles such as citizens in a technological world, teachers will need to know how to design curriculum and adapt their teaching so that it responds to their understanding, experience, and need, and also be relevant to family and community. Teachers can not develop all these qualities among their students unless and until they themselves are trained appropriately. Since the task of training of the teachers mainly depends on the teacher education institutions, their role in this context becomes very important.

The Ground Realities

(1) Today, the education sector has become very competitive and is also deregulated; it is modeled after the 'free-market' but with more pressure to assure that the future worker is prepared for some fluid jobs in the 'free-market of the 21st century'. Hence there is a lot of pressure on the teachers to train their students to perform in different walks of life.

(2) Due to commercialization the educational sector is no more considered a service sector; it is now better known as an education industry. The free market philosophy has already entered the educational sphere in a big way. Commercialization of education is the order of the day. Commercial institutions offering specialized education have come up everywhere. Many corporate universities, both foreign and Indian, are encroaching upon our government institutions. As the government teacher education institutions are limited in number, people have no choice but to go to private teacher education institutions which exploit the students in more than one way.

(3) In the current scenario, universities from different parts of the world aspire to join hands with Indian universities and be a part of India's lucrative economic strength. Partnerships by way of academic exchanges, joint ventures, research collaborations, etc. are the ways in which foreign universities are seeking a stake in India. Several reputed schools of the world are coming to India and they are being eagerly welcomed by the parents of upper and lower middle class of the society. Since these reputed schools require teachers with the calibre of international quality, the teachers have no option but to upgrade themselves to the required standards by developing their potentials.

(4) Large Industrial Organizations like Tata, Reliance, Wipro, Essar or Associations like CII, FICCI, SIAM and ACMA have undertaken an initiative to start institutes of excellence throughout India in collaboration with renowned institutes like Harvard School of Business, MIT in USA,

and London School of Economics. This situation has created a tremendous pressure on teachers to make their students competitive in the market.

(5) Privatization of higher education, particularly teacher education, has made education very expensive, which is beyond the reach of lower income groups.

(6) Because of strong hold of the English language in Multi-National Companies (MNCs) and corporate circles, there is a divide between those people who have fluency in English language and those who do not. It has been observed that people who do not have mastery on the content but have command over the English language get jobs easily in comparison to those who have command on the content but are not well versed in English language. The field of teacher education is not an exception to it. This has put extra pressure on the teachers as they need to gain mastery or expertise on the content and be well versed in English language too.

(7) As a result of globalisation, it is expected that we have to prepare teachers for global competitiveness. Our teachers are in much demand in UK for teaching English. Teachers are also in demand to teach different subjects in different part of the world. However it seems that teacher education institutions are not ready yet to take this challenge.

(8) Teacher education is facing a serious challenge from the rising demand for qualified and competent teacher educators. It has been the observation of the author that in the last fifteen years the quality of teacher education institutions is continuously deteriorating. There has already been crisis of qualified teacher. The insistence of National Council for Teacher Education (NCTE) on two years compulsory B.Ed course has added to the woes. Moreover, the teacher education institutions have a very stereotyped syllabus which have failed to transform students into more employable or industry-ready individuals.

(9) The increasing number of teacher trainees rushing towards other sector of jobs is a serious challenge to the teacher education institutions. Earlier students from other sectors were coming to get the teacher training but now the trend has changed and it is very troubling. The author has also experienced that a lot of seats allotted to private colleges in UP, MP, Chhattisgarh, Jharkhand, Bihar and West Bengal are vacant and a number of seats are also vacant in the education departments of various central universities. When enquired, the students responded that since they got admission in MBA, MSW, Ph.D. and other job and scholarship oriented courses, there was no need for them to continue and pursue the course in the education department and waste two years in completing B.Ed. course. They were also of the view that teacher education institutions in our country have continued to lack the expected qualities as they are very slow at learning and adapting to new technology and methodology in the

teaching and learning processes. Also the infrastructure facilities are inadequate. The failure in retaining talented students in the teacher education institutions may pose serious problems in the growth of the country.

(10) The good teacher education institutions are generally located in big cities. It has been observed that a few big cities like Hyderabad, Chennai, Pune, Noida, Gurgaon, Bhopal, Indore, Jaipur, Raipur, Amritsar, Jammu, Lucknow, Ranchi, Patna and Bangalore etc have good teacher education institutions, while small cities and rural areas have inferior institutions. Sadly, this concentrated growth of quality teacher education institutions in cities was primarily due to the profit motive of private actors who targeted only the upper-income groups of the society living in big cities. This trend has been detrimental to the interests of a vast majority of the Indian population who live in either very small cities or villages. It is also a fact that demand for good education institutions has remained very low in rural areas. As a result, the educational imbalance between the cities and villages has become alarmingly dangerous.

(11) Today, quality is a very important issue. It is a bitter truth that the quality of teacher education in our country is very poor. Most of the pass outs from teacher education institutions lack the required calibre to deliver in a competitive environment and corporate culture of the schools. This is very much evident from the poor passing rate of Central Teacher Eligibility Test (CTET).

The author of this paper has also a very bad experience of being a subject expert in various selection committees where the students perform very poorly and give the excuse that it is not their area. Moreover various types of imperfections exist in the teacher education system, including lack of uniformity in products, i.e., various courses/degrees being offered by educational institutions; conflicting objectives of providers (profit maximisation, maximisation of social benefits, prestige maximisation of the institution); wide heterogeneities among consumers (students) with regard to purchasing power; lack of knowledge about the providers; and price and quality of the product.

(12) Teacher education institutions are facing a severe manpower crisis. The government of India has been forced to adopt such a policy leading to the phasing out of grants, ban on recruitments and non-review of manpower requirements in the field of higher education. As various states declared higher education a "non-merit" area, private players and commercial entities started self-financing courses (even in public/aided institutions) and established self-financing institutions. They have been acquiring "deemed-to-be" university status and creating private universities through state legislation.

(13) There is a mismatch between supply and demand, and most of the teacher education institutions functioning today lack basic facilities and teachers have no access to the latest developments in their disciplines. These institutions churn out students as outcastes even in their own chosen area of knowledge. Thus the education offered by these institutions is unacceptable to the children of the fast growing affluent Middle Class Indians.

(14) The teacher education institutions are alienated from their various social responsibilities and are busy in producing only such youths who are suitable to the market. These institutions do not bother to inculcate values in their students, which has resulted in value crisis in the society. Besides, it is focusing only on the cognitive development of students and neglecting the affective and psychomotor domains of human behaviour.

(15) Experts say that teacher education should follow its best tradition, and it should remain practical, flexible and child-centered. It is expected that the next generation of learners will get the support and skills they need in life during their schooling years from their teachers. Hence there is an urgent need of a generation of teachers who will aim to develop their students as learners; help them to become independent learners (learning to learn); motivate them and awaken their interest in life-long learning.

The Changing Role of the Teacher Education Institutions in the Knowledge Society

Teacher education is a continuous process of imparting knowledge, developing skills, inculcating values and promoting the overall personality development of the prospective teachers. Imparting quality teacher education is greatly influenced by different factors viz. curriculum, teachers, information sources, teaching methods, examination systems, evaluation mechanism and infrastructure. Among all the components, teachers assume greatest significance in ensuring a quality teacher education.

Due to long and continuous domination of religious and spiritual features of Indian life, the teacher has been playing the key role in Indian education, and even in the modern educational system the teacher is considered as the most important component of the education system. 'Guru' (teacher) was revered as a guide and an imparter of knowledge. In the present context also, his/her role remains as critical as ever and plays a major role in implementing the policies and schemes formulated to achieve a breakthrough in the quantitative expansion and qualitative improvement of teacher education.

Continuous enhancement and upgradation of conceptual knowledge, practical skills and competencies of teachers in their respective specialised subjects to ensure quality teacher education to younger generation has become a great concern for teacher education institutions across the globe today. Against this background, it has become mandatory for all the teacher education institutions to recruit highly qualified teachers; providing them adequate facilities and infrastructure; and ensuring such conditions and climate in which they are highly satisfied and committed to the quality of teacher education. Besides, the teacher educational institutions have to play the following roles to satisfy the increasing expectations of a knowledge society:

1. Preparing the Prospective Teachers to be Reflective Practitioners

Traditional responsibility of a teacher is to pass on to the students the correct information, knowledge and understanding on essential subjects during their studies. This leads to the traditional role of the teacher as one of provider of information in the lecture context. Lecture remains as one of the most widely used instructional methods. It can be a cost-effective method of providing new information not found in standard texts, of relating information to the local curriculum and of providing the lecturer's personal overview or structure of the field of knowledge for the student. Good teachers can share with the students their thoughts as a reflective practitioner, helping them to develop the power of decision making. Hence, it is imperative for the teacher education institutions to prepare the teachers to be reflective practitioners in the society.

2. Enabling the Prospective Teachers to Behave as Role Models

The importance of the teacher as a role model is well documented. The teacher as a model exemplifies what should be learned. Students learn not just from what their teachers say but also from what they do in their practice and the knowledge, skills, behaviour and attitudes they exhibit. Teachers serve as role models when they teach students as teachers in the classroom, whether it is in the lecture theatre or the small discussion or tutorial group. The good teacher can describe in a lecture to a class of students, in a way that captures the importance of the subject and the choices available. The teacher has a unique opportunity to share some of the magic of the subject with the students. In this context it is very important for the teacher education institutions to enable the prospective teachers to behave as role models in the society.

3. Equipping Prospective Teachers with Required Abilities to Facilitate Learning

The teacher education institutions should focus on equipping their students with required abilities to facilitate learning. The move to a more student-centered view of learning requires a fundamental shift in the role of the teacher. No longer is the teacher seen predominantly as a dispenser of information or walking tape recorder, but rather as a facilitator or manager of students' learning. The introduction of problem-based learning with a consequent fundamental change in the student-teacher relationship has highlighted this change in the role of the teacher from one of information provider to one of facilitator. Besides, the role of mentor is an additional role of the teacher. The mentor is usually not the member of the staff who is responsible for teaching or assessment of the students and is therefore off-line in terms of relationship with the student. Mentorship is less about reviewing the students' performance in a subject or an examination and more about a wider view of issues relating to the student.

4. Training the Prospective Teachers to Assess the Students' Performance in an Objective Manner

The assessment of the student's competence is one of the most important tasks facing the teacher education institutions. Though the NCTE has issued certain directions in this context, things have not improved. Examining does represent a distinct and potentially separate role for the teacher. Assessment of learning and assessment for learning are different. To keep the trainees out of stress, to arouse interest in learning, to provide them quick and prompt feedback, to tell them about the areas where they have to excel and where they have to improve, besides encouraging the self esteem of the students, is a challenge. A lot of change has taken place throughout the globe in this context. Semesterisation, grading system, choice based credit system (CBCS), online exams, etc are important among them. Thus it is imperative for the teacher education institutions to experiment on them and if found suitable, make them an important feature of their evaluation system.

5. Planning the Curriculum of Teacher Education in a Proper Way

Curriculum planning is an important aspect of the teacher education institutions. NCTE has issued certain guidelines in this context. It has made few portions compulsory whereas in some portions it has given liberty to the teacher education institutions to adopt according to their environment, local needs and interests of the students. Most of the teacher education institutions are affiliated to some universities which have Board of Studies/Academic Councils and are responsible for planning and implementation of the curriculum. Teacher education institutions are expected to make a contribution to curriculum planning by involving their teachers. Thus curriculum planning presents a significant challenge and requires both time and expertise for doing the job diligently.

6. Developing the Resource Material for the Students

An increased need for learning resource materials is implicit in many of the developments in the field of teacher education. The new technologies have greatly expanded the formats of learning materials to which the students may have access, and make it much easier for them to take more responsibility for their own education. The role of the teacher as resource creator offers exciting possibilities. At least some teachers possess the array of skills necessary to select, adapt or produce materials for use within the institution. The production of Study guides is the further role of the teacher. Study guides suitably prepared in electronic or print form can be seen as the students' personal tutor available 24 hours a day and designed to assist them with their learning. Study guides tell the students what they should learn: the expected learning outcomes of the course, how they might acquire the competencies necessary, the learning opportunities available, and whether they have learned it. The students assess their own competence. The author himself has been a member of various committees in Bhopal to develop such study materials. The result of it is very satisfying and successful.

7. Focussing on Developing Mastery among the Prospective Teachers in the Concerned field/area of Specialisation

The teacher education institutions need to be aware that a teacher in the modern times will be respected only if he/she has honed the appropriate skills and knowledge of the concerned discipline according to the changing trends in scholarship. The teachers need to avoid mechanical repetition of the same lesson every year, lacking new insights or freshness of approach. They need to read/refer to latest books and research journals, for imparting additional knowledge and latest information to their students. The teacher ought to motivate to keep the students engaged in whatervever they are learning. Teaching, research and scholarship should be conducted in full accordance with the ethical and professional standards and should, where appropriate, respond to contemporary problems facing the society, as well as preserve the historical and cultural heritage of the world.

8. Enabling the Prospective Teachers to make Teaching a two-way Process

Teaching should be a two-way process – a constant interaction between the teacher and the students. Learning has shifted from monologue to dialogue. Participative learning has taken a lead, and education is seen as a right and a mechanism for self actualization. The goals of learning have transformed from acquisition of facts and information to higher levels of cognition, acquisition of the psychomotor skills and effective qualities of values, attitudes, emotions, etc. Hence, the prospective-teachers should behave like a facilitator, a communicator of ideas to be developed by the students. In the process, the perspective teachers should be guided by the highest professional ethics and personal values. This is essential particularly in the present times of dehumanization and fragmentation resulting in absence of values at both the professional and personal levels.

Besides, to stimulate logical, coherent and systematic thinking, the perspective teachers should be encouraged to interact with their students. Further, seminars and discussions should be organized by the teacher education institutions to build self confidence among prospective teachers, and also to encourage them to analyze the concepts and issues in a much broader perspective. Further the prospective teachers should also be encouraged to solve critical and new problems and undertake projects in the fields of their interest. Assignments, quizzes and seminars must be organized to provide a first hand and latest information to the prospective teachers related to their courses.

9. Giving Sufficient Knowledge of Educational Technology to Prospective Teachers

Educational technology prescribes a multi-channel learning to suit learning needs of different people at different times to optimize human learning. It includes technologies like TV, radio, film projector, pictures and tables, internet, etc. As time progressed, quite a few educational networks/software/satellites emerged, such as:

(a) *EDUNET* or Education Network enables a teacher to interact with one and all of his students through network and allows the transmission of his screen to each and every student's machine connected with the network. The teacher can also take control of the keyboard and mouse of student's computer while demonstrating the practicals.

(b) *E-campus* is complete campus management software for educational institutes. It helps the staff to handle students in a better way. Besides, the profile and performance of students in exams can be had instantly. It is used for online attendance, campus security, access control, etc. It also supports absenteeism notification, fee payment reminder, book return request, voice mail, college schedules and other routine chores.

(c) *EDUSAT* or Education Satellite was launched by Indian Space Research Organization (ISRO) on 20th Sept, 2005. With the help of it, the classes are beamed to predestined areas on TV; students can ask questions to the teachers who conduct classes through SMS, email or other modes of communication. In addition, these classes are also recorded on a CD and converted into a computer file and made available on the net. For future need, they are available in the archives.

If the teachers are not well versed with the latest technology, they will not be able to impart knowledge with the modern methods of teaching. This fact should be completely emphasised upon by the teacher education institutions.

10. Preparing the Prospective Teachers for Open Learning

The Open University System for open learning was initiated in the country to augment opportunities for higher education as an instrument of democratizing education and also for making it a lifelong process. The open universities provide education to students who are either economically weak or have no traditional qualifications for entering into higher education. Such students have no other opportunity to make up for the lost time. It also provides opportunities to students who are in the lower ranks of their careers and looking for opportunities to improve their qualifications, professional competence and new skills.

Since India is a very big country and its higher education institutions cannot cater to the needs of all the aspirants of higher education, Open and Distance Learning (ODL) can be a better alternative to the formal higher education system. The teachers may convince about this in a better and effective way to their students and may avoid some of the problems faced by their institutions concerned with the admissions. Besides, open learning may be a good source of professional growth for the teachers, and the teacher education institutions should motivate the prospective teachers to use open learning as an opportunity for professional growth.

11. Focusing on Conducting Research

Prompt initiatives should be taken by the teacher education institutions to concentrate on research activities and research-oriented programmes in accordance with the professional responsibility and subject to nationally and internationally recognized professional principles of intellectual rigour, scientific inquiry and research ethics. They have to base their research on an honest search for knowledge with due respect to evidence, impartial reasoning and honesty in reporting and observing the ethics of research involving humans, animals, the heritage or the environment. Higher-education teachers should undertake professional activities outside their employment, particularly those that enhance their professional skills or allow for the application of knowledge to the problems of the community. Besides, they should also be trained to conduct action research to solve day-to-day problems related with learners and learning process.

12. Enabling the Prospective Teachers to Evaluate their own Strengths and Weaknesses

Continuous self evaluation will undoubtedly help the teachers build up their strengths and overcome weaknesses in the teaching and research areas. Besides, it will serve three more purposes: first, it will enhance student and demand-oriented education so that the quality of teaching and learning process is no longer taken for granted by the teachers. Second, the association between faculty members and administration will be strengthened since parameters such as positive attitude, research aptitude, sense of cooperation, extension activities, regularity in attending meetings; use and maintenance of properties, work culture and discipline are major components to be used by heads/deans while assessing faculty members. Finally, the relationship among faculty members would be made more productive. The congenial relationship among peers and friendly atmosphere in departments will directly or indirectly affect the performance of faculty members. In this context, the teacher education institutions are required to train the prospective teachers to use SWOTA to analyse their own strengths and weeknesses.

13. Collaborating with the Excellent Institutions and Industries

Strong network, preferably between the mediocre teacher education institutions and institutions of excellence should be developed and strengthened. The growing presence of multinational corporations in India coupled with the boom in IT field holds considerable promise for partnerships in areas such as curriculum development, equipment donations, industrial visits and faculty training and student scholarships. Such interface between the teacher education institutions and industries may enhance application-oriented education and employability of the students. Finally, more focus should be laid on entrepreneurship development, innovation and leadership. These three qualities are needed most in the field of teacher education. The use of Internet technology to a greater extent would provide a platform for the perspective teachers to interact with successful entrepreneurs, leaders, innovators, teachers and other students within the country and abroad.

14. Familiarizing the Prospective Teachers with Ground Realities

The first and foremost thing is that the teachers should accept the existing realities of the world. Privatization has entered educational system and they cannot deny it at any cost. The nation at such a juncture will have to depend on private participation in education system of the country. In such a situation there is a need to draft such teacher education courses that have totally specialized knowledge, specialized skills and inherent code of ethics. It can be done by having good theoretical base. Moreover, from an ancient civilization, India has emerged as a modern hub of outsourcing. In this context the teacher education institutions should convince the prospective teachers that expectation from them is more than ever to produce quality students and if they will fail in the cause and will not give the required performance, then definitely, they will be worthless.

15. Developing some Specialized Skills among the Prospective Teachers.

The teacher education institutions should focus on developing some specialized skills among the prospective teachers that add quality to their professional functioning. Such skills mean having hard, technical expertise along with softer interpersonal capabilities. Skills of quality teaching and quality assessment are most desired. Quality teaching skills involve the process of making students work hard and become independent learner. Similarly, the assessment requires teachers to assess the students with respect to their thinking process and learning styles. In the same manner, the skills related to feedback have to be developed amongst the prospective teachers so that the feedback is accepted open mindedly by the students.

16. Convincing the Prospective Teachers to make Continuous Efforts for their Professional Development

Professional development of teachers refers to the generation of all those updated skills required to execute a task of teachers in academic teaching-learning situations. It means by which members of academic community maintain, improve and broaden their knowledge and skills and, develop the personal qualities required in their professional lives. Professional development may also come in the form of pre-service or in-service professional development programs. These programs may be formal, or informal, group or individualized. Individuals may pursue professional development independently, or programs may be offered by the teacher education institutions. Professional development opportunities can range from a single workshop to a semester-long academic course, and varies widely with respect to the philosophy, content, and format of the learning experiences. But, at the heart of professional development is the individual's interest in lifelong learning and increasing their own skills and knowledge.

Professional development has always been important for the teachers and has been associated with their professional efficiency. In today's context, it has come to occupy special significance because more and more foreign students are coming to India. Knowledge is increasing at a very fast pace as information and communication technology have given easy access to knowledge. Hence the teacher education institutions should enthuse the prospective teachers to become professionally competent.

17. Training the Prospective Teachers to Provide Guidance and Counseling to their Students

With the continued expansion of technical and professional education at secondary and senior secondary level of education, the range of choices available to the learners is becoming more comprehensive. Hence, the possibility of selecting their own missions is becoming difficult day by day. Moreover the students are required to be more flexible, innovative and creative and they must be trained to work in team. The teachers in the schools are supposed to provide proper guidance and counseling to the students so that they may be free from conflicts and cope with stress and anxiety. For that they have to teach their students effectively within the means provided by the institution and the state, and have to be fair and equitable to male and female students, belonging to different races and religions, as well as those with disabilities. They also need to encourage free exchange of ideas between themselves and their students, and be available to them for guidance in their studies. But this is a very challenging job and it will not be effectively discharged in the absence of proper training. The teacher education institutions can play an important role in this regard.

18. Enabling the Prospective Teachers in Creating Awareness among their Students about their Civic and Social Responsibilities

The role of teachers in providing an enabling environment for inculcating civic and social responsibility amongst their students has become more important than ever before. In today's world which is more divided and polarized, human security has come under siege. We find constant threats to human security in the form of narcotics trafficking, illegal migration, environmental degradation and abuse of human rights. An important development which has taken place in the recent decades is an increase in the problems which are faced by society as a whole: energy crisis, feeding and educating an ever growing population, controlling pollution, global warming, ozone layer depletion, climate change, restless youth, growing intolerance in the society, new life styles, extra modernization, rising consumerism, deforestation for the sake of establishing industries and housing projects, illegal mining, unsustainable development, corruption by public officials, impatient youth taking shortcuts for success and rising expectations of the people. All these must be discussed by the teachers in the class rooms, formally or informally, and awareness must be developed in them about their future roles and responsibilities. In this context also the teacher education institutions can provide a platform for discussions among the prospective teachers for enabling them to chalk out suitable strategies in their classrooms.

19. Fulfilling the Expectations of Global Society

The teachers must rise to the occasion and be ready to fulfill the needs, aspirations and expectations of the evolving concept of global society. They can play a catalytic role in promoting a global perspective, based upon universal brotherhood and sisterhood, cutting across the cultural and national boundaries. Mere economic growth and development is no guarantee of the well being of an individual or society. Much depends upon fostering a global perspective based upon the holistic development of one and all. Therefore, the teachers have an important role and social responsibility in providing harmonious and peace oriented high quality education leading to humane and sustainable development. They can also resolve some of the dilemmas like 'digital divide', 'wide economic and regional disparities', 'dehumanisation of individuals', 'social fragmentation', ' marginalization', and 'degradation of certain groups', etc. In this context, the teacher education institutions can enthuse and send the right message to the prospective teachers for fufilling the expectations of the global society.

20. Organising Training Programmes, Seminars, Symposia, Workshops for in-Service Teachers

The teacher education institutions can prove their worth to the society in more practical terms by organizing various teacher training programmes, seminars, symposia, workshops etc for the in-service teachers. They may also bring the school and community closer by organizing such type of programmes and thereby bring to an end the isolation of the teacher education institutions.

2

Rich Site Summary (RSS)

The Technology to Revolutionize Higher Education

Noushad Husain

RSS has become a valuable technology for everything from casual web users to webmasters. According to a recent Yahoo survey only 12 per cent of internet users are aware of RSS and a mere 4 per cent have knowingly used RSS. RSS exists as a means to gather and display information quickly and easily. RSS is a web technology that allows us to see at a glance what areas of our site have been updated, without having to visit our site. An RSS feed is basically a webpage that is designed to be read by a computer program instead. RSS feeds are used in conjunction with a news reader. News readers are software applications that can take an RSS feed and turn it into content that we can read. There are many different versions of news readers; some are available through a web browser interface, allowing we to check our feeds from anywhere in the world, whilst others are software applications that need to be downloaded and installed to our computer.

What is RSS?

RSS stands for 'Rich Site Summary', 'Real Simple Syndication' or 'RDF Site Summary' and is a standardized format that allows users to subscribe to a website's content using tools such as newsreaders or aggregators. According to Wikipedia, "RSS is a family of XML (http://en.wikipedia.org/wiki/XML) file formats for Web syndication (http://en.wikipedia.org/wiki/Web_syndication) used by (amongst other things) news websites (http://en.wikipedia.org/wiki/Website) and web logs (http://en.wikipedia.org/wiki/Weblog)...The technology behind RSS allows internet users to subscribe to websites that have provided RSS feeds; these are typically sites that change or add content regularly"(Wikipedia, 2005). RSS is firstly originated in weblog software and then now used in many other web sites such as news and journal sites. Weblogs (and other RSS-enabled web sites) have a code in a programming language called

XML. This code is generally referred to as a feed, and these feeds can be received by right-clicking the symbols – such as XML, + newsgator, , RSS – in the web sites. In order to use a feed, one has to install a software tool known as an aggregator or feed reader – such as Bloglines, Google Reader or Pageflakes – on his or her computer. By just copying the feeds to the aggregator, readers can subscribe to the content of either a weblog or a web site they are interested in.

The RSS information available from blogs and other frequently updated websites is usually referred to as a feed. A feed lists site content that has changed or is new. Feeds are collated for the user by an aggregator. When subscribed to a feed, users no longer have to visit many individual sites in order to obtain up-to-date information about their content; instead, the updated information from the subscribed sites is collected and organized by the aggregator. The benefit of RSS is that you can get the latest updates for a webpage without ever having to visit the site to see if the content has changed or is updated. You can view and read the feed by using an RSS feed reader. Figure 2.1 clearly shows the simplicity of RSS for information and knowledge searching.

Figure 2.1: Before and After the Arrival of RSS

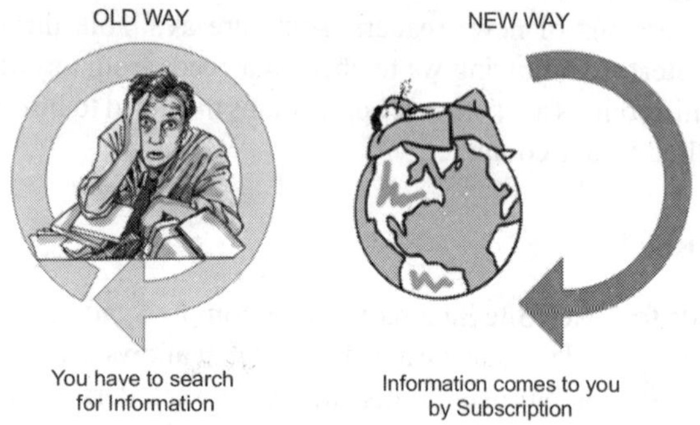

What is an RSS Feed?

RSS is an XML-based data stream that allows information from one website to be used across an unlimited number of websites. RSS Feeds are used to transmit a sort of "lite" version of a website's most freshly updated content. This "lite" version – called a "feed" – can be applied to any webpage by a website developer that knows about XML and XSL Transformation, or can be added to an RSS Aggregator's RSS Feed list for distribution. A single RSS feed can contain three things:

- Title (The headline)
- Description (very brief summary)
- link (link to the complete story or article)

Characteristics of RSS

The main characteristics of RSS are given below:

- As opposed to constantly checking for updates on your favourite websites, news sources and blogs, RSS allows for that material to come to you. This will save your time and help you to organize the wide range of resources on the web.
- Most websites have a RSS feed, which you can then subscribe to using a reader/ aggregator. This reader/aggregator will constantly check for new updates on all the websites you have subscribed to. It will then display these updates for you to see in one convenient location.
- A few effective and popular aggregators are Bloglines (http://www.bloglines.com), Netvibes (http://www.netvibes.com/) and Google Reader (http://www.google.com/reader).
- Since readers/aggregators are housed online, you can access your feeds from anywhere with an internet connection.

How RSS Works?

You create RSS Feeds of your web content (a feed is a list of headlines, short descriptions of the articles and the links to the full text in XML format) and provide a link to the file from your website. Feed aggregators collect these feeds and create topical index of all such feeds available. Feed readers then read and display these feeds to web users in a similar format of headline, description and link. The user can then view all the updates on their PCs with help of these feed readers and select links which thy would like to read in detail and are then transferred to the selected website.

RSS Feed Publishers

RSS Feeds are generally news agencies, periodicals, blogs, or product catalogs. The people (or companies) that provide these RSS Feeds are called "Publishers". Generally RSS Feeds are updated regularly,

Figure 2.2: Working of RSS

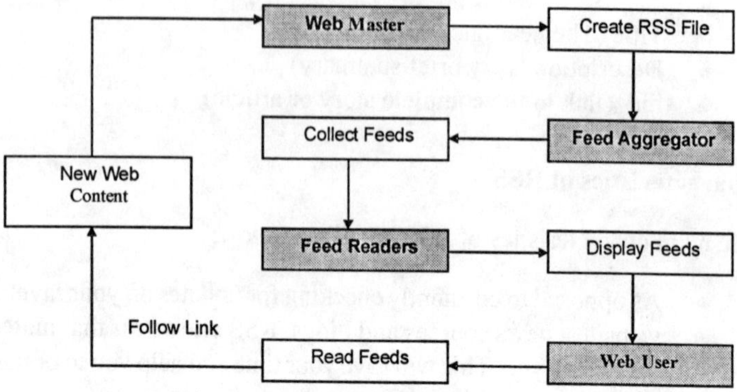

guarantee-ing the most fresh and current content for visitors. RSS Feeds broaden a publisher's reader base and help readers by focusing on the most relevant and current information – eliminating the need to look thru several sites and clutters to find they really want to read.

RSS Feed Aggregators

RSS Aggregators are places that collect many RSS Feeds for sharing and distribution. RSS Aggregators help web surfers organize their RSS Feeds for viewing – letting them scan the latest information from all the websites they regularly surf in a single page.

RSS Feed Readers

RSS feeds are used in conjunction with a news reader. News readers are software applications that can take an RSS feed and turn it into content that user can read. There are many different versions of news readers; some are available through a web browser interface, allowing user to check their feeds from anywhere in the world, whilst others are software applications that need to be downloaded and installed to the computer. Some important RSS feed readers are given below:

Google Reader

Google Reader is a free web based RSS feed reader. If we already have a Google or Gmail account, we automatically have a Google Reader account. We can access Google Reader at http://reader.google/com. Most websites also have a button to click on for Google Reader to subscribe to the site's feed. We can organize a feed from a site into folders. We can share our RSS feeds with others as an html page. We also can search through the feeds by using the search bar at the top. Google Reader also gives us the option to export all our feeds as an OPML list so if we decide to use another RSS Feed Reader, we don't have to start from scratch to add the feeds.

Bloglines

Bloglines is a free web based RSS feed reader. We can sign up for an account at http://www.bloglines.com. Most websites also have a button to click on for Bloglines to subscribe to the site's feed. We can organize our feeds into folders. We can search through the feeds by using the search bar at the top. Bloglines also gives us the option to post to our own Bloglines blog. We can save our blog post as clippings. We can make these clippings public, in case we would like to share it with our colleagues or public. We can export your RSS feeds from Bloglines into an OPML format. If we choose, we can import this OPML list into another RSS Feed Reader, so we don't have to start from scratch building out your RSS feed subscriptions.

Thunderbird

We can use the email client Thunderbird to read our latest feeds. Thunderbird allows us to set up RSS folders. All we need to do is go to File, New Account. In the dialogue box, select RSS News and Blogs. Press Next. Enter an account name and press Next. Then press finish. we can right click on the account name and select manage subscriptions. Then we can type in the RSS feed and subscribe to it.

Functions of RSS

The next step in RSS integration into education and e-learning practice is to present the benefits of using RSS as an information tool, while using this opportunity to expose faculty and students to relevant information resources in their course websites. Feeds provide critical benefits to any digital media and some of them are:

RSS provides the right platform to try out content distribution in many ways

- Content delivery can be categorized because RSS helps widen present distribution: it's nothing to worry about publishing a monthly or weekly publication;
- RSS enables to efficiently provide daily content updates to subscribers or as often as wanted;

- Providing useful content to subscribers from time to time, that helps building a deeper relationship and a better understanding, and creates a persistent link between publisher and subscribers;
- Easily providing better updates according to various interests or supply hard to find information to different target audience.

RSS drives quality traffic from other websites

Syndication is the process sharing content; therefore RSS allows to easily publishing content on other websites. Doing that, real profits will arrive for a long time because:

- giving the website the ability to gain new visitors from the different corners of the web it can very well reach new audiences of different interests;
- sharing the content with other similar websites it gains recognition as an expert in the field.

RSS can bring new targeted subscribers to the website because

- since most of the people today are reluctant to give out their email address (thanks to heavy spamming),
- RSS can act as a real savior;
- unlike email an RSS feed is zero maintenance, the messages will never get blacklisted or filtered and will always be delivered promptly, unless and until the subscribers choose to end the relationship;
- the messages, which are send out, will appear directly on the user's desktop in their favorite RSS reader because they want to receive new updates, being serious subscribers.

RSS improved search engine ranking

Since search engines seek to provide the best and the newest available information to their users, it's obvious they give a lot more priority to websites which update their content from time to time. It has already been proven that search engines frequently index websites, which have RSS feeds. RSS not only helps business gain more exposure through all the major search engines but also through RSS specific search engines and directories like Feedster.

The Power of RSS Feeds in Education

While RSS feeds started as a way to aggregate news into one application, the possible uses for educators go far beyond the basics. Web content became a powerful communication tool by the help of feeds. RSS feeds were most commonly found in news web sites or blogs but now it is natural to see them on any web sites that are updated frequently. There are also many directories dedicated to help finding RSS feeds on topics of specific and personal interests, like http://www.bloglines.com, http://www.technorati.com, http://www.ousub.com,http://www.syndic8.com. Teachers and students might think to embrace RSS as a means to educate (*Resources for Educators*). Academia, educational institutions are using RSS feeds in their daily routines and this fact demonstrates that RSS can be utilized in very different ways. Taking all these in consideration, the power of the RSS can be successfully used in the educational domain. The power of RSS feeds in education can be best understood with the help of the Figure 2.3.

Figure 2.3: The Power of RSS Feeds in Education

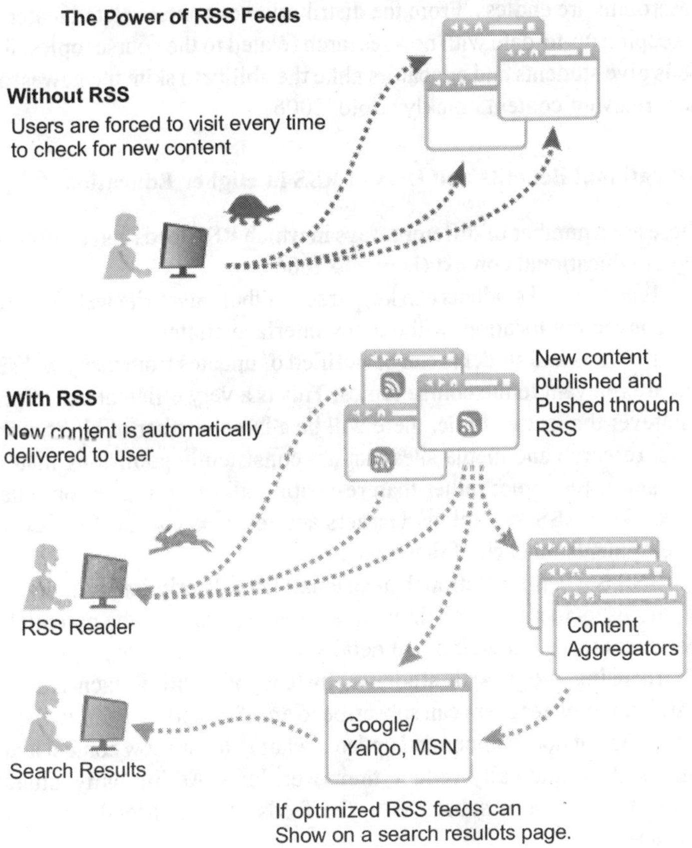

The Potential of RSS in Higher Education

Although RSS feeds were initially utilized by readers to create individualized, syndicated news pages (Asmus et al., 2005), their increasing popularity has brought the potential opportunities to the attention of educators. According to Joly (2006), a number of colleges and universities have already integrated RSS feeds into universities and colleges websites. RSS allows universities and colleges to effectively disseminate important information to all students, regardless of individual schedules or how students prefer to receive it. RSS feeds can serve several uses in a variety of educational settings and provide technology driven students with a plethora of opportunities to individualize their plans of study. With the content published in RSS feeds being immediately available to those with Internet connections with a few clicks (West, Wright, Gabbitas, & Graham, 2006), the possibilities for RSS in classrooms are endless. From the distribution of course related materials to keeping up-to-date with new research related to the course topics, RSS feeds give students and educators alike the ability to skim the newest and most relevant content quickly (Cold, 2006).

Educational Benefits and Uses of RSS in Higher Education

There are a number of different ways in which RSS feeds can be useful in higher educational context (Harrsch, 2006).

Teachers and students can keep track of their favourite websites from one convenient location, without any interface clutter.

Teachers and students can be notified of updates from many websites that are relevant to the course topics. This is a very efficient use of time. Whatever the lecture topic, there will be a large number of blogs, wikis, news, research and media sites that are consistently publishing material relevant to the topic; rather than re-visiting all of these sites on a daily basis, using RSS technology learners and teachers can easily track new developments on each of these sites.

RSS is a better solution than an email list subscription, as it does not require users to give out their email addresses, avoiding the potential for spammers to obtain their email details.

In using blogs with students, instead of visiting each student's individual blog teachers can subscribe to an RSS feed that allows them to obtain instant notifications and updates relating to any new content added. This will dramatically reduce their workload. Additionally, students themselves can also subscribe to the feeds of their friends, peers and teachers.

Teachers and students can establish RSS feeds relating to assignment topics and areas of research interest. This allows access to up-to-date content on a wide variety of subjects automatically.

From an administration perspective, higher education portals often offer targeted collections of links for students, staff, parents, visitors, and alumni. Most users start their portal experience with a time sensitive task to accomplish. Users typically 'pull' down information from a site. Within the RSS model users can have information 'pushed' to them that is customised to their personal interests.

RSS Promotes Research, Reflections and Collaboration in Higher Education

One of the most popular uses of RSS feeds in educational settings is to enable and improve student research. With the ability to gather multiple sources on one page and perform targeted searches, RSS can be a powerful research tool aiding educators and students in performing in-depth research with a few simple clicks (Asmus et al., 2005). It allows students to conduct their research as both individuals and collaboratively by sharing and combining feeds across various sources and encourages the sharing of information (Cold, 2006). A properly set up RSS feed aids the research process by notifying subscribers and saving the most recent posting of information and current events. They have been compared to conducting research 24 hours a day for seven days a week, only the RSS feed is doing all of the work for the researcher (Richardson, 2005). The use of RSS feeds in a classroom also allows for a more collaborative learning environment and enhances communication between educators and students, as well as between the students themselves, creating new networks of knowledge. Having a variety of resources available in one, easy to use location, RSS encourages sharing among peers and creates large repositories of knowledge that can benefit all users and subscribers (D'Souza, 2006). RSS feeds can keep track of discussions and conversation topics, wikis, newsgroups, interests, and web site updates, as well as build connections with others who have similar interests (Richardson, 2006). The combination of all of these items helps students to build a deeper understanding of the presented concepts and enhance their comprehension of the materials above and beyond what is offered in the classroom, creating more dynamic learning (West et al., 2006).

Classroom Applications of RSS in Higher Education

RSS can bring a revolutionize change in higher education. The classroom use of RSS in higher education is given below:

Simplifying Instructor's Research

For busy teachers who want to easily keep up in their field of study, RSS allows for access to all new research via news articles, blogs and websites through one simple interface.

Staying up to date with Student activities

If students have class blogs (such as one for group projects, discussion groups or lab groups) then RSS can keep teacher up to date with any new activities on their blogs. Teacher can check to see if the content is appropriate, comment on their posts or see the participation levels in discussions.

Allowing students to easily keep up with Course

If teachers have a course blog or website then they can allow students to use RSS to keep track of changes. This can allow teachers to give them information almost instantly about what is happening in their course and in their field. If other classes use RSS then students can compile all their class RSS feeds in one easy to access location.

Class/Social Bookmarking

RSS can be used to create a list of useful websites that the professor or the students have visited that relate to the class or a particular project. This can be done in class through a community class blog publishing web links or made easy and streamlined through the use of online applications built for social bookmarking which allow for rating and annotating.

Targeted Searching

RSS feeds can be used as a way to bring news on a certain topic for a paper or project to directly to reader/aggregator. All the information on a certain topic can be found by a search engine such as Google and then converted to a RSS feed and put into your reader/aggregator. Searching feeds can also allow for a wealth of useful research finds.

Strategies for Using RSS in Higher Education

There are a number of different ways that RSS feeds can add the knowledge base of teachers and help the teachers to communicate and make the teaching interesting and better. Figure 2.4 shows some uses of RSS in education.

Figure 2.4: Innovative Uses of RSS in Higher Education.

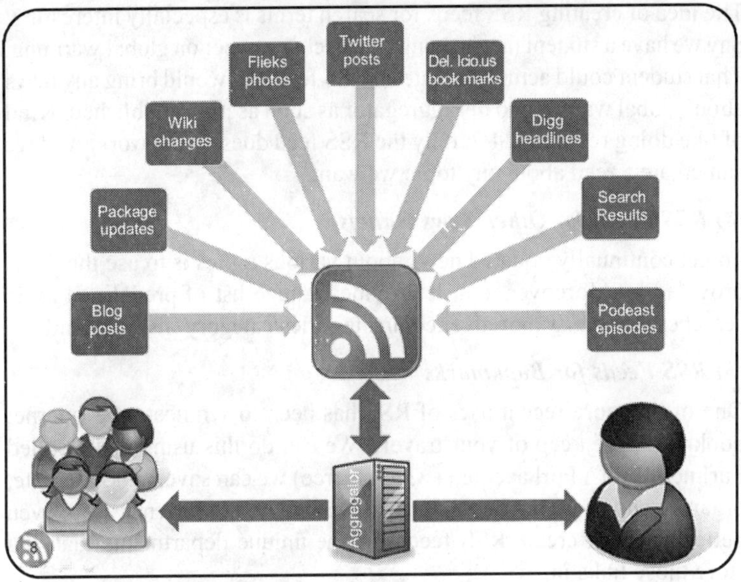

(1) RSS Feeds with Student Weblogs

If we already use Weblogs with your students, the uses of RSS should be pretty apparent. Instead of checking out all 25 (or 30, or more) student Weblogs every day, we could just collect their work in our aggregator using their RSS feeds. That way, we can scan through all of the class content in one place, make sure it's all appropriate and click through to a particular post if you want to comment on it. The use of student feeds in this way will drastically reduce the reading time and allow the teachers to make all of their classes paperless. In addition, we can provide individual student Weblog feeds to parents or counselors or whoever else might be interested in that student's work and be savvy enough to know about RSS. We can track just about everything going on in our student blogs using RSS.

(2) RSS Feeds without Student Weblogs

If our students don't have Weblogs, we may want to have them set up their own Bloglines account. With more and more news sources producing feeds for aggregation, the breadth of current events and even topic-specific research that students could collect could go a long way to assisting them with research or further study. And, if we use a Weblog, they can include your feed in their aggregator to stay abreast of what is going on in class.

(3) RSS Search Feeds

The idea of creating RSS feeds for search terms is especially interesting. Say we have a student that is doing a project or a paper on global warming. That student could actually create an RSS feed that would bring any news about global warming to his aggregator as soon as it was published. Kind of like doing research 24/7, only the RSS feed does all the work. And we can create a feed about any topic we want.

(4) RSS Feeds for Other News Outlets

To get continually updated news about various topics is to use the feeds provided by Moreover.com. It provides a huge list of predefined topic searches at http://w.moreover.com/categories/category_list_rss.html.

(5) RSS Feeds for Bookmarks

One of the more recent uses of RSS has been to syndicate the Internet bookmarks we keep of your travels. We can do this using a site called Furl.net. With a Furl account (which is free) we can save, annotate, rate, organize and share the best links that we find on the Internet. And, even better, you can create RSS feeds for the unique departments that you store those links in.

Every time you come to a site that has information on global warming, we can "Furl it" and save it into our global warming folder. (Instructions on how to do this are on the Furl site…it's easy!) Now, anyone who may be subscribed to the feed that Furl.net creates for that global warming folder (like, maybe, your students?) will get automatically updated when we add a new link to it. We set up a classroom Furl.net account and we and all of our students added links to a variety of topic specific folders as we found them. We could all keep track of those links by subscribing to the feeds that were most relevant in our Bloglines account. And Furl offers a whole bunch of other ways to share our bookmarks as well.

Another similar service is at del.icio.us. del.icio.us doesn't give us as many features as Furl, but it's really easy to follow what people are reading via RSS. At del.icio.us, people add tag words to whatever link they save and subscribing to all of the links under a particular tag is as simple as pasting the following into your aggregator: http://del.icio.us/rss/tag/blogs. In this case, you'd be following all bookmarks that were tagged with the word "blogs."

(6) Combining RSS Feeds

Suppose you have a classroom full of students who each have their own Weblogs. They also have set up accounts at Furl so that they can collect relevant Web pages for the work they are doing and they have a number of search feeds that they are tracking to collect even more information.

From a teaching standpoint, if we wanted to monitor all of that information flow, it would take quite a bit of time and work. But here is a way to combine all of those collective feeds into one so that we can keep all the related work together and get a clearer picture of a student's workflow.

Blogdigger.com (http://www.blogdigger.com) has a way to create what they call groups of feeds, blending as many different feeds as we want into one. Just go to the Blogdigger site, click on the "Groups" button, click on "Create a New Group," Fill out the information on the form that follows, then on the next page enter the various feed addresses that we want to combine. Blogdigger gives this new feed a unique address that we can then take and use in Bloglines.

(7) Including RSS Feeds in Your Weblog

Even though using Bloglines or some other aggregator is the easiest way to collect and view our feeds, with a little bit of work we can actually get feed results to show up on our Weblog or other Web page. Some Weblog packages have built-in ways to do this and the instructions vary.

How to Find Feeds to Subscribe

There are two places to look for a site's feed:

1. On the Site
2. In Your Browser

On Site Subscription

RSS is most commonly found in blogs or news web sites, but it is becoming more common to see on any web site that is updated frequently. Feeds help make web content a powerful communication tool. Over the last few years you may have noticed a lot of little buttons and widgets appearing on sites and blogs. These little orange buttons links to other web sites and blogs called RSS, XML, ATOM and many more. They come in all shapes and sizes. These buttons help us to quickly subscribe to the feed based on the aggregator of our choice. Here are a few one might have seen:

There are plenty more but any time you see any of these buttons or anything like them it means that the site one is viewing almost certainly has a feed that one can subscribe to. In most cases it's as simple as either copying and pasting the link associated with the button into our RSS Reader or clicking the button and following the instructions to subscribe using the feed reader of our choice.

Figure 2.5: RSS Buttons

Browser Subscription

Many internet browsers now have the ability to find and subscribe to RSS feeds built right into them. When we surf to a site, we can usually tell if it has an RSS feed by looking in the right hand side of address bar where we type in the site's URL. Here's how it looks for ProBlogger when we are using Firefox:

See the little orange icon on the right hand side? Click that and we will be locating ProBlogger's RSS feed.

Using Safari Browser it is a blue RSS icon:

Other modern browsers will have similar icons. To quickly and easily subscribe by clicking these icons we will want to set up our browser to do it with our feed reader of choice as by default they will probably subscribe us using the in-browser reader. We can do this by going to the 'preferences' to our browser and choosing 'Google Reader' or 'Bloglines' etc. as our feed reader. Once we have done this and have subscribed to a few feeds we will begin to see unread items in your Feed Reader and we can start reading.

We will also find many directories that exist to help you find RSS feeds on topics that interest you. Here are a few of the larger directories.

Figure 2.6: RSS Directories (Top Left http://www.bloglines.com/, Top Right http://www.technorati.com/, Bottom Left http://www.pubsub.com/, and Bottom Right http://www.syndic8.com/)

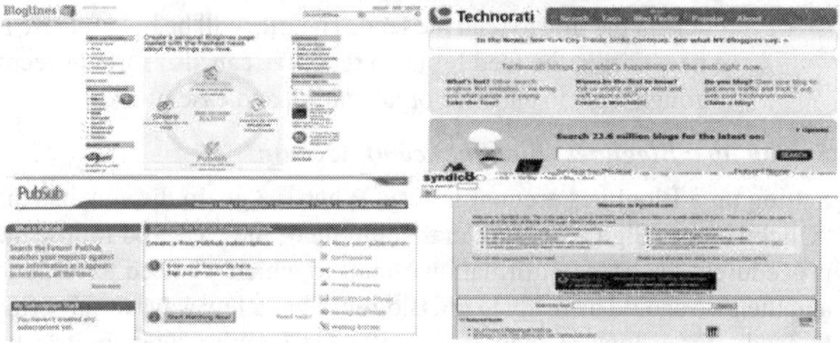

Get RSS by Email

We can also subscribe to any RSS feed by email. If we use RMail (http://www.r-mail.org/) or Squeet (http://www.squeet.com/) we can take any feed and convert it to an email subscription. When an update occurs to the feed we will be emailed the posting. If our email service supports rules and/or filters we can move all of these messages into a folder dedicated to the feed.

How to Get Started with RSS

First, we need to set up a reader/aggregator to collect your RSS feeds. This section will show that how to get started with a RSS reader/aggregator. How to set up an RSS feed reader/aggregator account in Google Reader and Bloglines is explained here.

Set Up a Google Reader Account

The following steps will be helpful to create an RSS account in Google:

1. Choose the reader/aggregator you wish to use. For Google Reader, visit http://www.google.ca/reader. It will ask to sign in with your Google account. If not have one we can click Create an account now.
2. Once we have created an account or have logged in with our pre-existing account we will be taken to our reader home page.

3. Once we have found a blog we like, go to their blog and copy the URL.
4. On our Google Reader click Add Subscription and paste the URL into the space provided. (We can use the Browse feature to also find blogs manually or to search for feeds of interest).
5. Our new feed will appear in the left hand panel where we can click on the title to read the feed. The title will be bold if there is a new post in the feed for us to read. We can also sort our feeds through tags, to enhance organization and ease of use.

Setting up a Bloglines (Bloglines.com) Account

Setting up a Bloglines account is easy. When we get to the site, use the "Click Here to Sign Up!" link in the middle of the page and follow the procedures. We get a confirmation e-mail to which we need to respond and then we should be ready to go. Bloglines has a few ways to subscribe to feeds. First, look at their listing of most popular subscriptions by clicking on the "Top Blogs" link under the "What's Hot" section of the Bloglines homepage. (Or, just go to http://www.bloglines.com/topblogs.) It will take us to a page of the 100 most subscribed to feeds among their users. One can preview the content and then, while logged in, one can subscribe to any on the list by clicking on the "Subscribe" link under each feed description. Then, click on the "My Feeds" link at the top left of the screen, we will see the feeds we subscribed to with the number of messages waiting to be read in parenthesis next to the name. Any time we come back, the feed name will be bold when new messages are waiting. The other way to subscribe to feeds is to manually add them to the list by using the "Add" link at the top of we subscription list. (See Figure 2.7) To use this, we will need to paste the address of the feed one wants into the subscribe form that appears on the next page. (Will Richardson, Online)

Once we paste in a feed, Bloglines will ask if you want to make a folder and whether or not you want other people to see your feed. And, when we have some feeds to work with, Bloglines lets we rename them

Figure 2.7: Bloglines Homepage

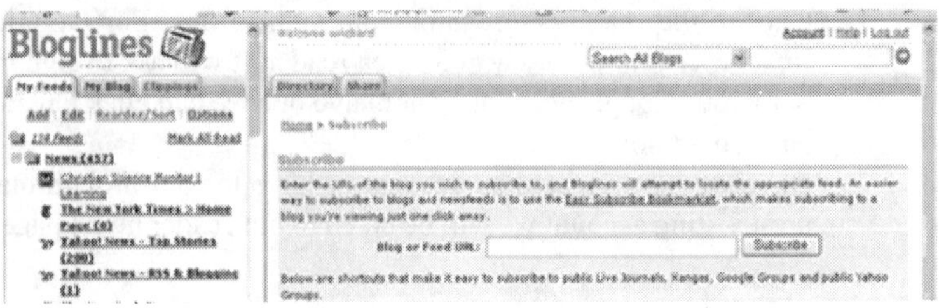

(among other things) by clicking on the "Edit" link at the top right of the right hand frame when we are viewing the results of one of our subscriptions. It's pretty intuitive and if we start getting quite a few feeds in our list, we might want to take the time to get organized. Finally, throw a link to Bloglines on your toolbar or in your Favorites folder. If we want up to the minute results, add the Bloglines notifier (http://www.bloglines.com/about/notifier) to the bottom of your screen which will let you know when new content has been posted to any of the feeds you are subscribed to.

Conclusion

RSS is well suited for the world of academia and educators have embraced it as a medium. Technology and communication have helped advance the educational field for years. RSS feeds are a natural fit for academics and it's obvious when we look at how teachers, students and professors are using it to further education. RSS will definitely be seen on every website and any service without RSS would lag behind. RSS is a great supplemental communication method that does not burden the publisher with maintaining lists or following strict privacy guidelines. RSS feeds are compiled according to the user's choices, removing any burden that is placed on publishers of email newsletters. Publishers no longer need to be concerned with spam, privacy policies, and age guidelines.

Any publisher using RSS as a communication vehicle is able to create keyword-rich, themed content, establishing trust, reputation and ongoing communication with current and prospective customers. Rarely in the last 10 years has there been a technology with so much potential to explode online exposure. A part of Web 2.0 has been the increasing popularity of RSS feeds and aggregation-syndication (Levine, A., Lamb, B., Norman, D, Online). Traditional education will not be replaced, but the RSS technology proves once again that the future of education will be based on online training and development. It is the learning trend of the 21st century.

3
Stress-Free Learning
Competitive to a Cooperative Learning

Mohd Shakir

Stress is one of the ways in which our body responds to the demands generated by the environment around us and our perceptions and interpretations of them. We experience stress in basically two forms- 'good stress' and 'bad stress'. 'Good stress' is that optimal amount of stress which results in motivation and enthusiasm. It encourages us to develop effective coping strategies to deal with challenges, ultimately contributing towards building resilience. 'Bad stress' occurs when our coping mechanisms are overwhelmed by stress to the extent that we are not able to deliver. Everyone involved in teaching-learning process is affected by stress and reacts to it in different ways. The students constitute the first target of this stressful environment. It is true that we cannot eliminate stress from our classrooms, but we always can reduce and manage it. There are numerous ways in which strategies can be build up to help the students in handling and coping with such stressful situations, for instance through proper relaxation, sound sleep, balanced diet and meditation. Author in this paper is trying to build up one such technique by employing the jigsaw method. The technique, it is hoped, would be of great help to the students in coping with the problems of stress, chiefly arising out of peer-competition, and other extraneous pressures, thereby creating comfortable educational environments for a better teaching-learning experience.

"The destiny of India is now being shaped in her classrooms", Kothari Commission Report (1964-66).

Justice Mohd. Shamim rightly remarks, 'there is no denying the fact that a man, in the absence of education, is nothing but a beast'. Education arms human beings to face the difficulties in life. An educated person can withstand problems in a better manner as compared to an uneducated person. He is calm, quiet and instead of getting worried he takes difficulties as challenge. He knows where his rights reside and is fully aware of his responsibilities. There is no doubt that education equips a man with a sense to distinguish good from bad and ugly.

The future of a country rests upon the shoulders of its younger generation, of which school children constitute a majority. Unfortunately the minds of these children are not free; they live and play with in highly stressful environments. Although, a small amount of stress, as experienced by the students before any examination, is a condition necessary for effective learning, higher stresses may lead to bigger problems. Not only that the students are unable to deliver their best, their performance also deteriorates; most of them go in to "underperformance" mode. Stressful situations often result from classroom conflicts where the students are constantly under the watchful eyes of their jealous peers. The classroom, therefore, becomes a level playing field of conflicts and counter-conflicts.

What is Stress?

School children's response to what is meant by stress is quite divergent. It is classified as "being under a lot of pressure"; "feeling angry or annoyed"; "too much on your mind and you can't take it anymore"; and "pressure and more stomach problems" (D'Autuono, 1998). It is defined as the state of psychological upset or disequilibrium in human beings caused by frustration, conflicts and other internal as well as external strains and pressures (Mangal, 1984). Richard S. Lazarus defines it as a condition or feeling, experienced when a person perceives that, "demands exceed the personal and social resources the individual is able to mobilize."

Stress is experienced by people as an innate reaction to everyday challenges or threats. It is normal and when experienced in brief episodes can act as a positive motivator. For example, it can help push a child to study for a quiz or test, or to complete his/her homework. However, when experienced for an extended period it can become debilitating and lead to difficulties within family, peers, and school work. It is sometimes a life event or situation that causes imbalance in an individual's life. An unhealthy response resulting from an excess to an individual's coping ability is also the cause of such stress. Self-control has much to do with the levels of stress; often things beyond our control constitute the reason of stress in our lives. Dohrenwend & Dhorenwend (1974) gave considerable evidence to show that there actually exists a relationship between life stress and physical illness. In the opinion of M Dash (2004), "stress refers to any adjustive demand that requires an adaptive response from us."

Is stress good or bad for us?: Stress in an individual's life can be categorized as "eustress" or stress needed to excel in life, whereas "distress" signifies serious reduction in the normal performance of a person.

Students, Under Stress and Distress

Students being a part of society are full of emotions and need adjustment in private and public life – at home, in school, on the playground or any other public place. For a child, proper expression of emotions is a necessity, more specifically as compared to an adult. Children are more prone to depression and stress if things do not follow their wishes. These effects are reflected in their academic achievements and fulfilment of their goals. A number of reasons can be given regarding stress. For instance, the behaviour of teachers, exam phobia, obtaining poor grade, change of seat in the classroom, poor methods of teaching by one or more than one teachers, any physical disorder or serious physical ailment, disability, poor economic condition, high expectations of parents and teachers, pressure of home work, peer group pressure, harmful home environment such as unhealthy relations of parents, remarriage, extra marital status, transfer of parents from one city to another, and death of loved ones, etc (Parvez & Jahan 2011). Studies demonstrate that children have identified a majority of stressful events in their lives, stemming from school-related problems. Peer relationship problems as well as home and family problems are major reasos of stress. (Henderson & Kelbey, 1992)

Symptoms of Students under Stress and Distress

- Lack of motivation
- Poor attendance
- Poor achievement
- Lack of energy
- Loss of interest in activities
- Irritability and anger
- Increased interpersonal conflicts
- Mood swings and short temper
- Hopelessness
- Frequent crying
- Frustration
- A feeling of being the target of other people's animosity
- Eating and sleeping disorder, i.e. eating too much or too little, and sleeping too much or too little
- Persistent back and neck pain
- Negative attitude

- Sense of loneliness and isolation
- Losing or gaining weight
- Thoughts of death and suicide

Suicide has become the second leading cause of death among students. Out of three suicide cases reported every fifteen minutes, one is committed by a student in the age group 15-29 (Sundaram, 2011). It is observed that college-life can be extremely stressful causing emotional difficulties and clinical depression, leading to suicide (Hart, 2010). Prof. Iqbal reports, "...increasing rate of suicide among students is because of examination stress, parental pressure and aspirations, curriculum that is beyond them and lack of teachers' competence and effective teaching and their harsh attitude" (Iqbal, 2012).

In most classrooms, the behaviour of students is generally appropriate and does not pose a challenge to the teachers. However, some students occasionally behave in an inappropriate and disruptive way, creating nuisance in the class. Disruptions in class are quite often problematic or inappropriate and difficult to be managed by the teacher. For handling these types of situations, the teacher needs to seek additional help from experts in order to develop better coping strategies in class.

What can be Done?

Long-standing suspicion, fear, and distrust among classroom students create an atmosphere of turmoil and hostility. Inter-group hostility fuelled by competitive environment of the classroom keeps it highly stressful. The author, as a matter of absolute necessity to help defuse this situation, views jigsaw technique as one of the best approaches for collaborative and cooperative learning. It is asserted that employing this jigsaw technique would help the students get along with one another and establish a congenial environment in the class room.

Cooperative Learning

Cooperative learning, as cited by Gocer (2010), is a conscious effort of the students of forming small groups with a common goal of learning a subject or performing a task collectively. It is basically a learning method that allows students to jointly achieve a given learning objective through division of labour (Watson, 1991).

In cooperative learning peers assist each other's learning by establishing proper communication among them. Students with different cultures, experiences and learning modes get together to achieve success towards a common goal by assuming responsibility of each other's learning processes. In simple words cooperative learning stands for 'making efforts by small groups of students and assisting each other in learning'. Studies show that cooperative learning increases students' motivation to do academic work (Johnson et al., 1986; Swortzel, 1997 cited in Adams, 2013). Many authors have identified Jigsaw technique as an efficient and frequently used technique in cooperative learning (Artut, & Tarim 2007; Moskowitz, et al., 1985).

Jigsaw Technique

This technique was developed by an American psychologist Elliot Aronson in 1971 to encourage a culture of shared goals and mutual support. The jigsaw method encourages listening, engagement and empathy by giving each member of the group an essential part to play in the learning process. Group members work together as a team to accomplish a common goal where each person depends on all the other members. Hence, no learner can succeed completely unless everyone works well together as a team thereby endowing a team spirit among learners of the group.

The jigsaw technique is a unique group-learning experience, in which the students are required to cooperate with each other so as to achieve a certain goal (Kagan, 1989). It is an effective cooperative learning strategy that has shown good results when applied to various subjects to teach (Slavin, 1995; Aronson & Patnoe, 1997). It not only increases and improves the performance of students, but also improves and promotes their communication skills and interpersonal relationships (Slavin, 1989). It improves academic performance of students (Walker & Crogan 1998); enhances the effectiveness of learning (Huang et al., 2014); promotes learner's participation and enthusiasm; stimulates students' motivation and increases enjoyment of the learning experience; and reduces students' reluctance and anxiety (Mengduo & Xiaoling 2010). It is indicated through studies that students actually improved their academic performance through the jigsaw technique (Carrol, 1986; Crone & Portillo, 2013). The study conducted by Adams (2013) reveals that through the use of the technique, students naturally developed an interest in working with their peers and started learning from each other in a much better way.

The jigsaw technique can be used to organize classroom teaching in such a way that makes learners interdependent on each other in order to succeed. They are not separate clusters rather they work as a unit. The technique splits classes into mixed groups to work on small problems which is collated into a final outcome. For example, a topic is divided into sub topics. Students are then split into groups known as home groups with one member assigned to each sub topic. Working individually, each student learns about his sub topic and presents it to his group. Next, students gather into groups divided by sub topics. Each member presents again to the sub topic group which is called expert group. In same sub topic groups, students reconcile points of view and synthesise information. They discuss thoroughly and conclude a final version. Finally, the home groups reconvene and listen to presentations and explanations from each member. The final explanation provides all group members with an understanding of their own material, as well as the findings that have emerged from sub topic expert group discussion.

We can understand this with the help of the following process: First, the problem is defined on which the class will be working, thereafter the class is broken randomly into groups of 4 to 5 students each, depending on the size of the class, and a number is assigned (eg 1 to 4) to students in each group. This is known as Home Group. Second, assigning each student/number a topic in which he will become an expert. The topics will be sub-topics of the main topic. For example, in a computer class the general theme might be hardware and the sub-topics might be central processing unit – assigned to student 1; memory – assigned to student 2; input devices – assigned to student 3; and output devices – assigned to student 4. Third, rearranging the students into expert groups based on their assigned numbers and sub-topics. Fourth, providing the experts with the materials and resources necessary to learn about their sub topics – the experts should be given the opportunity to obtain knowledge through reading and discussion. Finally, reassembling the original groups to be taught by experts.

In this system, each and every member of the class is involved in the process of cooperative learning. Each student becomes both a learner and a teacher, who achieves complete learning of a particular subject matter. In this congenial environment, all the students learn equally in the classroom.There is no conflict as there is healthy competition among the students in the class.

Conclusion

The jigsaw approach of teaching does not make the teacher the sole provider of knowledge because most of the work is done by learners (students) themselves, which leads to an efficient and effective way of learning. Learners take ownership in the work and achievement and therefore they are held accountable among their peers. This approach is very beneficial in teaching because learning revolves around interaction with peers, wherein the learners are active participants in the learning process and thereby help to build inter-personal and interactive skills among themselves. It is observed that the competitive nature of the classroom encourages students to discriminate against those who are in a way different from them. In order to counter this problem, students can be placed in diversified groups so that they would be required to work together and reduce the competitive atmosphere. Students often have difficulty in adjusting to the mixing of different groups in the classroom. Through this process, as employed by Aronson, the students have to pay attention and obtain information from other group members. This allows each member of the group to add a small piece to the larger picture. The method teaches the students to rely on each other and reduces their competitive attitude, making learning free from stress. They need everyone in their group to do well because their marks depend on the performance of other students, which marks a true shift from the erstwhile competitive environment of the classroom.

4

Stress Management

Nipping in the Bud

Anjum Ahmed

The family is the oldest form of institution in the history of mankind. It plays a significant role in the personality development and socialization of the child at different developmental stages. Any major disturbance in the functioning of the family can have adverse effect on the child. Today's children face stressful situations at a more early age. Stress has a huge impact on the child's personality and maturity and very much defines their coping ability for latter part of their lives.

Major life changes can cause stress in children. Even positive life events like change of home, job change, new baby, relocating or school change can cause stress in children. Other life stressors for children are death, divorce, marital conflict, violence, peer pressure. Only when the stress is more than what the children can cope with, it leads to imbalance in a child's life. The stress will then be noticeable as an unhealthy response. For children it becomes difficult to express or to understand that they are stressed. It can lead to emotional reactions – they may get aggressive, irritable, nervous, panicky or even start crying. They may complain about stomach ache or other psycho-somatic diseases. Thus, stress in children may also cause health problems.

Signs of Stress in Children

Children experience stress in a variety of ways. Some may just be over-tired and seem to cope very well. Others may have mood swings, changes in sleep patterns, or may revert to behaviours of a younger age (thumb sucking, bedwetting, clinging, etc.). There are many different signs of stress, but these are also signs of other conditions and illnesses. Any sudden change in behaviour of children that is not related to developmental stages is cause of concern. When stress interferes with a child's life to such an extent that the child feels overwhelmed, depressed, or physically ill, it may be time to see a professional (the child's doctor, a school counselor, or a therapist).

Signs of Stress: Up to 5 Years Old: Young children can't often tell you that they are feeling stressed. Their behaviour, however, can reveal their level of stress. Infants, toddlers, and pre-school children demonstrate stress by clinging to a parent, crying more than usual, throwing temper tantrums, displaying regressive behaviours (thumb sucking, bedwetting, fear of the dark, etc.), rocking, biting, and having toilet accidents. Crying, temper tantrums, and wakefulness at night can also be a normal response to a developmental stage.

Signs of Stress in 6 to 11 Years Old: Children of school age develop a better ability to express their stress. They may express it verbally or through abnormal physical gestures. Stressed school children often complain of stomach aches, headaches, respiratory tract illness, sleep problems, over or under appetite. Their recovery from illnesses is slow. They need to go to the bathroom more than required; they may also grind their teeth, especially in their sleep. Stressed children may also lie, bully, defy authority, express anger, be irritable, or engage in disruptive behaviour, hit other children, refuse to go to school and start bringing home poor school results.

Signs of Stress in 12 to 18 Years Old: Pre-adolescents and adolescents (a stage of storm and stress), though the most able to communicate of all of the ages of childhood, often are the least communicative. They may also deny that anything is affecting them and refuse to talk. When stressed, teenagers may behave in many ways like elementary school age children undergoing stress. Their regressive behaviour, however, may not include bedwetting and baby talk. It may manifest in different other forms like unwillingness to accept more adult responsibilities or overpowering desire to play more. They may not want to go to the University for attending classes.

Causes of Stress in Children

One of the main reasons for stress in children is the demand made on their time and potential. Apart from academics, most parents today push their children into a plethora of extracurricular activities. Most kids nowadays have crammed schedules with almost every minute accounted for and barely have any time for relaxation or play.

Family plays the most important role in a child's life. Children are especially sensitive to even the most minor changes in the behaviour of family members towards each other. If parents argue or adolescent siblings are in a bad mood, a child will perceive it almost immediately. Sibling rivalry, if it gets out of hand, will play on a child's mind almost all the time in the same way that adults obsessively think of their worries. Constant criticism of a child's shortcomings can lead to resentment and fear. If there is a breakdown or lack of communication between parent and child, the latter tends to feel unloved, unwanted and unimportant. An unstable home environment shatters a child's sense of security as well as his self-confidence in the long run.

Any kind of trauma, like the death of a loved one, a natural disaster, emotional abuse, violence, alcoholism or drug use by a member of the household, can have a detrimental effect on any human being's state of mind. Children are especially susceptible. A child's inability to cope with the extreme emotions born of tragedy can lead to various stress-related psycho-social disorders. One of the unusual sources of stress is caused by school children. Bullying and insensitive remarks from school children or playmates can cause low self-esteem. Peer pressure can result in a state of conflict and make a child feel embarrassed about his clothes and other possessions, his intellect, or the way he looks.

Pressure to excel leads to tremendous stress in children. The frustration over not being able to meet expectations in school or at home can lead a child to believe that he is stupid or worthless. This leads to stress, because of which the child may be unable to function normally, thus adding to the pressure and leading to higher levels of tension.

Role of Parents and Teachers

In the first 18 years of life, children are often exposed to many stressful situations – going to school, making friends, rejection, dating, puberty, adjustment to impending adulthood, etc. These are harmful not only in their physical development but also in their psychological development, leading to mental health problems. A child can be helped at any age to cope with stressful situations. Role of parents and teachers are very important, who can remove stress in children in the following ways:

- The perfect mode to relieve stress in children is to sit with them and encourage them to share their problem. They should be comforted, supported and motivated to take part in different activities
- Communication is the key to any relationship. Children who are not open with their parents have difficulty in dealing with stress. Parents should not promote any kind of barrier between them and the child and give them quality time. Patrents should iclosely interact with their children about school, studies, and their friends to know if anything is creating stress in their lives.

- Parents should maintain healthy diet schedule for their children. Healthy body helps children in keeping illness far away from them.
- Children can be encouraged to do exercises.
- Children should be told about the facts of life, and how some experiences in life are unavoidable. In cases like divorce or death in the family, children should be provided emotional support. The easiest and surest way to remove stress in children is to take complete care of them in their formative years.
- Parents should maintain their own stress levels. Stressed parents affect children more than is evident.
- Parents and teachers need to be vigilant about the stress in children. They should formulate a plan of action for stressed children.
- Teachers can encourage students by appreciating them for what they do and help them in the growth of their self-esteem. They should deal with them optimistically and train them how to turn negative situation into an opportunity to succeed in life.
- The parents should teach the children that it's normal to feel angry, upset, sad, lonely, etc. They should be made aware that as children, their parents too had undergone severe stress.

Recognizing Stress

Before one can help a child avoid stress, one needs first to recognize signs of stress in children. The child could be:

- Frequently tired
- Moody for no reason
- Unable to concentrate
- Unable to sleep
- Fearful, but doesn't know why
- Hungry all the time
- Not hungry at all
- Less enthusiastic than normal

Look for changes in their schedule, try to notice if they have different friends, and pay attention to their school results to see if they are doing badly. All these can be indicators of something stressful going on in their lives.

Effects of Stress

Body: Stress is something that most people encounter on a daily basis. It can be work related, home related or caused by something else in one's life. The important thing is learning to live a less stressful life because stress can adversely affect the body in many ways. Once we are stressed, our body immediately begins to react. Humans have innately developed a "fight or flight" response to stressful or threatening situations over the years. Several things happen under stress:

- Heart rate increases
- The blood flow to the brain and muscles increase dramatically
- Digestion temporarily stops to allow for more energy
- Muscle tension increases
- Memory functions are heightened
- Breathing becomes more rapid as muscles require more oxygen

Sometimes these responses can be good, but most of the time it harms physical and mental health. When we are under stress, we often tend to abuse our body. This can include poor lifestyle choices such as eating fatty and greasy food, drinking too much caffeine or alcohol, or even taking drugs.

Emotions: Emotions are triggered by the central nervous system. This is in response to an external situation or can even be caused by memories of a previously stressful time. In many cases, just because the stressful time is over, does not mean that the emotions related to that time do not still exist within the mind of the person who experienced them. All this is associated with the "fight or flight" reaction to harmful or potentially harmful situations. This is a primal reaction that causes humans to fight or flee from a dangerous situation. When either choice is made, several physical and psychological reactions and emotions take place automatically without our even being aware of the response.

Fear: Many times, when confronted with stressful situations, we react with emotions of fear or anger. For example, a person who is robbed at gunpoint is probably going to react to this stressor with an emotion of fear. The person may fear for personal safety or even life. This event may even lead to post traumatic stress disorder if the person is not able to return to normal state after a certain period of time.

Anger: Whether life threatening or not, many people react to stressors with anger. One such example of this is road rage. Road rage occurs when a driver resorts to violent behaviour while behind the wheel. For example, while driving down the road, if one driver thinks another driver has overtaken him forcefully, he may react by driving aggressively – too fast or too recklessly – to get back at the other driver, to essentially teach him a lesson.

Crying: One emotion that many people feel during times of extreme stress is crying. Women are especially prone to crying when they feel overwhelmed or feel helpless in any situation. Crying during times of stress is not necessarily a bad thing. Sometimes, it can help release the pent up emotions and actually make one feel better.

Mind: Stress can affect physically as well as emotionally. Sometimes the two are interconnected and result in sleeplessness. If a person is too stressed because of a big project at work, he/she may not be able to sleep. Lack of sleep affects concentration and decision making abilities.

While Post-Traumatic Stress Disorder (PTSD) is perhaps a more severe form mental disorder, there are other serious disorders of the mind. Stress can cause stuttering (or stammering), panic attacks, lack of sexual desire or poor performance, depression or mood swings, anger, racing thoughts, feelings of loneliness or worthlessness, nervous habits such as fidgeting or tapping, crying spells, defensive or suspicious behaviour, social isolation, and fatigue. Stress can also result in extreme behaviour, like excessive drinking, smoking or even eat more. Thes provide temporary relief to stress.

Spirit: Cumulative stress can affect every aspect of our lives – physical, emotional and spiritual. Chronic stress can begin to erode an individual's concept of self. Some people begin to lose confidence in their abilities and strengths. This self doubt begins to erode relationships with others and with the person's trust in how the universe works. People begin to lose their ability to laugh or find humour in the world. They also lose their creativity and the joy of living, leading to depression. Depressed people do not think of their loved one's needs or feelings. Their emotions can explode, and they can lash out at others. They can transfer their own tension by being intolerant of others actions. They can also exhibit mood swings.

As depression and isolation begins to take its toll, individuals under stress become demotivated. This lack of purpose and meaning soon leads to lack of hope, which is the real soul killer.

Global Stressors

People in most parts of the world are fearful and feel uneasy and uncertain about their future. They are fearful of natural disasters, war, or terrorism. Adults, especially children in war torn areas or places devastated by natural disasters, experience fear and uncertainty about the future. Though this level of general anxiety may not be felt intensely in safer areas of the world, it certainly is felt to some degree by nearly everyone. This kind of Outer Stressor is often called a *Global Stressor.*

Every area of the world has some inbuilt environmental stress during a specific part of the year. These stressors affect people differently. For example, compounding concern about natural disasters is the problem of global warming. This phenomenon projects that the Earth will heat up and a wave of unprecedented natural disasters will occur throughout the world. Though some people are reacting by formulating strategies to deal with such events, others can only feel the added stress it causes.

Television reporting of crime and violence has brought stress to cities, homes, schools, and between communities. In addition, people also feel Global Stressors as they watch world news on television. The actions of other political leaders in other countries can put their own personal safety at risk and the security of their own countries. The threat of terrorism anywhere in the world has changed the way most people perceive war and their personal safety. Since suicide bombers and other portable nuclear devices could be brought into any country, war is no longer something that occurs somewhere else. The threat of nuclear disaster significantly adds to the stress.

Techniques for Reducing Stress

Prayers: Whether we like it or not, stress is usually a part of our daily lives. We are so busy with children, spouses, jobs, extracurricular activities, etc that we rarely have any downtime and that means our stress level is often very high. Using prayer as a means of stress reduction is an excellent way to focus on what is truly important in life as well as focusing on the health and welfare of others. More and more people are turning to prayer that allows them to reflect on the positives in their life. Through prayer one can evaluate the problems and reflect on likely solutions.

Reflexology: Reflexology is the holistic practice of applying pressure to certain points of the feet, hands, and even sometimes the ears in order to have a beneficial health effect on a certain part of the body. These points correspond with a system of zones, so therefore reflexology is sometimes known as zone therapy. There are reflexology maps of the feet, hands, and ears, which tell you what part of the anatomy will receive a corresponding therapeutic effect when that point is massaged. For example, massaging the bottom centre of the big toe is supposed to stimulate the pituitary gland. The pituitary gland is often known as "The Master Gland" because it can affect metabolism, blood pressure, reproduction, and other vital functions. It is believed that reflexology works by unblocking an imbalance in the body that often follows illness, stress, injury, or disease. Using reflexology to return the balance to the body can help restore and maintain the body's natural equilibrium and promote healing.

Yoga: Many of us are not sports minded or gym friendly. There are other forms of movement that can help us relax. Hatha yoga is one of them. It is a system of asanas or postures which combined with proper breathing can help us destress and relax the body. Kripalu Yoga is a physical exercise that can stretch and tone without adding more tension to an already stressed body. Deep Breathing helps raise the level of oxygen in the blood, stimulates blood flow, and improves the delivery of nutrients to the cells. This is particularly important when a body has been dealing with stress. The deep belly breathing that accompanies the postures helps to turn off the flight or fight response and also helps to focus the mind on the body and the breath, and not on stressful issues. Stretching and Balance also emphasizes on stretching and balance. By moving the body in a series of postures, we can stretch the muscles and keep our joints supple.

Acupuncture: Acupuncture is an ancient method of treatment which requires inserting small needles to the ailing part of the body. I alleviates certain pains and relaxes the body. Acupuncture originated in China thousands of years ago. There are also Japanese, Tibetan, and Korean versions of acupuncture.

Conclusion

Stress is something almost all of us have to deal with at some time in our lives. Some of us learn the art of leading a relatively stress free life, while others have difficulty in coping with it. Stress can affect not only our physical health but also our emotional and mental health. Stress can come from many sources. These sources are called stressors, which can be found in all areas of our lives. One of the biggest stressors is 'time'. As everthing is timebound, it is a major cause of stress in humans. However, we need to maintain a good balance of mind and body and keep away from stress of all kinds.

5

TQM Practices in Teacher Education Institutions

A Review

Nupur Sen and *Seema Gupta*

There is a close link between the prosperity of a nation and the quality of education it provides for its people. Quality education improves standard of living of people by enhancing the performance of engines of economic development. Quality assurance is one of the central issues among teacher educators and teacher education institutions. The serious problem includes assuring the quality of adverse academics of teaching, admission and infrastructure. Accessibility and quality improvement is inseparable dimension with respect to construction of curriculum, methodologies of teaching – learning, infrastructural facilities and administration. Over-emphasis on one at the cost of another would be unproductive. Emphasis on quality parameters become all the more necessary in the light of mushrooming growth of private institution with the opening of the economy. Recent emphasis on quality excellence among teacher educators has been mostly on manpower development and mainly focus on skilled manpower development. The prerequisite to plan for a better future is an understanding of the changes and their impact on the teacher educators and their quality assurance.

Education is a process through which a nation develops its self-consciousness by developing the self-consciousness of individuals who compose it. It is not mere public instruction, it is social institution, which provides mental, physical, ideological and above all training to individuals of the nation so as to enable them to have full consciousness of their mission, of their purpose in the life and then to achieve that purpose (AIOU, 2002).

Quality is one of the most important issues in education. It is recognized that there are problems with today's education system. Students leaving or graduating from high schools and colleges are unprepared to meet the demands of society. These students are product of an education system that does not focus on quality and is a cause of increase in social welfare cost. Quality management is a vehicle to which professionals can use to cope with the "forces of change" (Arcaro, 1997).

Quality in higher education is a multidimensional concept, which includes all related functions and activities that form the part of academic life in an institution. Therefore, any framework for assessment of quality should take into account the quality of teachers, infrastructure provided to students, student support services, curricula assessment and resources (Isani and Virk, 2005).

What is TQM?

Total Quality Management is a people driven process. It involves change in people's attitudes primarily. In addition, it deals with process orientation and continuous improvement of the process. It strives for empowerment and autonomy of the people involved in using processes of production. It asks people to continuously look for new ways to adapt to the changing environment. It is a continuous improvement plan, with an effort to bring out the best for the stakeholders as well as for the institution.

TQM in Education

If TQM has been relevant for the industry in the second half of the twentieth century, it is relevant in the field of education in the twenty first century. People interested in education have to take on the leadership of applying TQM concepts and tools for a continuous improvement plan for educational institutions. Such people are those who are endowed with a commitment to education and a passion for work associated with such commitment, and can guarantee total quality in education.

The Gurukula System of education was probably the best example of quality management in education. In the Gurukula (Gurukula means Preceptors family) system, students lived with the Guru in his family until the time they completed their study. The Gurukula tradition of total quality was successfully transferred to the early Indian Universities like Nalanda and Takshasila.

The expertise of visionaries also in institutional planning should be a part of planning the academic curriculum. The concept of Total Quality Management should not be left to the corporate world. It should extend its reach to educational institutions too. Now some computer education institutions have obtained ISO 9001 to assure their clientele (the learners enrolling in their institutions) of quality education. This phenomenon should be extended to schools, colleges and universities. The governing body awarding accreditation should review the status of institutions periodically to ensure quality learning.

TQM can be defined as a general management philosophy and a set of tools which allow an institution to pursue a definition of quality and a means for attaining quality, with quality being a continuous improvement ascertained by customers' contentment with the services they have received (Michael et al., 1997). According to Witcher (1990), TQM is composed of three terms: *Total* – every person is involved, including customer and suppliers; *Quality* – customer requirements are met exactly; and *Management* – senior executives are committed. TQM may also be defined as "doing things right for the first time, striving for continuous improvement, fulfilling customers need, making quality the responsibility of every employee etc.

Objectives of Education and Quality

The total quality management framework of any institution is derived from its broad objectives. Therefore, the right objectives of education must be set, both at the national as well as institution levels before implementing the total quality management. The objective may broadly be classified in the following three categories:

(a) *Social Excellence*: Social norms are the foundation of a country's culture and provide longevity to its social values. Many religions and/or polities systems attempt to provide such norms. Different groups/counties have chosen different models for their community affairs and ethics, e.g. Islamic ethics, Christian ethics, Hindu ethics, socialism, etc. The believers of these religions derive their social norms from their religions.

(b) *National Excellence*: Unity and integrity among the countrymen cannot be taken for granted. It must be designed, developed and groomed through the educational processes. It can easily be lost with unplanned and borrowed literature of other counties. For this to be a strong objective, every mean must be used, including education, media, and the law. The subject of Social Studies taught in schools is specifically designed to achieve this goal. These values are also normally embedded in many other subjects like literature. Similarly, many extra-curricular activities are also designed to achieve this goal, e.g. the morning assembly in schools, the national anthem in all public functions, national integrity in classes, defence training in schools and colleges, etc.

(c) *Academic Excellence*: This focuses around academic outcome, i.e. results of academic learning. This is creation of the right capabilities of the subject matter/discipline, e.g. engineering, medicine, chemistry etc. Its quality, usually measured, also include Industry Feedbacks,

Employability, Career Progression, Job Retention Rates, Accessibility, Affordability, and fulfilment of National, Economic and Defence Priorities, etc. Total quality Management assurance function for the objective of academic excellence includes activities like: employers-needs analysis, designing needs-based courses and academic standards focusing on "Application", practical orientations in schools, research in colleges/ universities that leads to the development of industrial and national requirements, systems which measure the quality and performance of education (both at institution and country levels), process control of the teaching and learning activities to ensure the quality of faculty, curriculum students, teaching environment, and learning activities to ensure the quality of faculty, curriculum, students, teaching environment, and placing a system of customer satisfaction.

Changes in the Vision of Quality

The vision of quality of education is very much a function of the mission of the education system, educational training, social insertion, preparation for work, and for citizenship. These are occurring, in particular, in historical, ideological and political contexts. Additional missions are expected from the education system, thus altering our vision of quality.

Four major trends of relevance leading to the alteration of the vision are:

1. Globalization of Societies

Globalization of societies will require a common share of an international system of values; account has to be taken of local and national cultural identities, as well as universal moral and ethical consideration of tolerance, solidarity and human rights. In this situation the education system has changed the goals of education system along with vision of quality of education.

2. Globalization of Economies

Due to globalisation of economies, the tasks for different skill development and the priorities attached to the different skills development significantly change the vision of educational quality.

3. Shifts in the Tasks Distributed among Protagonists System

One of the major trends in recent years is that state is losing its monopolistic responsibility for education and its role is changing. The consequences of the vision of quality are, needless to say, multifarious.

4. Fast Scientific and Technological Development

The combination and parallelism of the fast evolution and progress of science and technology, and of the massive and universal development of information and communication, have numerous consequences on the vision of quality of education. It is vital to remind ourselves of the humanistic or moral ideal of quality of education which is to elevate the mind and personality, as those ideal remains consistent with, and will ultimately condition, the future development of contemporary societies (UNESCO, 1996a).

One response to the twenty-first century challenges to traditional higher education, from globalization, from an increasingly competitive higher education sector, and from perceived initiatives of information technology and media companies, has been launched in 1997 by Universities 21, which is an association of major research-intensive international universities. Its objective is to assist its members to become global universities and to advance their plans for internationalization (Scott, 2000).

It was generally viewed that quality lies in business organizations, but due to rapid change in social needs, it has become prime agenda of the countries worldwide. In the changing context marked by expansion of education and globalization of economic activities, education has become a national concern with an international dimension. To cope with this changing context, countries have been pressurized to ensure and assure quality of higher education at a nationally comparable and internationally acceptable standard. Consequently, many countries initiated "national quality assurance mechanisms" and many more are in the process of evolving suitable strategy. Most of the quality assurance bodies were established in nineties and after a few years of practical experience, they have started rethinking many issues of quality assurance (UNESCO, 2002).

According to Mukhopadhyay (2005) quality in education is a massive challenge since it deals with the most sensitive creation on earth, i.e human beings. Education only changes the human propensities to evolve and unfold it till the last breath, a process that covers the human journey from "womb to tomb". Education facilitates this very evolution of the individual. No wonder then that the concept of quality in education has attracted scholarly attention. Education is no doubt goal and market oriented. The quality of education has been seen with reference to concepts like fitness of educational outcomes and experience for use, defect avoidance in education process, excellence in educational process, conformance of education output to planned goals, specifications and requirements, and value addition in education.

TQM in education surfaced in 1988, which has become increasingly popular in education, as evidenced by the plethora of books and journal articles since 1990 (Tucker 1992). TQM has also spread into mainstream of educational organisations. In support of the TQM initiatives in education, Crawford and Shutler (1999) applied Crosby (1984) model to suggest a practical strategy for using TQM principles in education. Their strategy focused on the quality of the teaching system used rather than on students' examination results. They argue that examinations are a diagnostic tool for assuring the quality of the teaching system.

To satisfy the educational needs of students, continuous improvement efforts need to be directed at the curriculum and delivery services. From such a perspective, various root causes of quality system failure in education have been identified. These include poor inputs, poor delivery services, lack of attention paid to performance standards and measurements, unmotivated staff and neglect of students' skills (Ali and Zairi 2005). One of the weaknesses of such a perspective is its concentration on the student as a customer whereas TQM in education should concern the customer beyond students.

Literature available, points to a growing interest in applying TQM in education for a wide variety of reasons (Thakkar et al., 2006; Temponi 2005). Some of the reasons include:

- pressures from industry for continuous upgrading of academic standards with changing technology;
- government schemes with allocation of funds, which encourage research and teaching in the field of quality;
- increasing competition between various private and government academic institutions; and
- reduction in the pool of funds for research and teaching, implying that only reputed institutions will likely have a chance of gaining access to various funds.

The TQM framework should be built upon a set of core values and concepts. These values and concepts provide foundation for integrating the key performance requirements within the quality framework. A set of fundamental core values forming the building blocks of the proposed TQM framework is: leadership and quality culture; continuous improvement and innovation in educational processes.

Quality in higher education is a multidimensional concept, which includes all related functions and activities that form the part of academic life in a university system. Therefore, any framework for assessment of quality should take into account the quality of students, teachers, infrastructure student support services, curricula assessment and resources

(Isani and Virk, 2005). Quality must be viewed in terms of outcomes. The educated person should display specific competencies in specific areas.

In the views of Winn and Green (1998), total quality management (TQM) is recognized as an important management philosophy and is widely used in development and acquisition of education. It recognizes the need for continuous development of the education system, whether students, faculty, or administration. TQM involves principles applicable to classroom teaching, administration, examination system, curriculum development, and faculty development, which means changing the culture of an organization.

According to (Harris 1994) there are three generic approaches to TQM in higher education.

- Firstly there is a customer focus where the idea of service to students is fostered through staff training and development, which promotes student's choice and autonomy.
- The second approach has a staff focus and is concerned with the value and enhancement of the contribution of all the members of the staff, effectiveness of an institution's operation and the setting of the policies and priorities. This entails a flatter management structure and the acceptance of responsibility for action by defined working groups.
- The third approach focuses on service agreements stance and seeks to ensure conformity to specification at certain key measurable points of the educational processes. Evaluation of assignments by faculty within a specified timeframe is an example.

Whitty (1992) emphasized that quality teacher education requires a genuine partnership between various stakeholders, a clearer definition of competencies required by teachers as reflective practitioners, monitoring of academic activities through a quality assurance system, administration of professional accreditation through a council for accreditation of teacher education with strong extra professional representation to ensure public accountability, sensitivity to local needs within this national framework.

Hillman (1995) concluded that more education faculty teaches about technology than with it. Teacher education programs must pay heed to the fact that teachers need consistent, pragmatic training in the use of various technologies for instructions. Over the past years, the public and politicians have become concerned with the quality of teachers in public schools. As a result of this concern, today's educational institutions are most interested in the level of preparedness of their teacher candidates.

Gore (2001) advocates a framework rooted in classroom practices with four components: intellectual quality, relevance, supportive classroom environment, and recognition of differences. In essence, Gore suggests that the knowledge base for teacher education should include the same elements that characterize effective teaching.

Naik (2001) has strongly suggested that bringing quality movement through application of TQM in Indian higher education will result in global recognition. He further suggested that a law should be made to have quality assurance cell in all academic institutions like in UK.

Akhtar (2002) conducted a research on "Self-financing in higher education public and private sectors: its prospects and implications". The objectives of the study were to critically examine the self-financing scheme in higher education in public and private sectors and also to visualize its future prospects and implications. The views of the students as the recipients of the higher education; the parents/guardians as the sponsors of their education; the faculty and management in universities as mainly responsible for the implementation of the self-financing scheme, etc were collected by using questionnaires and interviews as research instruments.

The recommendation of the study included that the fee structure needed to be rationalized and made accessible to students. The fee was slightly increased in professional subjects that have greater demand in the world of work. In public sector universities, efforts were made to generate scholarship opportunities with the cooperation of leading business firms in the country. Revenue earned by universities were meant to be used for infrastructural development.

Osseo-Asare and Longbottom (2002) in their model for TQM implementation in higher educational institutions, proposes enabler criteria, which affect performance and help organizations to achieve organizational excellence. These "enabler" criteria are leadership, policy and strategy, people management, resources and partnerships and processes. They also suggest "result" criteria, including customer satisfaction, people satisfaction, and impact on society and key performance results for measuring the effectiveness of TQM implementation. Non-implementation of TQM was due to institutions pre-occupation with funding agencies and non-embracement of continuous improvement culture. Proper education and training of those involved in the implementation process will help to mitigate this problem.

Iqbal (2004) investigated the problems and prospects of higher education in Pakistan. The main objectives of the study were: (1) to determine present profile of higher education in Pakistan; (2) to examine the past efforts done for the improvement; (3) to highlight the budget provision; and (4) to explore problems of higher education. The sample included eight universities of Pakistan. Four questionnaires were developed for data collection. 20 teachers and 40 students from each university were included in the sample. Thirty community leaders and 50 experts were also included in the sample. Data was tabulated and analyzed using the Likerts' five-point scale and Chi-Square.

The conclusions drawn from this study were: access was very limited in universities; quality was very low in the field of academics, administration, research and equipment; faculty and staff needed to develop adequate knowledge and skill; funds provided were inadequate and misappropriation was common; character building of students was ignored; there was no linkage between university and industry; examination system was faulty; good governance was non-existent and private sector was expanding without merit.

On the basis of the conclusions, the recommendations were: provision of facilities for increase in enrolment, enhancement in quality of all the elements and in-service training, increase in funds and linkage with industry, institution of more open universities and opening of night classes.

Mary (2004) studied total quality management in higher education. The objectives of the study were to look at the concept and meaning of internationalisations of higher education; to explore the issues of quality in the higher education sector and their relationship to the internationalisations process; and, finally, to provide an overview of quality assurance systems within the Australian and Swedish higher education sector. It was found that in order to survive in a fast-maturing marketplace, institutions of higher education now need to provide formal, transparent and credible systems of quality assurance in order to allow appropriate evaluation for interested parties, be it prospective students or other domestic or international institutions.

Pour and Yeshodhara (2004) studied the perception of secondary school teachers in Mysore city (India) regarding Total Quality Management (TQM) in education. It was an attempt to understand how these perceptions vary with demographic variables such as, gender and subject specialization (Arts and Sciences). Data were collected from 156 high school teachers in Mysore (India) on the Bonstingle's conceptualization of Deming's 14 points Total Quality Management (TQM) in Education (1992) and were analyzed using SPSS version 14.0. Analysis of Variance (ANOVA) was employed to find out the significance of difference between variables subscales. Significant difference was found between male and female teachers in the perception of total quality management. Female teachers had higher mean score than male teachers.

There is no significant difference between Arts and Sciences secondary school teachers in the perception of TQM in education.

Sangeeta et al. (2004) considers education system as a transformation process, comprising inputs of students, teachers, administrative staff, physical facilities and process. The processes include teaching, learning and administration. Outputs include examination results, employment, earnings and satisfaction. The study states that due to open competition, students are increasingly becoming customers and consumers and thus expected to pay a growing share of the costs of education. This leads to competitive forces that generate different programmers for different student groups. The conceptual problems include whether TQM in higher education should be people or problem oriented, difficulty in introducing the application and acceptance of TQM in higher education institutions which have not embraced tenets of TQM, team vs individual orientation towards TQM, maintaining the rate of innovation amongst others.

Srivanci (2004) in his article discusses about critical issues in implementing TQM in higher education which includes leadership, customer identification, cultural and organizational transformation. He believes that, unlike business organizations, chancellors and heads of higher educational institutions do not enjoy ultimate authority in hiring and firing of personnel and allocating resources. He continues by saying lack of necessary authority makes it difficult to deploy their values and goals through layers of higher education institutions. Deep rooted traditions dating back to centuries, a rigid departmental model, inter-departmental competition for resources, lack of market focus are the cultural and organizational reasons that makes it difficult to tune in with TQM transformation.

Jadoon and Jabeen (2006) presented a paper at the first International Conference on Assessing Quality in Higher Education, held at Lahore, Pakistan. The paper is based on the premise that there exists a positive relationship between human resource management and quality improvement aspects. Hence, an alignment between both is important for improving productivity and performance of an organization. To examine that relationship in the context of Punjab University, the logical and analytical framework is based on: (1) The concepts and tools of quality management are based on a comprehensive management philosophy popularly known as total quality management, which affects every aspect of organization, (2) The strategy and processes of human resource management are critical to the success of quality management initiatives. This means that traditional and bureaucratic type of system of managing people needs to be drastically changed, (3) Quality oriented human resource systems ensure the selection, development, motivation and retention of employees who are competent and willing to work in a team environment at all levels of organization, (4) Human resources management affects and is affected by organizational culture, (5) Quality initiatives and processes will be sustainable only if they are supported by a system wide organizational development and cultural change, and (6) Cultural change means change of attitudes and values in organizations as well as in society, which is undoubtedly a slow process.

Venkatraman, Sitalakshmi (2007) has written an article on "A Framework for Implementing TQM in Higher Education Programs". The proposed TQM framework with six core quality elements encompassing the seven-step course evaluation process flow provides a systematic guideline for an effective and efficient implementation of TQM in higher education. The paper fulfils the need for a systematic, feasible and cost-effective TQM framework for higher education. The new seven-step course evaluation process flow offers a practical guidance for academics to implement TQM in higher education programs.

Manivannan, M. and Premila, K. S. (2009) conducted research on "Application of Principles of Total Quality Management (TQM) in Teacher Education Institutions". The findings focus on the strong and weak areas of various teacher education institutions according to the quality indicators. The study recommends further strengthening of quality indicators, which are already strong, and the revamping of weaker quality indicators. It is also recommended that institutions should adhere to the quality standards set by national and international assessment and accreditation bodies. In conclusion, the global scenario expects skilled teachers to produce students with a versatile personality for which teacher education should be strengthened.

Murad and Rajesh (2009) studied status of higher education and emergent needs to enhance the quality of higher education. The objectives of the study were: to assess the quality and social relevance of higher education imparted in developing nations which remain quite low and deteriorating due to paucity of funds, to assess whether Total Quality Management (TQM) should be unavoidably common factor that will shape the strategies of higher educational institutions in a same manner, to find out if the development of higher education is correlated with the economic development, and to assess the study on the feasibility of different strategies for TQM in higher education. It was found that quality of education takes into account external environment in which institutions operate: internal environment where teaching learning takes place and home environment of learners. The systems approach to education comprises inputs, processes and outputs – all encompassed in an arbitrary boundary and the environment.

Satish, (2009) examines the role of quality management concepts towards enhancing classroom learning. The article talks about cooperative learning and how it can enhance the learning process among students as the teaching shifts from 'teacher oriented' to 'student oriented'. Collected data were analyzed using factor analysis to arrive at specific focus areas to improve learning. It was found that specific quality management concepts can assist towards increased classroom learning for students. This research broadened the scope of the applicability of quality management tools for enhanced students learning across varied cultural settings.

Arshad, Ahmad and Asaf (2010) conducted another research, a comprehensive case study of the University College of Education Chiniot, Punjab (Pakistan) with reference to Total Quality Management. The entire population, comprising 1 principal, 20 teachers and 120 students of B.Ed. class of this college, was selected as the sample of the study. The data regarding total quality management were collected through data sheet and three types of questionnaires. Responses were shown in simple percentage form.

The study found that most of the facilities were present in the institution, though they were not properly used. The Principal and the majority of the teachers and the students agreed that most of the aspects of total quality were neglected or not implemented in the college. The total involvement of stakeholders, basic facilities and teaching materials produced a satisfactory academic environment to get better examination results. However, the academic environment was not satisfactory for the Total Quality Management of this teacher training programme. The target of the traditional system is the examination results, not the specific competencies or skills of the students.

Doman, Mark S. (2010) has conducted a case study on "A New Lean Paradigm in Higher Education". This case study found that a small group of undergraduate students can quickly learn basic lean principles, tools and practices, and reinforce that learning by applying them in a team effort to significantly improve the administrative process of a university. The study found that with the changing higher education environment, where efficiency and effectiveness have become more imperative due to increase in budget and stiff competition, students can play a major role in the improvement of university administrative processes and also gain new knowledge and skills that are highly valued in the industry. This case study confirms an opportunity for universities to create a valuable learning experience for their undergraduate students, by involving them in improving the administrative processes of the university.

Flumerfelt, Shannon, Banachowski, Michael (2010), conducted a study on 'Understanding Leadership Paradigms for Improvement in Higher Education'. The study identifies six highly ranked, and seven highly associated leadership paradigms of concern. The one paradigm that was most highly ranked and most highly associated is confronting ambiguity. The findings highlight that improving leadership paradigms is important. The implications are limited to the higher education respondents' organizations. However, the results of the study provide some insight into the impact of leadership paradigms on improvement work in these higher education settings, where an average of 5.6 paradigms of concern and 114 paired associations were selected.

Kumaradas, M (2010) has conducted a study on the managerial skills of the Principals of colleges of education as perceived by teacher educators in Kerala State at Manonmaniam Sundaranar University. The study found a significant difference in the managerial skills and the dimensions of the Principals of colleges of education as perceived by male and female teacher educators in the state. It was observed that that was no significant difference in the managerial skills and the dimensions of the principals of colleges of education as perceived by teacher educators in the state with reference to locality, nature of institution, subject handled qualification, age, salary, publications and extracurricular activities. But there was significant difference in managerial skills – coercive autocracy dimension – of the Principals of colleges of education in Kerala as perceived by rural college teachers and urban college teachers in colleges of education in the state activities.

Chowdhary, (2012) in his paper talks about how the higher education sector characterized by diversity, students and course profiles are different and how universities can help to develop students with distinct characteristics and attributes. Universities are required to work in developing employability skills in their students by providing academic staff with relevant support and resources, integrating these skills into curriculum and course design, providing students with work placements and exposure to professional settings and providing advice and guidance through career services. The article also focusses on the importance of strategies related to programs so that employment skills can be formulated and monitored religiously.

Han (2012) talks about the challenge that the education environment faces today, which is to ensure that the quality of teaching and learning is maintained. One possible path for improving the quality of education lies in the application of the ideas of Total Quality Management (TQM) to the teaching and learning (T&L) process. Employing these TQM quality attributes in the education context creates value for educational institutions, employers and students. This paper focuses on the limited application areas of specific key components of TQM methods/tools in managing, scrutinizing and enhancing the quality of teaching and learning practices in the classroom environment.

Stukalina (2012) has researched on how to prepare students for productive and satisfying careers in the knowledge-based economy: creating a more efficient educational environment. The article talks about how globalization poses new challenges to higher education institutions. The main concern for educators is to provide their graduates with an extensive assortment of skills required for the new knowledge-based economy. To successfully address the emerging challenges, education managers have to create an efficient educational environment for providing a sustaining learning process. The integrated educational environment, where students have an opportunity to develop their creative potential, is an efficient means of preparing students for productive and satisfying careers in the knowledge-based economy. Realizing the importance of strategy, educational managers employ a variety of management practices.

Arshad (2003) researched on the attitude of teachers of higher education towards their profession. The purpose of conducting this study was to examine the attitudes of the teachers of higher education towards their profession. All the universities of Rawalpindi and Islamabad were included for the research study. The following conclusions were drawn: i) Teachers accepted challenges and extra workload if they received extra financial reward, ii) Most of the teachers tried in personal capacity to improve their knowledge and skills, iii) Teachers were helpful and approachable to their students and gave them spare time for guidance, iv) In order to have more respect and status in society, they wanted more incentives and facilities from the government and universities, v) Majority of the teachers discouraged and insulted students in front of the whole class due to lack of their maturity level, vi) The teachers showed their willingness to give relevant information to the students, vii) In general, the teachers were more keen to complete the syllabus rather than learning and attaining knowledge by students.

Hamidullah (2004) conducted a study on "Comparison of the quality of higher education in public and private sector institutions in Pakistan". The objectives of the study were to compare the quality of staff, quality of student, quality of infrastructure of higher education in public and private institutions. The sample of study included twenty universities/ degree awarding institutions, ten each from public and private sectors. The major findings of the study were that the teachers in private sector were more confident and competent than those in the public sector; the quality of students was better in private sector than in public sector; and private sector universities were far better than the public sector. However, the infrastructural facilities like playgrounds, common rooms, cafeteria, hostels, dispensaries and transport facilities were much better in the public sector universities. Regarding the quality of management, both sectors were weak.

The study focused on the analysis of examination system, teachers' attitude and factors affecting the development of higher education. It was observed that student's access to higher education is limited. The quality is low in the fields of academic, administration and research. The examination system moves around marks and selected questions are repeated successively. There is no proper system of training university teachers and students. Parents were not satisfied with the standard of teaching in the public sector. Thus, the private sector universities were considered to be better than the public universities.

Shirazi (2004) studied the analysis of examination system at university level in Pakistan. The major objectives of the study were: (1) to identify the defects of the present system of examination in Pakistan; (2) to discuss the merits and demerits of external and internal evaluation; (3) to determine the impact of examination system on teaching-learning process; and (4) to make recommendations for the improvement of examination system. The population of the study was all the working university teachers and experts of examination system. The university students were also included in the population. Eight universities were randomly selected as sample. 120 university teachers, 160 students and 45 examination experts were included in the sample. Three questionnaires were developed for collection of data. After validation of questionnaires, the same were administered. Data collected were tabulated, analyzed and interpreted by using Chi-Square. It was found that (a) examination enhances the command on subject in the teachers and they try to improve their instructions to meet the desired standards, (b) the examination system moves around the marks, (c) in the internal system the whole syllabus is covered in time. There are lesser chances of mal-practices in this type of examination, and (d) the pet selected questions were repeated in every examination. On the basis of conclusions, recommendations were made for the creation of efficient machinery for supervision, replacement of external examination with internal, continuous internal evaluation and maintenance of integrity of such evaluations, introduction of central marking system and question/item bank.

Madu and Kuei (1993) discussed the dimensions of quality teaching in higher educational institutions. They studied the difference between Total Quality Assurance and Total Quality Management, and recommended the changes to be made in colleges and universities in order to improve the quality of teaching.

Narula (2000) conducted a research entitled "Effective teaching in Higher Education". The major objectives of the study were to measure job performance of teachers on the basis of (a) quality of academic inputs in the teaching and learning processes; (b) job performance of teachers and financial performance of the two sample universities, namely Jawahar Lal Nehru University (JNU) and Jamia Millia Islamia (JMI). The major findings of the study were: in both the universities the mode of imparting knowledge was according to their missions and objectives; the hypothesis that the greater the level of qualification of teachers, the better would be quality of students was not supported; and teachers were working according to the mission, objectives and key inputs provided to them through the universities.

According to the study, there was wastage of nearly half of the resources and the overall efficiency of teaching faculty showed that none of the departments/teachers had completed their expected work load. The teachers' duty was confined only to traditional classroom teaching. The suggestions given were to improve academic standard and job performance of teachers, universities to be funded as teaching institutions, yearly exams be replaced by continuous assessment, facilities to teachers be expanded, and cost per student be lowered without affecting the quality and computerization of all the records of the university.

In his book Mukhopadhyay (2005) contends that a partisan or fragmented way of looking at quality in any academic sector is neither desirable nor feasible, for an action in one area sets out a chain of reactions in several other areas of management of an educational institution.

Sallis (2009) states that TQM is a philosophy and a methodology that is widely being used in business and increasingly in education to manage change or other processes. With the pressure for change and quality in education never more acute, this book provides an opportunity for readers in education to acquaint themselves with TQM.

Thapa, (2011) opines that Total Quality Management (TQM) is the latest in a parade of models, recipes, programs, frameworks, and slogans for guiding academic reform. It provides a tool to help ensure this quality. The management in TQM means that everyone is a manager of his/her own responsibilities, irrespective of status, position or role. Information and technologies have brought sea level changes in education and have therefore changed the interpretation of the term quality. TQM advocates that everything and everybody in the organization is involved in the academic institutions for continuous improvement. As it is applied to education, TQM faces new challenges due to diversity in nature of students and educators, large and multileveled classrooms, technological advances and new paradigms in educational content and delivery. Despite these issues education must maintain quality across classrooms, schools and institutions. This article highlights the need of TQM to improve the overall quality of education in Nepal.

Conclusion

By reviewing earlier researches, it is found that Total Quality Management can be a powerful tool in the educational setting even though it is developed with manufacturing processes in mind. The key elements of a successful implementation are: (1) gain the support of everyone in the chain of supervision, (2) identify your students, and (3) focus on refining the process. The final result will be a more efficient operation and a teamwork attitude rather than an 'us versus them' attitude between teaching, non-teaching staff and students.

The quality of education will improve when administrators, teachers, staff, and school board members develop new attitudes that focus on leadership, teamwork, cooperation, accountability and recognition. Therefore, quality is vital for education for improving existing set up, internal systems and procedure and teaching-learning environment.

Quality is creating an environment where educators, parents, government officials, community representatives and business leaders can work together to provide students with the resources they need to meet current and future academic, business, and societal challenges.

Hence, Total Quality Management as a necessary element always has a direct influence on human improvement. It can also lead to high commitment and spirit in work environment. Everyone in the teacher education institutions should be encouraged towards positive aspect of Total Quality Management and to take active participation to render quality education. Total Quality Management applied to higher education should be modified to fully recognize some unique aspects of education, *viz* education is a service industry with no visible, tangible "product".

6

Re-Defining Quality

Role of Madrasa Education System

K. Mohammed Basheer

The ultimate aim of education is preservation, transmission and transformation of culture. Madrasa education system is the largest non-formal education network in India with more than 2 lakhs Madrasas and 10 lakhs teachers. It has played a vital role in the field of inclusive education by providing education to the poor section of the society and in the development of Muslim education. Quality enhancement process was continuously progressing in the field of Madrasa education since the inception of the organized Islamic education system by Nizam-ul-Mulk Tusi (AD 1018-1092), who is considered to be the father of the Islamic public education system.

In India the quality enhancement efforts was initiated by the Mughal ruler Aurangazeb through the *Firanghi Mahal* by the scholar Mulla Nizamuddeen, the founder of *Dars-e-Nizami.* The Calcutta Madrasa (AD 1781) under the regime of Warren Hasting, the then British Governor, underwent various creative reforms. There came into being the *Darul Uloom Daeoband, Mazharul Uloom Saharenpoor* (1866) and *Darul Uloom Nadwathl Ulama* (AD 1894).

Government of India also extended needy support to the development of Madrasa education by providing funds through different minority schemes like 'Scheme for Providing Quality Education in Madrasa' (SPQEM), which was formerly known as 'Madrasa Modernization Scheme', launched in 1993-94. Indoctrination of value education as the major aim of madrasa, should be more concentrated over affective domain rather than cognitive and psychomotor domains of learning. For attaining this aim, varieties of teaching-learning experiences should be provided to the learners at the time of class room interaction. Unfortunately, most of the madrasas are following the traditional 'chalk and talk' system of instruction.

The present study will talk about the ways and means of quality enhancement of madrasa education system with the implementation of curriculum revision, teacher empowerment programmes, innovative instructional strategies, adoption of ICT in the learning process, etc.

The quality of a nation depends on the quality of its citizens; the quality of its citizens depends more than any other feature on the quality of education. As we know, the quality of education mostly depends upon the quality of teachers. The quality of teacher depends upon the quality of education and training s/he got. This is the reason behind the statement of Education Commission of India (1964-66): "No people can rise above the level of its teachers".

Globalization is consistently on its march and technology has brought the world closer. Knowledge has been recognized as the key driving force in the 21st century. India's ability to emerge as a globally competitive player has substantially depended on the management of its knowledge resources. However, under the impact of globalization, the educational system has been undergoing continuous change as a consequence of new international agreements, redefinition of the trade and intellectual property right conditions, innovations in information and communications, application of new technologies and the structural changes in labour market.

Madrasa is a traditional religious educational institution of Muslims. Literally it means a place where Dars (lesson) is given to the students. The history of Madrasa system of education began from the Masjid, in *Masjid al Nabavi* (Prophet's Masjid), wherein there was a platform called *al-Suffa* which was reserved for the learned people, known as *Ashab-al-Suffa*. So *al-Suffa* is the first Madrasa of Islamic Tradition.

The modern madrasa system originated in Eastern Iran in the tenth century and spread to major urban centers throughout the Middle East by the late eleventh century. The architect of the madrasa as a state-sponsored institution of higher education was Nizam-al-Mulk (died 1092 C.E.), the Prime Minister of the Seljuk empire. These residential colleges were designed by the ruling elite both as a training ground for state bureaucrats and as a Sunni Islam response to the propaganda of Ismaili Shi?ism wat al-Azhar, the theological learning center founded by the Fatimid dynasty in Cairo in 969 C.E. As part of Sunni Muslim religio-political agenda, the madrasas spread throughout the Islamic world. The madrasa system augmented already extant mosque-centered training sites for the study of religion and law. Unlike these centers, the madrasa forged links between the *ulama,* the religious scholars who directed Islamic education, and the ruling government authorities whose financial support made their control of the madrasa possible.

The madrasa system of education was linked to the mosque, which traditionally had been the place of instruction for Muslims in the Quran and the Hadith – the traditions that preserved the words and deeds of the Prophet Muhammad. The madrasa combined the site for education with student residences. Libraries and sometimes hospitals were adjoined to the madrasas. Financial support for the educational institutions was generated by the state in the form of a charitable endowment called *waqf.* The revenue on these endowments was spent on the maintenance of the buildings, stipend to students, and fee to the and instructors.

The various subjects of learning at the madrasa included the Quranic tradition, Arabic language, theology, arithmetic, geometry, astronomy and, often, medicine. The study of Islamic law *(sharia)* provided the core of the madrasa's rigorous curriculum. Initially, madrasas were founded to provide specialized instruction in one of the four Sunni legal schools. At a later stage, legal instruction in one or more of the Sunni legal schools were being offered in a single madrasa. The method of instruction relied heavily on memorization of the Quran and as many traditions as possible (Denise A Spellberg, 2009).

The word Madrasa includes four types of Islamic educational institutions prevailing all over the globe: *(i) Maktab, (ii) Madrasa,(iii) Darul Uloom,* and *(iv) Darul Qur'an.*

Maktab is a primary centre which functions in a Masjid or in a modest building and provides instruction in religious as well as some secular subjects. Madrasa is an institution that provides education generally up to senior secondary level. Darul Ulooms are institutions of higher learning providing instruction up to post graduation and specialization levels. Darul Quran are those madrasas that specialize in *Hifz* and *Thajwid* (memorizing the Glorious Qur'an and learning the art of reciting).

Madrasa has played a vital role in education of the Muslims. It has helped them to preserve their identity as Muslims. Through the Madrasas, Muslims not only managed to protect their Islamic identity but also influenced the Indian culture to a great extent and synthesised the Indo-Islamic culture. The Madrasa made great contribution during the Indian freedom struggle. From 1857 to 1947 they never compromised with the British rule and always upheld the torch of freedom. Madrasas were like NGOs promoting education among people. Monarchs as well as masses were educated in the Madrasas in the yesteryears. And even today Madrasa education in India plays a vital role in educating lakhs of Muslim children.

The importance of Madrasas lies in their potential to make education available to the underprivileged section of the society. The special characteristic of Madrasa is that it provides free education, free boarding and free books to its students. In contrast to the Madrasa system, the

Government of India has not been able to provide children free and compulsory education, even after the landmark legislation of RTE, 2009. Thus, the contribution of the Madrasas in the field of literary and academic work cannot be ignored.

Madrasa Education in India

Although no regular census of madrasa has ever been taken, government sources estimate that there are approximately 2 lakhs of such institutions in India. Every Madrasa follows its own pattern in educational structure and curricula. There is no uniformity with regard to subjects, books, specializations, or duration of various degrees. Its nature, structure, management, curriculum and degrees vary from state to state. Thus we need to understand the system of madrasa education in a wider sense.The community should be ready to make use of various minority schemes. The Madrasa modernization scheme, which was launched in 1993-94, has changed into Scheme for Providing Quality Education in Madrasa (SPQEM) and an amount of Rs. 500 crore was proposed for the scheme as per budget provision in the XII Five Year Plan. There are some schemes in Prime Minister's new 15 point programme for the welfare of Minorities. Maulana Azad Foundation has implemented many programs for the benefit of minorities.

Need for Quality Enhancement

The madrasas are standing amazingly in the floodlight of Globalization. Here we need immediate measures to transform the system of madrasa education to overcome the challenges of globalization. The only way is to enhance the quality of Madrasa education system. But the reform in the madrasa education system can be achieved only after taking the ulama into confidence.

Madrasas have been changing over time, although the pace and scope of these changes may not be as spectacular as some of us would wish. The syllabus of schools and universities keep upgrading/ modifying at the interval of every 5-7 years. The *dars-i-nizami*, syllabus of the madrasas has not been changed for last 3-4 centuries. There is need to modify Dars-i-Nizami madrasa syllabus, without altering its core subjects.

When we talk about reforming the madrasas we must keep in mind their basic goals and purpose. They are meant to train religious specialists and so reforms must be such that can help the madrasas better fulfill their purpose. Rather than the 'hard' sciences, we should be thinking in terms of incorporating the social sciences into the curriculum, along with basic

Mathematics and English. Teaching social sciences in the madrasas is important in order that the students can go on to interpret Islam in a socially and contextually relevant manner.

Employability and Skill Development

Ideally, although this is not always the case, one should choose to become an alim not for the sake of a job but as a religious calling. Imamat in a mosque or delivering sermons should not be a paid profession. It should be an honorary, voluntary thing. This is how it was in the distant past. For instance, Imam Abu Hanifa, whose school of law most South Asian Sunni Muslims follow, was not a professional alim—he earned his livelihood as a businessman. Today, however, the general feeling is that large sections of the ulama live off the donations of others. If one is dependent on others, how will one earn the respect due to him? The ulama can gain proper respect only when they are seen as providing benefits, in terms of proper leadership and guidance to others, rather than, as now, benefitting from them. For that, financial independence of the ulama is a must, including the introduction of vocational training in the madrasas. The reforms in madrasas aim to explore the development of new technologies that make madrasa students job-oriented. Knowledge of Information Communication Technology is inevitable in this globalized era. So there must be space for ICT in the curriculum as an effective learning aid. Vocational training should be included in the curriculum.

Paradigm Shift in Transaction Strategy

A thorough revision is needed in the instructional strategy for the upgradation of the madrasas. A shift from the age old method of comprehension and conversational competence is compulsory. Activity Centered Methods are highly useful in the class of jurisprudence. We are getting benefits from modern educational theories in our school classrooms. These strategies should be used in our madrasa system of education also. For this we should use new audio-visual methods, CDs, presentations, documentaries and so on.

Teacher Empowerment

As teachers play vital role in the education system, they should be adequately trained. Without appropriate training, they cannot do justice with the curriculum. Kerala is a role model in this regard. There is a Muallim Training Centre under Samastha Kerala Islamic Education Board, which runs 9200 madrasas and 300 higher Arabic Colleges. In addition to religious subjects, the Muallim Training Course curriculum includes English, History, Educational Administration, Organizational Training, Teaching methodology, Madrasa Internship Programme and Personality Development Training. The course is of two year duration and a person who completes matriculation along with Madrasa 7th class, can apply. In addition to that, different teaching-qualification tests are conducted, like Muallim Lower and Higher. 40 days in-service training course is also conducted by the Board. All the Arabic college students have to compulsorily undergo 40 days teacher's training. Institutes like these should be constituted throughout the length and breadth of the country. We could start with establishing a sort of central madrasa teachers' training institute, which could offer short-term courses, covering such areas as child psychology, pedagogy, and basic 'modern' subjects.

ODL System and E-Learning for Public Education

The booming of English medium schools eliminated the chances of religious studies for a majority of Muslim students. In order to compensate this, the possibilities of Open and Distant Learning System and E- Learning should be utilized. Each Madrasa has to cater to the students of its surroundings. In addition to providing scientifically and psychologically prepared study materials, weekly or monthly counseling sessions should be conducted. This will be also helpful for those who do not get the opportunity for primary religious education. The e-learning will particularly focus on the new generation.

Equivalency to the General Stream

Unlike the universities of the country, the madrasas are neither members of the Association of Indian Universities nor their degrees are recognized by it. Moreover, each university is an autonomous body and, hence, decisions of the Academic Council of a particular university do not have binding effect on others. That is why some universities like Aligarh Muslim University, Jamia Millia Islamia, New Delhi, etc recognize some degrees of a number of madrasas while other universities have no such provision. Jawahar Lal Nehru University also recognizes some madrasa degrees.

Utilization of State Schemes

The community should be ready to make use of various minority schemes. The Madrasa Modernization Scheme, which was launched in 1993-94, has changed into Scheme for Providing Quality Education in Madrasa (SPQEM) and an amount of Rs. 325 crore is proposed for the scheme as per budget provision in the XI Five Year Plan. There are some schemes in Prime Minister's New 15 Point Programme for the Welfare of Minorities. Moulana Azad Foundation has implemented many programs for the benefit of minorities.

Central Madrasa Education Board

Madrasa Education Board should be constituted not only in the states but also in the Centre. Some Madrasa Boards are well established and are working systematically, while they need to be constituted in other states. Without the Madrasa Boards, the problems of Madrasas like University Equivalency and Budget provisions, etc cannot be solved. The Central Madrasa Education Board Bill, which is under consideration in Parliament, should be passed after thorough discussions with Ulama.

Waqf for Madrasa Empowerment

The huge waqf property in India should be rightly utilized for the empowerment of Muslim education, as Prime Minister's high level committee led by Rajender Sachar Commission recommended. A number of Waqf lands and properties are misused and lost throughout the country. In this regard, a mass campaign against corruption needs to be organised by the Muslim Community. The Waqf property should be utilized for the rejuvenation of Madrasas in the globalized era.

Kerala Model of Madrasa Education

Kerala boasts of highest literacy rate in India. The Kerala Muslims, estimated around one fourth of the state's population, are the most well educated Muslim community in the country. The system of Islamic education in Kerala presents a considerable contrast to its counterparts in different states of India, who have been overtaken by a large and expanding network of reformed madrasas that have incorporated secular subjects and teaching methods to varying degrees. One of the major factors for the high literacy rate among Kerala's Muslims – who are among the most educated Muslim communities in India – is the vast network of educational institutions that Muslim community leaders have established across the state.

Religious education provisions for Muslims of Malabar can be divided into five distinct styles: 1. Othupalli are single teacher schools set up in neighborhood mosques, 2. Dars is the mosque centric residential learning system, 3. Madrasas are parallel to General School system from primary classes to senior secondary, functioning in the morning (from 1st to 12th standard), 4. Arabic colleges in which students studying both Islamic and Material subjects in residential campus, and 5. Islamic University affiliated to International Islamic Universities, provide research level courses.

There is no Madrasa Board in Kerala at Government level. 90 per cent of the Madrasas are affiliated to Samastha Kerala Islam Matha Vidhyabhyasa Board (SKIMVB). "The Community should provide basic Islamic instruction to all boys and girls in maktabs as in Kerala and rationalize the Madrasa system for quality education and for producing the Islamic scholars it needs. This, it can do on its own" (Syed Shahabudhddin, 2001).

Madrasa system prevailing in Kerala state is a highly effective machinery for imparting basic religious education to the growing generation upto plus two levels; which is run in a smooth manner with well defined aims and objectives supported by a well planned curriculum, syllabi and other tools required for an educational system in the modern period. It is designed as such that a student can pursue his religious studies together with modern education in schools. Though the students here are generally undergoing both types of learning simultaneously, they do not fall behind others in schools. Hence the Madrasa system of Kerala, through which almost every Muslim child passes upto adolescence, does not hinder in any way their achievements and progress in the field of modern education. On the other hand, this systematic religious education contributes to their all round development, adhering to moral values and ethics.

Samastha Kerala Islam Matha Vidhyabhyasa Board

To improve the condition of the Othupallis and Dars systems of education, one of the organizations namely Samastha Kerala Jamiyyathul Ulama (SKJU) started a madrasa board called Samastha Kerala Islam Matha Vidyabhyasa Board (All Kerala Muslim Educational Board) in 1951. The Board has 9636 (Dec, 2013) madrasas registered to their board in which 11,13,806 students are learning. They have one hundred thousand teachers working in these madrasas. The salary of the teachers and all expenses of the madrasas are met by the villages where these madrasas are situated. The Board takes care of the pension of the teachers when they retire and also deposits money in their welfare funds. The Board itself is funded by exam fees. Public Examinations are conducted at 5th, 7th, 10th, and 12th grade levels. The madrasas are co-educational. The Board also has 7 Master Trainers, 6 (Qari) Reciters, 5 Muballig

(Organizers), 107 madrasa inspectors who are constantly on the move and continuously check the quality of education being imparted in board affiliated madrasas. In recent years the Board has spread its wings and now it has 384 madrasas in Karnataka, 38 in Tamil Nadu, 12 in Andaman Islands, 11 in United Arab Emirates, 3 in Oman, and 4 in Malaysia. Board officials informed that their text books are being translated in Urdu but did not report any Urdu medium madrasa affiliated with the Board.

Various Teacher Empowerment Programmes

There are various provisions for the training of teachers comprising pre-service and in-service courses. The majority of teachers in Madrasas have passed out from the Arabic Colleges with degree/titles like Baqawi, Faizee, Darimi, Anwari, Rahmani, Asharafi, Yamani etc. Most of them are working in Madrasas. For preparing them for teaching, a special training of 40 days is given to them in the final year of their 8-10 years of study. Only those who have received teacher's training and Hizb training (Quran Recitation) are eligible for various welfare schemes by the teachers association, SKJM. There is a well equipped Mu alim Training Centre and provisions for on job training for In-service training and qualifying examinations like Lower, Higher, Hizb training.

Conclusion

Madrasas are one of the largest non formal education systems in India, with a wide network all over the country. However, they need to be strengthened with modern pedagogic practices in order to enhance and improve their quality to achieve inclusive education. The teachers of the madrasas too need to be trained academically to meet the challenges of the modern times.

The system of Madrasa education has come a long way since the early days of *Othupalli* system. It requires major changes to sustain itself in the present competitive environment. Kerala model of Madrasa is worth emulating not only in India but all over the world. (Huda, 2010).

Today, a growing number of Muslims in other parts of India, including several "ulamas" are advocating reforms in the Madrasa system, following the footsteps of their counterparts in Kerala (Sikand, 2004). Healthy practices for the development of quality culture in Madrasa education can be implemented through identification, implementation, institutionalisation, internalisation and dissemination of best practices.

7

Capacity Building of Muslim Minorities

Role of NIOS

Mohammad Hanif Ahmad

India is a country of diversities inhabited by various ethnic, cultural, linguistic and religious groups. The Indian Constitution defines the term 'minority' on the basis of two criteria, viz. religion and language. The National Commission for Minorities in India has identified Muslims, Christians, Sikhs, Buddhists and Parsees which constitute 18.8 per cent of the total population of the country as religious minorities, whilst Hindus are the majority group (according to the census of Government of India 2001). Among these, Muslims, the largest minority community in the country constituting 13.4 per cent of the population, are seriously lagging behind in terms of most of the human development indicators. While the perception of deprivation is widespread among Muslims, there has been no systematic effort since independence to analyze the condition of religious minorities in the country.

The development of any nation depends on its educational system and it is proved that education is the key to human progress and social change. Education is a powerful tool for empowerment of individual. It is one of the most powerful factors for political, social, economic or spiritual development of individuals and communities. It helps individuals to acquire the confidence and capability to match the levels of those who are in the mainstream society and helps in developing the individual and community their own capacities, inherent strengths to shape their lives, and thus enhances the inner strength – intellectual, political, social and economic – against oppression, exclusion and discrimination.

Empowerment is the enhancement of the political, social, economic or spiritual strength of individuals and communities. Empowerment envelops developing and building capacities of individuals and communities to make them part of the mainstream society. Education is the means by which societies are known in history, to grow out of oppression to democratic participation and involvement. It is a powerful tool for the empowerment of individual. It is intrinsic to human personality. It carries both intrinsic as well as instrumental values.

Importance of Education in Islam

According to First Report on Religion, Census of India 2001, Lakshwadeep recorded the highest proportion of Muslims: a staggering 95 per cent followed by Jammu and Kashmir, Assam, West Bengal, Kerala, Uttar Pradesh, Bihar, Jharkhand, Karnataka and Delhi, making it to the list of top ten. In recent times, the question of Muslims' educational backwardness has been an important element of political and social rhetoric in India. Although Muslims are not alone in reflecting educational backwardness, yet recent statistics show that they are one of the most backward communities in the field of education and literacy in the country. This fact is, no doubt, astonishing for those who know that the very first declaration of the Qur'an – 'IQRA' (to read) is about 'education'. And the Prophet of Islam, Mohammad (SAWS) termed education as basic obligation for every individual – male and female – the very first time in the history of mankind, in 610 (AD).

Muslims' Contributions towards Indian Education

Education in India, before the advent of Islam, was considered to be the monopoly of Brahmins. They excluded the lower class people to acquire knowledge because they thought themselves to be superior. There were mass revolts against this notion resulting in the shape of Buddhism and Jainism, but soon these religions grew weaker and the previous condition returned. Although none can deny the glory of Nalanda and Taxila universities of India, the fact cannot be over looked that the common people were always deprived of education in early Hindu periods. When Islam came to India, it had to fight this mindset that prevailed. Ultimately, due to the efforts of Muslim rulers every citizen of the country, whether Muslim or Hindu, man or woman, rich or poor, was enshrined with the right to acquire knowledge.

Problems of Post Colonial Indian Muslim

The current situation of Indian Muslims has alarmingly deteriorated despite the fact that they make up nearly 15 percent of the national population and have a glorious history of several centuries of enlightened rule that put India firmly on the world map, and are the second largest Muslim community in the world today. Although, thev are improving day by day for the last two decades and are learning to stand on their own feet, they have been deliberately placed in harsh social, educational and political conditions, ever since the historic defeat of Indians in 1857 Revolt against the British till this day. For instance, the number and percentage of Muslims in all government sectors of India has steadily declined from 31 percent in early 1947 to only 2.3 percent in 2001. The ruling class puts the blame on the Muslims, while the facts are different in view of the gradual isolating trend imposed on the community. A graphic picture of Muslim deprivation also emerges from the studies done in recent years by the National Council of Applied Economic Research (NCAER). The findings have been summed up in two sentences: "Muslims in India have a poor human development status. Widespread illiteracy, low income, irregular employment, implying thereby a high incidence of poverty is all pervasive among the Muslims." To me, the study of the NCAER fails to penetrate deep into the depth of these problems; it misrepresents facts and falsifies perceptions, which is a new hindrance towards accurate diagnosis of real problems.

Major Problems of Indian Muslims

There are some major problems which are real obstacles in the educational, economic and socio-political asspirations of the Muslimcommunity:

1. *Absence of true Muslim leadership from the post-partition period till today*: The present Muslim leadership is either a puppet of the leading parties or it has no knowledge of the problems the Muslim community is actually facing in India. In the post 1947 India, the majority of the Muslim politicians have proved to be ineffective by the community which has voted them to power.

Maulana Abul Kalam Azad's famous address to the Muslims of Delhi on October 23, 1947 set a new political trend for Indian Muslims. The occasion demanded leadership of a bruised and bewildered community; the Maulana chose to lace his advice with taunt and reproach, a very different approach from the one he had taken in his presidential address to the Ramgarh session of the Indian National Congress in 1940. His bitterness over the turn of events, as he penned down in his book 'India wins Freedom' is understandable. The painful fact remains that he chose not to lead when leadership was most needed for the Muslim community.

2. *Lack of security:* Riots, communal violence have become a sad reality of India's life and the majority of the victims of riots in India have been Muslims. The political milieu in the post independence and partition period made Muslims feel so demoralized that they could not dare to ask as to why the doors of defence forces were barred for them under the

policy directions of the Nehru Government. The Muslim Civil Servants similarly were not to be appointed on sensitive posts and extra caution had to be used for issuing passports to them.

3. *Poverty*: Poverty and and lack of genuine financial recourses are hampering socio-educational development of the community at every step.

4. Most painful problem of Muslim Indians is the discriminatory attitudes of the majority community towards them in all walks of life.

The Concept and Definition of Open and Distance Learning (ODL)

ODL is a way of providing learning opportunities that is characterized by the separation of teacher and learner in time or place, or both time and place. It is a type of learning that is certified in some way by an institution or agency and uses a variety of media, including print and electronic. There is a two-way communication that allow learners and tutors to interact, occasionally even face-to-face. There is a specialised division of labour in the production and delivery of courses. The characteristics of ODL are as under:

(a) Separation of teacher and learner in time or place or in both time and place. It is institutional accreditation, wherein learning is accredited or certified by some institution or agency.

(b) Use of mixed-media, including print, radio and television broadcasts, video and audio cassettes, computer-based learning and telecommunications.

(c) Two-way communication for learners and tutors, which is different from passive receipt of broadcast signals. Communication can be synchronous or asynchronous.

(d) Possibility of face-to-face meetings for tutorials, learner–learner interaction, library study and laboratory or practice sessions.

(e) Use of industrialised processes in large-scale open and distance learning operations. Labour is divided and tasks are assigned to various staff who work together in development teams.

Vocational Education

Vocational education consists basically of practical courses through which one gains skills and experience directly linked to a career in future. It helps students to be skilled and in turn, offers better employment opportunities. These trainings are parallel to the other conventional courses of study (like B.Sc., M.Sc. etc.). Time management and meeting deadlines play an important role while studying any vocational course.

During their studies, the students normally produce a portfolio of evidence (plans, reports, drawings, videos, placements), which is taken as a demonstration of students' capabilities for a job. After completing their studies, students are often offered placements in jobs.

Vocational trainings, in a way, give students some work related experiences that many employers look for. According to a National Sample Survey Organization (NSSO) Report (No. 517, 61/10/03), two types of vocational trainings are available in India: a) Formal, b) Non-formal. Formal vocational training follows a structured training program and leads to certificates, diplomas or degrees, recognized by State/Central Government, Public Sector and other reputed concerns. Non-formal vocational training helps in acquiring some marketable expertise, which enables a person to carry out her/his ancestral trade or occupation. Through such non-formal vocational training, a person receives vocational training through 'hereditary' sources. Non-formal vocational trainings are also received through 'other sources'. In such cases training received by a person to pursue a vocation, is not ancestral and is different from the trade or occupation of his/her ancestor.

Capacity Building Definition and Concept

Community Capacity building, also referred to as capacity development, is a conceptual approach to development that focuses on understanding the obstacles that inhibit people, governments, international organizations and non-governmental organizations from realizing their developmental goals while enhancing the abilities that will allow them to achieve measurable and sustainable results.

> "A Planned development of (or increase in) knowledge, output rate, management, skills, other capabilities of an organization through acquisition, incentives, technology, and/or training."

NIOS: A Brief Introduction of National Institute of Open Schooling

A mighty banyan tree that provides shade and shelter to thousands grows from a humble seed. Similarly, NIOS (National Institute of Open Schooling) has grown from a modest project in the Central Board of Secondary Education to an institute of national importance, catering to the educational needs of disadvantaged, or the masses that are unable to access formal school education due to various reasons. Govt. of India has always given due importance to education, and has made sincere efforts towards providing quality school education to all, particularly for lower middle class and poor families. It is necessary to design, create and establish alternative educational provisions for such prospective learners. As a result of experimentation and initiatives in Open and Distance Learning (ODL) the open schooling systems emerged as an alternative system.

NIOS, an "Open Schooling Institute", was started as a project with in-built flexibilities by the Central Board of Secondary Education (CBSE) in 1979. In 1986, the National Policy on Education suggested strengthening of Open School System by extending open learning facilities in a phased manner at secondary level all over the country as an independent system with its own curriculum and examination, leading to certification. Consequently, the Ministry of Human Resource Development (MHRD), Government of India set up the National Open School (NOS) in November 1989. The pilot project of CBSE on Open School was amalgamated with NIOS through a Resolution (No. F.5-24/90 Sch.3, dated 14 September 1990, published in the Gazette of India on 20 October 1990). The National Open School (NOS) was vested with the authority to register, examine and certify students registered with it up to pre-degree level courses. In July 2002, the Ministry of Human Resource Development amended the nomenclature of the organization from the National Institute of Open Schooling (NIOS) with a mission to provide relevant continuing education at school stage, up to pre-degree level through Open Learning system to prioritize client groups as an alternative to formal system, in pursuance of the normative national policy documents and in response to the need assessments of the people, and through it to make its share of contribution to universalisation of education, greater equity and justice in society, and the evolution of a learning society.

Main Features of NIOS

The National Institute of Open Schooling (NIOS) provides opportunities to interested learners by making available several courses/programmes of study through open and distance learning (ODL) mode. It provides for Open Basic Education (OBE) Programme for Children (upto 14 years), adolescents and adults at A, B and C levels that are equivalent to classes III, V and VIII of the formal school system respectively. It also provides for Secondary Education Courses, Senior Secondary Education Courses, Vocational Education Courses/Programmes and Life Enrichment Programmes.

NIOS provides flexibility in the choice of subjects/courses, pace of learning, and transfer of credits from CBSE, CISCE (Council for Indian School Certificate Education), various Board of School Education and State Open Schools to enable learner's continuation. A learner is allowed as many as nine chances to appear in public examinations spread over a period of five years. The credits gained are accumulated till the learner clears required credits for certification. The learning strategies include learning through printed self-learning material, audio and video programmes, participation in personal contact programmes (PCP), and Tutor Marked Assignments (TMA). Enrichment is also provided to the learners through the half yearly magazine "Open Learning". The Study Material is made available in English, Hindi and Urdu mediums. The On-Demand Examination System (ODES) is in operation at Secondary and Senior Secondary stage. NIOS offers 27 subjects in seven mediums (Hindi, English, Urdu, Marathi, Telugu, Gujarati, and Malayalam) for Secondary Examinations and 24 subjects in Hindi, English and Urdu mediums for Senior Secondary Examinations. In addition there is provision for the learners to take 1 out of 10 vocational subjects at Secondary stage and 1 out of 20 vocational subjects at Sr. Secondary stage in combination with academic subjects.

Vocational Education Courses are imparted through a network of Accredited Vocational Institutes for imparting skill based training to its learners. The existing institutions like ITIs, Jan Shikshan Sansthans, Krishi Vigyan Kendras, Schools, Colleges, District Institutes of Education and Training (DIETs), Universities, Paramedical Training Centres, NGOs and several other Voluntary Agencies are partnering with NIOS in imparting Vocational Education.

Admission to vocational education courses of NIOS is open round the year. During the year 2011-12, admission in various courses was done through a network of about sixteen hundred AVIs all over India. The NIOS programmes pay special attention towards requirements of the first generation learners, physically, mentally and visually challenged learners and those from disadvantaged sections of the society. NIOS is providing the facility of On-Line Registration for admission and examinations under NIOS Online. The NIOS Online is aimed at increasing educational access through the use of technology.

Role of NIOS in Capacity Building and Promoting Education of Muslim Minorities

The objective of capacity building programmes is to develop effective manpower resources for open schooling system, because nurturing the personnel associated with open schooling is as important as nurturing the learners of open schools. To reach out to the minority communities of the society, a one day meeting was held under the Chairmanship of Mr M.C. Pant, the then chairman of NIOS, at Indore on 13th November 2006. Twenty representatives of minority communities from Indore attended the meeting. The Chairman NIOS highlighted various employment generation programmes being offered by NIOS under its vocational educational programme. Another meeting of Project Co-ordinators of NIOS and the local community leaders of Orissa for Minority Education Programme of NIOS was held on 29th January, 2007 at Puri. Mr M A A Fatmi, Minister of State, MHRD presided over the meeting, Prof. Najma Akhter of NUEPA, Mr. Devendra C. Mishra, Commissioner, Madrasa Education, and Mr. D S Bist, Secretary, NIOS were the prominent participants. The Chairman, NIOS emphasized the need for education of minorities and suggested that the Project Co-ordinators should identify the unreached areas and contact the Madrasas of their region for effective implementation of various programmes.

In another attempt, mass sensitization programmes were organized by the minority education cell of NIOS. The gathering informed about various academic /vocational programmes offered by NIOS and the benefits of distance learning.

Minority Cell for Capacity Building

The Minority Cell was created in 2006 to look after problems of minority communities. The cell plays an important and vital role for implementation of NPE 1986, and Programme of Action (POA) 1992. It is making efforts to bring *out of school* Muslim children within the fold of education through alternative schooling by accreditation of Maktabs and Madarsa. The Minority Cell has therefore become a major instrument of policy intervention for Government of India for improving educational access of Muslim Minorities at school level in the light of the recommendations of Sachar Committee and Prime Minister's 15 Point Programme.

The Minority Cell of NIOS grants accreditation on relaxed norms, especially developed for Minority Institutions. This has helped to link traditional educational institutions of Muslims like Madrasas, Maktabs and Darul-Ul-Uloom into mainstream education. The Minority cell conducts Advocacy programmes for grant of accreditation and for minority education:

- Centrally Sponsored Scheme for Providing Quality Education in Madrasas (SPQEM)
- Project HUNAR for Muslim Girls in Bihar
- Project HUNAR Phase II
- Project HUNAR Delhi

Centrally Sponsored Scheme for Providing Quality Education in Madrasas (SPQEM)

National policy on Education (NPE) has adopted the concept of national system of education, which means inclusion of all children for the purpose of quality education up to certain level/class, irrespective of caste, creed, language or sex. The national policy on education commits itself to provide all possible means for the upliftment of the educationally backward minorities. In order to provide them with access to education in modern subjects, the Central Government has been implementing the Area Intensive and Madarsa Modernisation Scheme. The National Monitoring Committee for Minorities Education (NMCME) was constituted in 2004 to look into all aspects of education of minorities. The Expert Committee has suggested that the madarsas should be provided a linkage with the National Institute of Open Schooling (NIOS) to provide for certification of academic levels, linkage with vocational education, improving the quality of education in modern subjects.

The objective of the scheme is to encourage traditional institutes like Madarsas and Maktabs to introduce Science, Mathematics, Social Studies, Hindi and English in their curriculum (by giving financial assistance). However, the process of modernization of traditional madarsas and maktabs will be voluntary. Maktabs/Madarsas/Dar-ul-uloons can opt to become accredited study centers of the National Institute of Open Schooling for offering Senior Secondary level programmes as well. The scheme will also seek to provide opportunities for vocational training of children studying in madrasas, who wish to enter the job market. This scheme will also encourage entrepreneurship.

The SPQEM is a demand driven scheme. It will endeavour to cover a total of about 4,500-6,000 Madrasas and provide honorarium to about 13,500-18000 teachers in Madrasas all over the country during the 11th plan period. Each full time graduate teacher teaching Science, Mathematics, Social Studies, Languages, Computer Application and Science, will be paid salary for 12 months @ Rs 6000/-p.m. For strengthening the libraries / book banks at primary / middle/ secondary and senior secondary level,s one time assistance upto Rs.50, 000/-followed by an annual grant of Rs.5,000/- will be provided to each madrasa. For purchase of Maths and Science kits, a grant up to a maximum amount of Rs.15000/- will be provided. Financial assistance for establishment of science/computer labs in Madrasas at the Secondary/Sr. Secondary levels, a maximum of Rs.10,000 will be provided. Financial assistance will be provided to meet registration fees, examination fees and cost of study materials supplied by the National Institute of Open Schooling (NIOS) up to 100 per cent for each student opting to study through NIOS at Secondary and Senior Secondary levels. Madrasas can also opt for vocational courses offered by NIOS after fulfilling the norms and standard set by NIOS.

Madarsas which have been in existence at least for three years and registered under Central or State Government Acts or Madarsa or with Wakf Boards or NIOS shall be eligible to apply for assistance under this programme. All madarsas opting to be covered by distance education mode and availing of government grant will need to be accredited with the NIOS. Madarsas applying for financial assistance under the scheme to the State Government would have to provide documentary evidence of their affiliation /accreditation to the State Madarsa Boards/NIOS. The madarsas would for this purpose send an application for accreditation/ affiliation to NIOS. The Central Government will provide 100 per cent funding for the scheme during the 11th plan. The financial assistance will be given yearly under the scheme through state governments/union territory administration in whose jurisdiction the institution is situated.

Project HUNAR for Muslim Girls in Bihar

NIOS started Project Hunar in Bihar in collaboration with Bihar Education Project Council (BEPC) to impart skill training to Muslim girls in seven vocational courses, from 2008-09 session. A total of 13768 Muslim girls have been imparted skill training in courses like Gram Sakhi, Cutting, Tailoring and Dress Making, Basic Rural Technology, Jute Production, Bakery and Confectionery, Beauty Culture and Early Childhood Care and Education. For phase I, a tripartite MOU has been signed with three Nodal Agencies to collaborate and co-operate with NIOS in identifying and recommending institutions which could be granted accreditations by NIOS for running the project. Out of 13768 girls, 11347 girls passed the examinations and got certificate in respective trades. It is interesting to mention that not even one learner dropped out of this programme.

Project HUNAR Phase II

Seeing the success of this project, the Government of Bihar offered NIOS to make it a continuous programme for phase II with a target of 50,000 more Muslim girls. It also targeted SCs, STs and the most backward communities for the session 2010-11. About 45,298 students enrolled and 12,252 appeared in the examinations held on 23rd and 24th July 2011. Apart from 298 accredited institutions under

Hunar Phase I, 723 new OBH study centres have been accredited for running this programme. These 723 OBH study centres are model cluster schools, institutions and NGOs as recommend by the BEPC.

Special Initiatives of NIOS to Promote Education amongst Minority Groups

Following the directive of the Government of India, NIOS set up a Minority Cell in June 2006, under the overall supervision of the Secretary, NIOS. The objective of the Minority Education Programme of NIOS was to expand the outreach and impact of NIOS programmes and policies amongst the minority communities, especially girls and women, by undertaking active advocacy programmes to establish linkages with existing Minority Educational Institutions. The NIOS was identified as a lead institution for providing a linkage between traditional educational institutions like Madrasas with mainstream education. NIOS attended several meetings held in minority dominated areas and initiated advocacy programmes for their awareness about NIOS. Some of the special initiatives taken by NIOS to expand the number of schools in remote as well as Muslim dominated areas are as follows:

- Granted accreditation to institutions affiliated to/ recognized by various Madrasa Boards.
- Made relaxation in conditions regarding infrastructural requirements on need basis.
- Engaged Project Coordinators for different regions like Uttar Pradesh, Bihar, Rajasthan, West Bengal, Jharkhand, and Delhi.
- Presentations by the Chairman, NIOS and the Secretary, NIOS on Minority issues before leaders from minority groups were facilitated.
- Proactive advocacy programmes like meetings, seminars, surveys, mass sensitization and awareness programmes in remote/hilly and backward areas for increasing awareness among downtrodden and unprivileged sections of the society regarding utility of NIOS programmes in the field of school education were undertaken.
- Regional Conference (Eastern Region) of the NIOS Co-ordinators and Leaders of Minority Institutions/Madrasas of Orissa, were organized for promotion of minority education (2007).
- Seminars were organized at Munger in collaboration with Rahmani Foundation, Munger, Bihar (2007).

- Advocacy meeting was organised in District Kannauj (UP) on 19th March 2008. About 25 Minority Institutions and Madrasas attended the programme.

To establish partnership with Minority Educational Institutions, the following steps were taken:

- Translation of Academic and Vocational courses in Urdu Medium. Development of Multimedia programme for Urdu Medium (ICT interventions).
- Introduction of a language course in Arabic at the Secondary level. It also initiated Persian language at the Secondary level.
- Facilitated setting of question papers in Urdu and also permitted the learners to answer question papers in Urdu language. It also made arrangements for getting the Urdu answer scripts evaluated. Due to this particular initiative taken by the NIOS, the number of AIs, AVIs and OBE, AAs, etc in minority institutions has increased.

Increase in genderwise, coursewise, yearwise and religionwise enrolment showing popularity and acceptability of open distance learning in capacity building of all communities can be seen in the Tables 7.1 and 11.2.

Majority of technical workers like tailors, carpenters, barbers, welders, motor mechanics, electricians, washermen, plumbers, watch mechanics, painters belong to the Muslim minority, but they are untrained and unskilled. The courses offered by NIOS are job-oriented and suitable to the Muslim minority, as they are engaged more in technical work rather than high profile official and administrative jobs. By popularizing the courses among the Muslims, we can make them skilled so that they could perform professionally, and their capacity of work would also increase. This can be done through awareness programmes, advetisements, involvement of social activists, NGOs, and Madrasas.

Challenges before the Muslim Minority in India

Some of the challenges faced by the Muslim Minority are lack of support from parents, religious leaders, Government, and the Muslim community leaders. There is also lack of supportive environment at the Government level. There is problem in public schools as well because the teachers and administrators are not well educated about the beliefs and lifestyle of Muslim students. Frustrated over being neglected and not being considered in the development process of the community, the Muslims

Table 7.1: Enrolment Profile – Genderwise, coursewise and religionwise during last 5 Years

Year	*Vocational*			*Academic*			*Total*		
	Male	*Female*	*Total*	*Male*	*Female*	*Total*	*Male*	*Female*	*Total*
2007-08	11558	12116	23674	235649	104693	340342	247207	116809	364016
2008-09	10450	13030	23480	261063	110562	371625	271513	123592	395105
2009-10	11511	7693	19204	294158	125544	419702	305669	133237	438906
2010-11	8902	13877	22779	319556	138499	458055	328458	152376	480834
2011-12	9972	26354	22779	343978	149556	493534	353950	165938	519888
Total	52393	63098	115491	1454404	628854	2083258	1506797	691952	2198749

Table 7.2: Religionwise Enrolment in Academic courses

Year	*Hindu (X)*	*Muslim (A)*	*Other Minorities (B)*	*Total Minority Y = (A)+(B)*	*Total (X + Y)*
2007-08	277560	27925	34857	62782	340342
2008-09	304364	36154	31107	67261	371625
2009-10	331846	42163	45693	87856	419702
2010-11	379334	39797	38924	78721	458055
2011-12	413841	42661	37032	79693	493534

find it hard to maintain their values and beliefs in public life. They have multiple identities and live in a bubble between their parents and Mainstream cultures. Lack of understanding of the religious leaders about the reality of the youth and their needs, makes the Muslim youth feel unfit in society, leading to serious behavioural disorder. Without the collective action and collaboration of educators, religious leaders, organisations, and Muslim institutions with one another, it would not be possible to find solutions.

Suggestions and Recommendations

The following recommendation can be made for economic empowerment of Muslims of India in the light of the Sachar Committee findings and recommendations. The recommendations of the report for economic gain and growth of the community emphasize on the the following points for capacity building of Muslims through which NIOS can make their policy and can play an important role in the vision 2020:

- Mechanisms to ensure equity and equality of opportunity to bring about inclusion should be such that diversity is achieved and at the same time the perception of discrimination is eliminated.
- Creation of a National Data Bank (NDB) by NIOS, where all relevant data for various SRCs are maintained, is recommended.
- An autonomous Assessment and Monitoring Authority (AMA) is needed to evaluate the extent of development benefits which accrue to different SRCs through various programmes.
- An Equal Opportunity Commission (EOC) should be constituted to look into the grievances of the deprived groups.
- A carefully conceived 'nomination' procedure should be worked out to increase inclusiveness in governance.
- The idea of providing certain incentives to a 'diversity index' should be explored. A wide variety of incentives can be linked to this index so as to ensure equal opportunity to all SRCs in the areas of education, government and private employment and housing.
- In the Muslim Dominated areas there is need to establish more NIOS study centres of vocational courses with some relaxations in the norms for studies for the Indian Muslims. This is so because the issue of growth and development of Indian Muslim Community is a complex one and needs an in depth study and analysis.

- There is need to take initiative for establishment of NIOS study centres in the backward Muslim concentrated 55 districts. The existing NGO's could be trained so that they could become effective vehicles of benefits of private philanthropy and public sector schemes (15 Point Programme) to the marginalized people. It may be noted that actual NGO interventions in this field has brought about wonderful results. There is no reason why Muslims NGOs can't play a positive role in economically uplifting Muslims of India.

The submission made above is no way exhaustive. Much more can be written and deliberated. Empowerment is possible only by disempowering the process of destitution.

8

Education to Achieve Sustainability

Raisa Khan

Today every country in the world aspires to develop in the best possible way. In India, it is essential to remove barriers like poverty and corruption to reach the destination of success. It is also necessary to achieve sustainable development rather than mere development. Here we discuss sustainable development in the area of education.

Education is a life long process as we receive education from various sources. It is necessary for the overall development of the child to adjust with the environment. Education makes an individual a complete man and enables him to apply acquired knowledge and experience in real situations. However, individuals are more concerned about their own happiness and prosperity rather than the needs of others. Education not merely develops the individual but also promotes social development. Thus, the needs of the society can be fulfilled by education.

Education is a dynamic process. Whatever change we require in a society can be achieved or applied through education. It is an urgent requirement that our future generations should be motivated to live in harmony with nature, family and society as well. Thus education becomes an important means to maintain harmony and promote awareness towards sustainable development.

Sustainable Development – An Introduction

Sustainable development is a process in which every member of the society progresses not as an individual but as a whole. Every individual becomes an integral part of the society. Every individual is responsible to fulfill his needs without exploiting the needs and requirements of others. The main aim of sustainable development is to secure all the available resources for future.

According to Brundtland Commission, sustainable development "is a development that meets the needs of the present without compromising the ability of future generation to meet their own needs" (World Commission on Environment and Development, 1987, p. 43).

Dimensions for Sustainable Development

The concept of sustainable development relies on three dimensions that are also correlated with each other. These dimensions are social, economical and environmental sustainability.

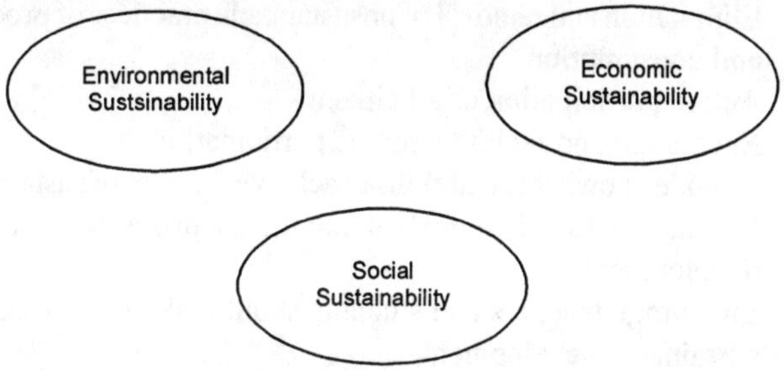

Environmental Sustainability

It demands the commitment of all human beings to secure the the resources available on this planet as human life cannot survive without natural resources, water or food. Factors like over-population, urbanization, pollution, etc are degrading our natural resources beyond redemption. It is necessary to preserve our natural resources for the survival of the present and the future generations. Thus it becomes the bounden duty of every member of the society to use these renewable resources in a sustainable manner.

Social Sustainability

Society is a group of people living together with some common character. All the members of the society are interdependent on each other, having common goals. As an integral part of the society, every individual needs to make sincere effort to meet the needs of the society. Social sustainability also depends upon environmental sustainability.

Economic Sustainability

Economic sustainability relies upon social and environmental sustainability. Meeting the target of social and environmental sustainability will lead to economic sustainability. Through economic sustainability, we will be able to meet our social and environmental needs.

Thus, it can be said that all the dimensions for sustainable development are linked together. To meet the needs of the present and the future, we need to maintain balance between social, economical and environmental needs.

Principles of Sustainable Development

(1) Every individual has a right to live with harmony

(2) Development should focus on both the present and future needs.
(3) Preservation of environmental resources.
(4) Provide equal opportunities to progress
(5) Equal distribution of resources
(6) Elimination and removal of unsustainable practices of production and consumption.
(7) Active participation of all citizen
(8) Encourage and facilitate public participation
(9) Provide knowledge and skills to achieve the goal of sustainability.
(10) Education as an important means to promote sustainable development.
(11) Encourage teachers and students should take up initiatives for sustainable development

Role of Education in Promoting Sustainability

Prepares skilled manpower: Development of the country depends upon its citizens. More skilled manpower means more development. Skilled manpower is necessary to support economic development of the country. As a result there will be no need to depend on other countries for international trade, which leads to exploitation of natural resources.

Develops wide vision to understand: Education is not merely a process to acquire knowledge. It also empowers an individual to understand the social, economical and environmental issues with brought vision.

Enriches logical and critical thinking: To maintain harmony and balance, it is necessary that each and every citizen thinks rationally and critically. Educated person is more efficient to think rationally as compared to others.

Facilitates decision making: An educated person is capable of taking logical decisions based on facts and data.

Modifies and improves behavior and attitude: Education develops the ability to modify behavior in a desirable manner and helps in bringing about attitudinal change.

Value orientated: One of the functions of education is to enrich social and national values like love, respect, sympathy etc. It enables students to understand their needs without compromising the needs and requirements of others.

Recommendations for Sustainability through Education

(1) Integrated curriculum with social, economical and environmental issues.

(2) Reorientation of education at all levels of learning i.e. primary, secondary and higher.
(3) Promotion of group and team learning.
(4) Encourage participation among teachers and students.
(5) Promotion of activities related to social, economic and environmental issues.
(6) Promote co-operation.
(7) Universalization of education.
(8) Promotion of girl education.
(9) Gender equality at all platforms.
(10) Organization of seminars and workshops to discuss national or international issues.
(11) Development of skills like questioning, critical thinking, analyzing etc.
(12) Training to implement sustainability programs
(13) Collaboration of formal education with informal and non-formal agencies of education.
(14) Encourage parents and community participation through awareness programs.
(15) Value orientation and enrichment.

Issues to Implement Educational Sustainable Programmes

How to integrate sustainable programmes in to curriculum?

Curriculum is a planned way to assist educational instruction. It includes all the activities which are required for the systematic growth of the child. Many subjects like math, science, social science have diffic;lty in integrating sustainable programs with existing curriculum. Teachers and students both can face difficulty in maintaining equilibrium.

How to create awareness?

Successful implementation of sustainable programs requires developing awareness among educational community. Educational experts and policy makers should be aware about the linkage between sustainability and education. For this purpose it is necessary to create awareness for reorientation of education.

How to encourage community participation?

Sustainability cannot be possible without community participation. Hence efforts should be made to make the communities participate in activities

How to develop skills?

Smooth functioning of sustainable programs require responsible and innovative leaders. These leaders will be able to introduce educational reforms leading to social and economic development without compromising on environmental issues.

How to describe sustainable development?

Economical development depends upon national or international trade. To fulfill our economic needs, we compromise with our environmental safety. Thus it is very difficult to describe or understand the contradictory dimensions of sustainable growth.

How to arrange resources?

To achieve sustainability through education we require to achieve the target of 100 per cent literacy rate. Orientation of education is required at all levels. More trained teachers are required for fulfilling the task of arranging resources. Funds for seminars, workshops and training program are also required. Thus it is necessary that government should take initiative to arrange funds for the implementation of sustainable programmes.

How to remove barriers?

Sustainable development is a collaborative effort which cannot be achieved individually. The feeling of oneness and togetherness is required. There are some barriers like caste, class, religion etc. Thus it is necessary to develop the ability to think and imagine beyond the boundaries of these barriers. It can only be possible through education and community participation.

How to share responsibility?

Education is an important means to achieve sustainability. Teachers and students are the main sources to implement sustainable programs. However, this does not mean that only education department is bearing the responsibility. It is equally the responsibility of each and every citizen of the country and all are accountable for this.

9

Reforming Evaluation System in Higher Education

Shaheen F., Khan and *Reema Singh*

Education is considered as an investment in human beings in terms of development of human resources, skills, innovation, knowledge and the like. The quality of education depends largely upon the quality of instruction provided in the classroom. To assess quality of education, evaluation of both the processess and products of education becomes imperative. The purpose of education is to make judgement about the quality, reach and relevance of evaluation. The diagnostic element of the evaluation serves us as an inbuilt monitor within the system of education to review from time to time, the progress in learning and to provide valuable feedback about the strength and weaknesses of the system. It must also give guidance to teachers on modifications in teaching methods and materials.

The terms evaluation has been introduced by educationists for the examination system. Traditionally, the examination process is the last phase of teaching and learning and it has been a very tough exercise, fearful enough for students.

A glimpse over the present examination system shows the following shortcomings:

1. The assessment is often done in a rush, to meet the given deadlines and is really carried out under the best of conditions.
2. Assessment is often done by people tired of reading the same answers to same questions and seeing the same mistakes.
3. The traditional paper and pencil test measures only the recall of facts and information ie. It lays emphasis only on the growth and development of scholastic aspects like decision making skill, judgment skill, personality which are no less important.
4. Almost all assessment processes in common foster learner competition rather than collaboration. Only a certain proportion of learners are allowed to receive higher scores or first class honours degrees.

With changing times the procedures of conventional examination should change. The modern concept of examination should become progressive, scientific, logical, practical, and fruitful. In order to consider as to what type of evaluation system should be implemented and how the evaluation system should work, a look at Chester F. Mc Nermly's view about evaluation will give a clear picture, "The purpose of any programme of evaluation is to discover the needs of the individuals being evaluated, and then to design learning experiences that will solve these needs.Evaluation is an important and delicate process, not only from the stand point of determining the needs and growth of programmes and individuals, but also from the standard point of what it does to the individuals being evaluated. An evaluation cannot adequately be made by using a single checklist, an isolated anecdotal record or a battery of examinations; a complete evaluation will require use of many techniques." It is necessary that teachers must use assessment results for evaluating students' progress in learning and for planning curriculum improvements and not just for generating grades.

Good assessment should include data from many sources besides paper pencil tests. It should assess not only knowledge but also higher order thinking and content related values and dispositions. A broad view of assessment will help to ensure that assessment component includes authentic activities that provide students with opportunities to synthesise and reflect on what they are learning, to think critically and creatively about it and to apply it to problem solving and decision-making contents.

Results should be scrutinized to identify learner's needs, misunderstandings that may need attention to suggest potential adjustment in curriculum goals, instructional material or teachings methods and to detect weaknesses in the assessment practices themselves.

So, a well constructed evaluation system can motivate teachers to present appropriate materials in their instruction and improve the much talked quality of education.

In light of this, some suggestions are given for reforming the evaluation system and which if considered would certainly change the scenario of the teaching learning process.

- Firstly, alignment of curriculum should be such that it is divided into smaller units each with specified learning objectives. Along with objectives, the means to achieve them should also be mentioned or suggested. Some units should incorporate learning aids such as videos, slides, models and other structured learning materials.
- Secondly, besides assessable quantities, unassailable qualities

should also be included in the agenda of evaluation. For this, a clear description of such competences which learners need to be able to demonstrate should be formulated. What kind of evidence needs to be looked into and how the demonstration of that evidence can be built into assessment procedure should be decided accordingly. The orientation of teachers is a must.

- Lastly, the evaluation system should increase the proportion of assessment schedules allocated to continuous assessment. A battery of evaluation techniques must be used to assess the 'is doing' competence rather than 'did once' competence.

In view of all the mentioned concerns of evaluation system and suggestions given, an innovative approach is suggested which could meet a wide variety of needs of our evaluation system. The credit semester evaluation system prevalent in reputed institutions of our country and a popular personalised system of instruction known as Keller Plan developed in late 1960s by Professor F. S. Keller of Columbia University in the U.S.A., if both are modified and adapted together, it would certainly produce drastic result. In this approach, the whole course is divided into a number of units, each with specified learning objectives.

Credits are given to the courses as per time devoted to these units in each semester. About 20-25 credits are considered equivalent to one semester. For example, to pass M.A./M.Sc. course, a candidate must have courses covering 60-70 credits. Students work largely at their own pace, using a range of instructional material.

For a postgraduate course of four semesters, students are required to cover courses carrying a total of about 80 credits, including credits for means of achieving objectives like assignment, class discussion, seminars, tutorials, projects, laboratory work, etc. Typically, each unit represents roughly one week's work carried out by a student at his/her own pace. The students are free to discuss problems associated with the units with their teachers at any time. In certain circumstances 'peer teaching' can be incorporated into this approach. This means that a third year student can be instructed to help a first year student in certain parts of the course.

When the students feel they have mastered a given unit, they have actually achieved the objectives identified and can demonstrate competences specified, and can present themselves for assessment. Here various assessment techniques can be used apart from essay type test. These are:

- Practical test in which various types of test can be used to test how the task should be performed. It may include project assessment where a student may be assessed in terms of his/her cumulative work over a period of time or only on the end result of the project.

- Skill tests which are common in training courses can be incorporated or situational assessments which involve assessment of non cognitive skills (decision making skills, leadership quality, personality, conflict management) in a real or simulated environment can be included.
- Unobtrusive assessment is a technique which can take place without the student necessarily being aware that he is in fact being assessed. Such techniques can be important in assessing a student's commitment and attitude to work rather than simply his ability to perform tasks under controlled conditions of more formal assessment. Video techniques are used for recording the performance of a student; including analysis and assessment of personal skills and traits.
- The students should be assessed according to Relative Grading System instead of Absolute Grading where student performances are first quantified as marks. The teacher assigns the letter grades like A, B, C, D etc. Here teachers need to ensure that they shoulder this responsibility with care. Any carelessness in this respect would not only provide an incorrect picture of students' calibre, but also result in the loss of confidence in students. If the students pass the test upto a specified standard, they move on to next semester. There would be no penalty for failing and students can reappear in the failed unit as many times as necessary.

The essential features of this approach are independent study, individualized learning, self pacing and tutor support. A bright student may cover the courses in three semesters only, instead of the usual four; whereas a slow student may complete in 5 to 6 semesters. It may also happen that a student completes only 20-25 credits and has to leave the university in the midst of his/her studies. After a gap of some years if he again finds time and wants to complete his studies, he is allowed to complete the remaining credits and earn his degree.

This will put an end to the fear psychosis among the students about their performance in examination as they can appear again in the subjects they have not been able to perform, This approach, however, demands devotion, commitment and sincerity on the part of teachers.

10

Issues and Challenges for Higher Education in India

Nasrin and *Mandira*

India's higher education system is the world's third largest in terms of students, next only to China and the United States. Unlike China, however, India has the advantage of English being the primary language of higher education and research. India educates approximately 11 per cent of its youth in higher education as compared to 20 per cent in China. The main governing body at the tertiary level is the University Grants Commission (UGC, India), which enforces its standards, advises the government, and helps coordinate between the center and the state. Universities and its constituent colleges are the main institutes of higher education in India.

At present (in 2011) there are 227 government-recognized Universities in India. Out of them 20 are central universities, 109 are deemed universities and 11 are Open Universities and rest are state universities. Most of these universities in India have affiliated colleges where undergraduate courses are being taught. According to the Department of Higher Education, Government of India, 16,885 colleges, including 1,800 exclusive women's colleges are functioning under these universities and institutions and there are 4.57 lakh teachers and 99.54 lakh students in various higher education institutes in India. Apart from these higher education institutes, there are several private institutes in India that offer various professional courses in India. Distance learning is also a feature of the Indian higher education system.

Some institutions of India, such as the Indian Institutes of Technology (IITs), have been globally acclaimed for their standard of education. The IITs enroll about 8,000 students annually and the alumni have contributed to both the growth of the private sector and the public sectors of India. However, India has failed to produce world class universities like Harvard and Cambridge. According to the London Times Higher Education (2009) World University rankings, no Indian university features among the top 100. But universities in East Asia have been included in the first hundred. Hong Kong has three, ranked at 24, 35 and 46; Singapore too ranked at

30 and 73; South Korea ranked at 47 and 69 and Taiwan one in the 95th position. Notably, China's Tsinghua University and Peking University are ranked at 49 and 52 respectively. There is no Indian university in the rankings from 100 to 200. It is only when one moves on to the next 100 that we find the Indian Institute of Technology, Kanpur at 237; IIT Madras at 284 and the University of Delhi at 291.

A recent evaluation of universities and research institutes all over the world, conducted by Shanghai University, has not a single Indian university in the world's top 300, while China has six. The Indian Institute of Science, Bengaluru, comes in somewhere in the top 400 and IIT, Kharagpur, makes an appearance after that. Yet these decisive edges also have its shortcomings. Besides top rated universities which provide highly competitive world class education to their pupil, India is also home to many universities which have been founded with the sole objective of making easy money. UGC and other Regulatory Authorities have been trying very hard to extirpate the menace of private universities which are running courses without any affiliation or recognition from regulatory authorities like BCI, NCTE and AICTE. Students from rural and semi urban background often fall prey to these institutes and colleges.

Today knowledge is power. The more knowledge one has, the more empowered one is. According to the University Grants Commission (UGC), India needs 1,500 more universities with adequate research facilities in the coming years in order to compete in the global market.The country lacks the critical mass in higher education. Its gross enrolment ratio (GER) is a mere 11 per cent compared to China's 20 per cent, the USA's 83 per cent and South Korea's 91 per cent. This means that in comparison to India, China has double the number of students pursuing higher education. The Eleventh Five Year Plan envisaged increase in the Gross Enrolment Ratio (GER) in higher education to 15 per cent of the population in the age group of 18-24 years by 2011-12, but this did not happen. It required a substantial increase in the number of institutions and consequently adequate number of teachers for imparting education.

India aspires to increase enrolment in higher education. The country intends to raise gross enrolment ratio in higher education to 30 percent by the year 2020, which means almost tripling the enrolment from the present 14 million to about 40 million. There is no point in debating that higher education has been accorded priority in our country but to take this aspect on a serious note. Universities of the country, existing and the new ones, will have to be very responsible for achieving this dream target.

The overall scenario of higher education in India does not match with the global quality standards. Hence, there is enough justification for an increased assessment of the Quality of the country's educational institutions. Traditionally, these institutions assumed that Quality could be determined by their internal resources, viz., faculty with an impressive set of degrees and experience detailed at the end of the institute's admission brochure, number of books and journals in the library, an ultra-modern campus, and size of the endowment, etc., or by its definable and assessable outputs, viz., efficient use of resources, producing uniquely educated, highly satisfied and employable graduates.

Critical appraisals undertaken by the governmental committees and independent academicians have highlighted the crisis confronting the system: '*increasing educated unemployment; weakening of student motivation; increasing unrest and indiscipline on the campuses; frequent collapse of administration; deterioration of standards; and above all, the demoralizing effect of the irrelevance and purposelessness of most of what is being done.*' While the politicians and policy makers have often spoken about the need for radical reconstruction of the system, what has been achieved in reality is nothing but only a sublime reform.

At present, the world-class institutions in India are mainly limited. Most of the Indian colleges and universities lack in high-end research facilities. Under-investment in libraries, information technology, laboratories and classrooms makes it very difficult to provide top quality instruction or engage in cutting-edge research. This gap has to be bridged if we want to speed up our path to concrete development. The University Grant Commission, which was supposed to be revamped to University Developmental Council (UDC), is not only the lone grant giving agency in the country, but also responsible for *coordinating, determining and maintaining the standards* in institutions of higher education. The emergence of a worldwide economic order has immense consequences for higher education more so under the changes that have taken place in the recent past with regard to globalization, industrialization, information technology advancement and its impact on education aided to these are the policy changes that have taken place at the UGC, All India Council for Technical Education (AICTE), Distance Education Council (DEC), Indian Council for Agriculture Research (ICAR), Bar Council of India (BCI), National Council for Teacher Education (NCTE), Rehabilitation Council of India (RCI), Medical Council of India (MCI), Pharmacy Council of India (PCI), Indian Nursing Council (INC), Dentist Council of India (DCI), Central Council of Homeopathy (CCH), the Central Council of Indian Medicine (CCIM) and other such regulatory bodies, from time to time to accommodate these development and yet maintain quality students in higher education. It is high time for all those who are concerned with policymaking, planning, administration and implementation of Higher Education to revitalize the very thinking on the subject and put it on the right track.

After recording handsome growth rate for the last few years, India is now considered to be one of the most promising economies of the world. While, higher education gives India an edge in the world economy as evident from the availability of the skilled manpower, and research scholars working abroad, *overpopulation, unemployment, illiteracy and relative poverty,* continue to be the major deterrents to realize her potential in human resources.

The taskforce constituted by World Bank and UNESCO during 2000 has also observed that higher education helps increase wages and productivity that directly enrich individuals and society. The prospects and development in the higher education sector in India needs a critical examination in a rapidly globalizing world. Expansion, inclusion and excellence were the three major objectives of higher education policy of the Government of India. The government had taken many steps to increase student enrolment in higher education and quality improvement in higher educational institutions.

Keeping in view, the Government has constituted a Knowledge Commission to suggest measures to alleviate the problems that higher education sector is afflicted with and make India a knowledge based Super Power in the global economy. But the Government is at a crossroad. While there is a need for an expansion of the higher education sector, resource constraint for both the center and the states poses challenge to ensure quality education even in the existing institutions. Everyone is aware about the vacant posts that are now and then a subject of wide debates. The government after pursuing neo-liberal policies for the last so many years is keen to open the higher education sector to the private providers, either through public-private participation or foreign direct investment in higher education.

The society is divided. While one section is opposed to commodification of education, the other section thinks that involving the private sector is the only way out. How would the higher education sector evolve in response to these challenges is a crucial issue for us to understand and anticipate. How is the sector contemplating changes to engage with the world? If India is to be a global economic powerhouse, it is essential to nurture this higher education sector.

Critical Issues in Indian Higher Education

As India strives to compete in a globalized economy in areas that require highly trained professionals, the quality of higher education becomes increasingly important. So far, India's large, educated population base and its reservoir of at least moderately well trained university graduates have aided the country in moving ahead, but the competition is fierce; from China in particular. Other countries are also upgrading higher education with the aim of building world class universities. Even the small top tier of higher education faces serious problems. Many IIT graduates, well trained in technology, have chosen not to contribute their skills to the burgeoning technology sector in India; almost half leave the country immediately upon graduation to pursue advanced studies abroad, and most do not return, thereby inflicting a severe "Brain Drain". A stunning 86 per cent of Indian students in the fields of Science and Technology who obtain degrees in the United States do not return home immediately following their graduation. A body of dedicated and able teachers work at the IITs and IIMs, but the lure of jobs abroad and in the private sector makes it increasingly difficult to lure the best and brightest to the academic profession, thus creating a void, difficult to fill.

The present system of higher education does not serve the purpose for which it was started. In general, education itself has become so profitable a business that quality is lost in the increase of quantity of professional institutions with quota system and politicization adding fuel to the fire and spoiling the system further, thereby increasing unemployment of graduates without quick relief to mitigate their sufferings in the job market of the country.

So, the drawbacks of the higher education system underscore the need for reforms to make it worthwhile and beneficial to all concerned. Most observers agree that Indian higher education system, the significant and impressive developments of the past few decades notwithstanding, faces major challenges in both quantitative and qualitative terms. Perhaps the clearest and boldest statement of this issue can be found in the "Report to the Nation 2006" of the National Knowledge Commission which concludes that there is 'a quiet crisis in higher education in India that runs deep', and that it has to do with both the quantity and the quality of higher education in India.

Recognizing and emphasizing this double challenge, the former Indian Prime Minister, Mr.Manmohan Singh, severely criticized in a speech the serious qualitative deficiencies in Indian higher education while at the same time announced plans for a major expansion of the system. The coming up of several central universities in last few years is a small step towards that commitment. Reflecting on the findings of a confidential report by the National Assessment and Accreditation Council (NAAC), which is affiliated to the University Grants Commission (UGC), he expressed his concern over the fact that two thirds (68 per cent) of the country's universities and 90 percent of its colleges are of "poor quality" and that well over half of the faculty in India's colleges do not have the appropriate degree qualifications. Knowledge is the base for overall growth and if the nation has to be competitive and to be at par with the globalization pace, we will have to respond to the market forces.

According to a study, only 25 per cent of engineering graduates are directly employable *(Infosys, an IT giant, some years back sorted through 1.3 million applicants only to find that around two percent were qualified for jobs).* Quality of education delivered in most institutions is very poor. While India has some institutions of global repute delivering quality education, such as IIMs (Indian Institute of Management) and IITs (Indian Institute of Technology), we still do not have enough of them. There is clearly a lack of educated educators and teaching is not an attractive profession. It's a last choice in terms of career. Number of PhDs produced each year is very low, and those required by academia is far higher. In fact, in many institutions fresh graduates are employed to teach.

Most of the educational institutions in different states such as Maharashtra are owned by politicians. Thus the education system which is highly regulated by the Government has been set up to benefit politicians. The growth of higher education in India has been largely guided by the serviceable prerequisite of the economy. After independence, the role of the state in planning out a development path and also in building higher education institutions was guided by mutuality of purpose. Most observers of higher education in India feel that performance of higher education institutions has been less than satisfactory in terms of access, equity and quality. Now there is an urgent need to work for the development of the educational sector to meet the need of the emerging opportunities, increasing younger generation population and challenges of the 21st century.

Challenges of Present Higher Educational System in India

Ever since we have attained independence, we are facing challenges to establish a great and strong education system. Various governments came and went. Of course, they tried to establish new education policies in the system but they were not sufficient for our nation. Still we are facing problems and challenges in our education system. India recognizes that the new global scenario poses unprecedented challenges for the higher education system. The University Grants Commission has appropriately stated that a whole range of skills will be demanded from the graduates of humanities, social sciences, natural sciences and commerce, as well as from the various professional disciplines such as agriculture, law, management, medicine or engineering.

India can no longer continue the model of general education as it has been persisting for the bulk of student population. Rather, it requires a major investment to make human resource productive by coupling the older general disciplines of humanities, social sciences, natural sciences and commerce to their applications in the new economy and having adequate field based experience to enhance knowledge with skills and develop appropriate attitudes. Responding to these emerging needs, the UGC stated: "The University has a crucial role to play in promoting social change. It must make an impact on the community if it is to retain its legitimacy and gain public support". It seeks to do so by a new emphasis on community based programmes and work on social issues. Concepts of access, equity, relevance and quality can be operationalized only if the system is both effective and efficient. Hence, the management of higher education and the total networking of the system has become an important issue for reaping effective results. The shift can occur only through a systematic approach to change as also the development of its human resource, and networking the system through information and communication technology.

There are many basic problems in higher education in India today. These include inadequate infrastructure and facilities, large vacancies in faculty positions and poor faculty thereof, low student enrolment rate, outmoded teaching methods, declining research standards, unmotivated students, overcrowded classrooms and widespread geographic, income, gender, and ethnic imbalances. Apart from concerns relating to deteriorating standards, there is exploitation of students by many private providers. Ensuring equitable access to quality higher education for students coming from poor families is a major challenge. Students from poor background are put to further disadvantage since they are not academically prepared to crack highly competitive entrance examinations that have bias towards urban elite and rich students having access to private tuitions and coaching.

Education in basic sciences and subjects that are not market friendly has suffered. Research in higher education institutions is at its lowest ebb. There is an inadequate and diminishing financial support for higher education from the Government and from the society. Many colleges established in rural areas are non-viable, under-enrolled and have extremely poor infrastructure and facilities with just a few teachers. A series of judicial interventions over the last two decades and knee-jerk reaction of the Government – both at the center and state level and the regulatory bodies without proper understanding of the emerging market structure of higher education in India has further added confusion to the higher education landscape in the country. There is a definite absence of a well-informed reform agenda for higher education in the country. A few efforts made now and then are not rooted in the new global realties based on competition and increased mobility of students and workforce.

Some of the leading challenges before the higher education system are *continuous upgradation of curriculum to keep in pace with rapid growth of science and technology; globalization and the resultant challenges from the international universities; grooming of many private institutions without any method of ensuring maintenance of quality and standard; need for adequate funding to meet the demands of various novel innovative programmes; developing a meaningful and purposeful inter-face between the universities, establishing National Research Laboratories, industries, fine tuning between the government and society, etc.* ICT in higher education policy may not be able to completely overcome all these challenges though it may play an important role in information and resource sharing. There are so many people in various parts of country who are still out of reach. This is despite the fact that there has been increased emphasis on our education programs, and efforts have been made to reach them to far off places.

The Government has to rethink on these areas to implement more on the policies. Money also plays a vital role for the education system which needs to adhere to globally recognized syllabus and curricula. Our constitution specifies that it is the responsibility of central and state government to build good education system. For that we need to have funds. The Central government prepares policies and plans while the responsibility of State government is to run those policies on ground. The standard education facilities are better in the states that are richer. There is need to remove such defects from the education system of the country which can only be influenced by increasing funding and providing better facilities to students. We know there is always an increase in the fund for the education system but never implemented in the area. So we have to work in this area. Government tries to make different policies which are implemented but quality is never checked. Majority of fund goes to the pockets of officials working for this. There is an urgent need to improve the quality and standard.

The time has come to modernize our education system so that our country can get more technically graduate citizens. This will to a large extent help the country to become a developed state. Today's youth are more inclined towards foreign shores for their higher education as they have much better facilities and the quality is also better. Can't we get that quality in India? We have to stop this brain drainage so as to stop students from leaving the country. Our Government is trying to meet these challenges but there is no substantial outcome. Thus we need to work hard to overhaul the higher education system in India.

Suggestions for Improving Quality of Higher Education

There is immense expectation from the Government, industry, educational institutions, parents and students for improving the quality of higher education. Some suggestions have been made for improving the quality of higher education:

1. *Towards a Learning Society:* As we move towards a learning society, every human activity will require contributions from experts, and this will place the entire sector of higher education in sharp focus. Although the priority of the Government is 'Education for All', the country will have to take the extra mile and gear up to invest more and more on higher education. Simultaneously, appropriate measures will have to be taken to refine, diversify and upgrade higher education and research programmes.

2. *Industry and Academia Connection:* Industry and academia connection is extremely necessary to ensure that curriculum and skills imparted in educational centres are in line with actual requirements. Skill building is really very crucial to ensure employability of students. Besides, it is also important to ensure that good jobs are generated (Knowledge + skills + global professional skills = good jobs).

3. *Incentives to Teachers and Researchers:* Both the industry and students are expecting specialized courses to be offered so that they get the latest and best in education.The job seeker needs to be industry ready and employable. Vocational and diploma courses need to be made more attractive to facilitate specialized programs being offered to students. Incentives should be provided to teachers and researchers to make these professions more attractive for the younger generation.

4. *Innovative Practices:* The new technologies offer vast opportunities for progress in all walks of life. They offer opportunities for economic growth, improved health, better service delivery, improved learning and socio-cultural advances. Though there is need to improve the country's innovative capacity, yet it is felt that this should be done in light of new understanding of research innovations.

5. *Mobilization of Resources:* The decline in public funding in the last two plan periods has adversely impacted the educational standards due to ever increasing costs on non-salary items, emoluments of staff, etc. Measures will have to be adopted to mobilize adequate resources for higher education. There is also need to link the fee structure to the payment

capacity of students. The students at lower economic levels can be given subsidized or fully subsidized education.

6. *Coming of Information Age:* As the world is entering into an Information Age, the developments in communication, information and technology will open up new and cost-effective approaches for providing higher education to the youth of the country. It will also endeavour to meet the needs of those who require continuing education for meeting the demands of explosion of information, fast-changing nature of occupations, and even lifelong education. Knowledge, which is at the heart of higher education, is a crucial resource in the development of political democracy, struggle for social justice and progress towards individual enlightenment.

7. *Student-Centered Education and Dynamic Methods:* Methods of higher education should cater to the needs of learning to learn, learning to do, learning to be and learning to become. Student-centered education and employment of dynamic methods of education will require from teachers new attitudes and new skills. Methods of teaching through lectures will have to become subordinate to the methods that will lay stress on self-study, personal consultation between teachers and pupils, and dynamic sessions of seminars and workshops. Methods of distance education will have to be employed on a vast scale.

8. *Public-Private Partnership (PPP):* This is most essential to bring in quality in the higher education system. Governments can ensure PPP through an appropriate policy. University Grants Commission and Ministry of HRD should play a major role in developing a purposeful interface between the Universities, Industries and National Research Laboratories (NRLs) as a step towards PPP. Funding to NRLs by the Government should ensure the involvement of institutions of higher education engaged in research activities to facilitate availability of latest sophisticated equipment.

There has been some effort both by the Government and the private education institutions to develop the teaching staff at various levels. However, this needs to be intensified with appropriate attention to all the aspects related in order to prepare quality and sufficient number of educational staff. Such efforts need a very serious structuring for the research based institutions. We need to be optimistic to believe that private-public partnership and the industry interface will take place in the field of education at all levels, particularly in the backward regions. To achieve excellence, we thus need to create a real partnership between Government, Educators and Industry. This kind of partnerships will provide the high-tech industries with skilled workers, capable of meeting their standards.

9. *To Provide Need Based Job-Oriented Courses:* All round development of personality is the purpose of education. But the present day education is neither imparting true knowledge of life nor polishing talent of students by which they can achieve laurels in the field of interest. So, combination of humanities and computer science and sciences or literature should be introduced so that these courses could be useful for the students to do jobs after recruitment in some companies which would reduce unnecessary rush to higher education. The programme must be focused on graduate studies and research and developing strategies and mechanisms for the rapid and efficient transfer of knowledge and for its application to specific national and local conditions and needs. Meritorious doctoral students should be recognized through teaching assistantships with stipends over and above the research fellowships. Finally, based on knowledge only vision of the future life and work can be had; based on this vision only a broad ambition can be fixed for oneself; and based on this ambition only one can lead interesting life doing satisfying job to do remarkable achievements in some field in the world.

10. *International Cooperation:* Universities in India have been a primary conduit for the advancement and transmission of knowledge through traditional ways, such as research, innovation, teaching, human resource development, and continuing education. International cooperation is gaining importance as yet another function. With the increased development of transport and communication, the global village is witnessing a growing emphasis on international cooperation and action to find satisfactory solutions to problems that have global dimensions, and higher education is one of them.

11. *Towards a New Vision:* India realizes, like other nations of the world, that humanity stands today at the peak of a new age of a large synthesis of knowledge, and that the East and the West have to collaborate in bringing about concerted action for universal development, lasting peace and unity. In this age, great cultural achievements of the past have to be recovered and enriched in the context of the contemporary advancement so that humanity can successfully meet the evolutionary and revolutionary challenges and bring about a new type of humanity and society marked by integrated powers of physical, emotional, dynamic, intellectual, ethical, aesthetic and spiritual potentialities.

12. *Cross Culture Programmes:* After completing education, an extensive tour of countries across the world, possibly with the cooperation of the Government, is necessary in order to understand different cultures, arts, literatures, religions, technological developments, and the progress of human society globally. It is also essential to take a tour of the country, to understand the diverse nature of the Indian society.

13. *Action Plan for Improving Quality:* Academic and administrative audit should be conducted once in three years in colleges by external experts to ensure quality in the educational field. The self-finance colleges should come forward for accreditation and fulfil the requirements of accreditation. But this should not be done the way it is being done by most private colleges and universities. Institutes should realize the need for quality education and come forward with action plan for improving the quality in higher educational institutions.

14. *Individuality:* Undue interference of parents in the education of children should be done away with. Parental guidance is necessary but it should not interfere in the creativity or individuality of the students. It is relevant to note that despite the prevalence of the obsolete type of education system, some students are achieving spectacular results in sports, music, dance, painting, science and technology in the world. This is primarily because of the encouragement of parents and dedicated teachers in the educational institutions. Higher education is necessary for everyone to achieve excellence in the chosen line. But one should be selected for higher education on the basis of merit only. Further, fee for education in general should not be high; especially, the fee for higher studies should be within the reach of every class of people in the nation.

15. *Privatization of Higher Education:* In any nation education is the basic necessity for the socio-economic development of the individuals and the society. In reality only 20 per cent of the population is educated in India. Therefore, improved standard of education should be offered to the majority by the governmental authorities with sincere political will. Privatization of higher education – a necessary evil – is absolutely necessary in a vast country like India. It is not possible for the Government alone to take care of the educational demand of the huge population in India.

16. *Quality Development:* Quality depends on the type of facilities provided in teaching and academic programs, research and scholarship, staffing, building facilities, equipment, services to the community and academic environment. For upkeep of quality, higher education should incorporate international dimensions: exchange knowledge, interactive networking, mobility of teachers and students, international research projects, etc while taking into account the national cultural values and circumstances. The level of education and knowledge being imparted by many colleges is not up to the mark. Instead of concentrating on quantity, these institutions should concentrate on quality. The approach of doctoral research in social sciences needs to be more analytical and comparative and related to society, policy and economy. A study conducted on 'Social Science Research Capacity in South Asia (2002)' showed that the share of

the Indian universities in the special articles published in the Economic and Political Weekly was only about 25 percent. This too was dominated by only three universities, namely Jawaharlal Nehru University, University of Mumbai and University of Delhi.

17. *World Class Education:* Indian Government is not giving priority to the development of high standard in education. It is very important that India aspires for international standard in the field of education. Many Universities in USA, UK, Australia, etc. allow studies in higher education for foreign students through correspondence courses. In the same way, Indian Universities providing world class education can offer courses to foreign students, taking advantage of globalization. In order to achieve the goal, it should adopt uniform international syllabus in its educational institutions.

18. *Personality Development:* Finally, the purpose of education should be flowering of personality, not suppression of creativity or natural skill. In the current globalized world, opportunities for the educated people are naturally ample in scope. As a result, business process outsourcing (BPO) activities have increased competition in the world trade leading towards the production of quality goods and their easy availability everywhere in the world market. That is the way the world can be developed for peace, prosperity and progress by able and skilful men.

19. *Status of Academic Research Studies:* If we see the number of researchers engaged in Research and Development activities as compared to other countries, we find that we have merely 119 researchers, whereas Japan has 5287 and US has 4484 researchers per million of population. Even in absolute terms, number of researchers in India is much smaller compared to US, China, Japan, Russia, and Germany. Numbers of doctoral degrees awarded in all subjects are 16, 602 out of which 6774 are in Arts and 5408 in science and rest in other professional subjects. India has a little over 6000 doctorates in Science and Engineering, compared to 9000 in China and 25000 in US. It increased rapidly from a little over 1000 in 1990 to over 9000 in recent years in China. In comparison, there has been a modest increase in India. National Science Foundation (NSF) – Science and Engineering Indicators (2002) – shows that in the US, about 4 per cent of the Science and Engineering graduates finish their doctorates. This figure is about 7 per cent for Europe. In India this is not even 0.4 per cent. Data on doctorates, particularly in Science, Engineering and Medicine suggests that only a few institutions have real research focus. In Engineering, there were merely 650 doctorates awarded in 2001-02. Of these 80 percent were from just 20 top universities. In science, 65 percent of the doctorates awarded were from the top 30 universities.

20. *Stipend to Research Fellows:* The number of quality research in

Indian Universities should increase. This should be seen in the context of extremely low fraction of Ph.D.'s in India in relation to M.Sc. /B.Tech, as compared to what it is in USA, UK, Germany, Japan etc. Meritorious doctoral students should be recognized through teaching assistantships with stipends over and above the research fellowships. Identifying talented, meritorious students and encouraging them through recognition is very important to attract students into research and teaching.

21. *Fair Quality Assurance System:* Colleges and private institutes should set up *Internal Quality Assurance Cell* (IQAC) and must follow a minimum standard for giving degrees. The quality assurance system must be independent of political and institutional interference and it must have a basis in the legislation. There should be operational, financial and academic autonomy, coupled with accountability. There is a need of an independent accreditation agency with a conglomerate of government, industry, academia, society etc. All stakeholders in education should ensure that the stakeholders, particularly the students, are not taken for a ride. They should be able to know whether a particular institution delivers value or not, then things can be under control to some extent. It is also important that all institutes of higher learning must make public the acceptability of their courses and degrees (the status, recognition and acceptability of their courses by other institutions).

22. *To increase Quantity of Universities:* We need more universities because we are quite substantial in population and the present number of universities is too less. On 13th June, 2005 Government of India constituted a high level advisory body known as *National Knowledge Commission (NKC)* to advise the PM about the state of education in India and measures needed to reform this sector. It was headed by Sam Pitroda, and it submitted its report in November 2007. NKC has recommended setting up of 1,500 universities in the coming years so that gross enrolment ratio increases to the level of some of the advanced countries. It has also called for establishing an 'Independent Regulatory Authority for Higher Education (IRAHE)' to monitor the quality of overall higher education in India.

23. *Examination Reforms:* Examination reforms, gradually shifting from the terminal, annual and semester examinations to regular and continuous assessment of student's performance in learning should be implemented.

24. *High-tech Libraries:* Our university libraries have a very good collection of books, but they are all in mess. A library must be online and conducive to serious study. Indian universities should concentrate more on providing quality education which is comparable to that of international standards.

Conclusion

After independence, there has been tremendous increase in institutions of higher learning in all disciplines. But has the quantitative growth been able to attend to the core issue of quality? Perhaps, not. India is one of the fastest developing countries of the world with the annual growth rate going above 9 per cent. In order to sustain that rate of growth, there is need to increase the number of institutes and also the quality of higher education in India.

To reach and achieve the future requirements, there is an urgent need to relook at the financial resources, access and equity, quality standards, relevance and at the end the responsiveness. To attain and sustain national, regional or international quality, certain components are particularly relevant, notably careful selection of staff and continuous staff development in particular, through the promotion of appropriate programs for academic development, including teaching/learning methodology and mobility between countries, between higher education institutions and the world of work, as well as student mobility within and between countries. Internal self-evaluation and external review must be conducted openly by independent specialists, if possible with international experts.

Report of the National Knowledge Commission, if properly implemented can help boost education sector in India. We are moving towards an era which would be defined by the parameters of knowledge and wisdom. India, in order to become a developed nation by 2020 and knowledge power in the coming years, will have to work very hard. The decisions that are going to be taken on these are likely to hold the key to India's future, as the main center of knowledge production. We need highly educated people with skill and who can drive our economy forward. If India can provide skilled people to the outside world, then we can change our country from a developing nation to a developed nation very easily and quickly. According to our Ex-Prime Minister: 'The time has come to create a second wave of institution building and of excellence in the fields of education, research and capability building'.

Thus, we need an education system that is modern, liberal and can adapt to the changing needs of a changing society, a changing economy and a changing world. The thrust of public policy for higher education in India is to address these challenges. However, one university can't make much difference. If the Government welcomes more such initiatives, the future will be ours. We will be able to match and compete with other nations and the dream to be the world's greatest economy will not be difficult to achieve.

11

ICT in Higher Education

K.C. Vashishtha and *Pravendra Singh Birla*

Information and Communication Technologies (ICTs) are increasingly utilized by higher education institutions worldwide. ICTs are emerging as a part of on-campus delivery as well as open and distance modalities of higher education delivery. UNESCO actions in this area focus on assisting Member States to develop robust policies in ICTs and higher education.

ICTs in higher education are being used for developing course material; delivering and sharing content; communication between learners, teachers and the outside world; creation and delivery of presentations and lectures; academic research; administrative support; and student enrolment. Higher education institutions in developing countries are on the whole making the most of computers and software available to them even though challenges including insufficient telephone and telecommunication infrastructure, lack of training resources for teachers, and lack of skilled and experienced information technology specialists to assist with development, maintenance and support of ICT usage in higher education institutions (HEIs) remain.

Positive ICT policies and investments are clearly beneficial to HEIs, even though ICTs have not replaced classroom-based modes of learning or teaching. Undoubtedly, ICTs can provide greater access for different target learners, and have become vehicles for enriched pedagogical experiences, particularly for distance educators and learners, separated by time and space.

Higher education systems have grown exponentially in the last five decades to meet the demands of quality education for all. This aspect has further gained momentum due to swift advancements in Information and Communication Technology (ICT). Demand for skilled and competent labour is ever-increasing in the contemporary globalised society. In this backdrop, access to quality in higher education for all has emerged as determining factor of economic growth and development. In order to increase the access to higher education and improving its reach to the remotest parts of the country, contribution of open and distance learning

Fig. 11.1: The Power of ICT

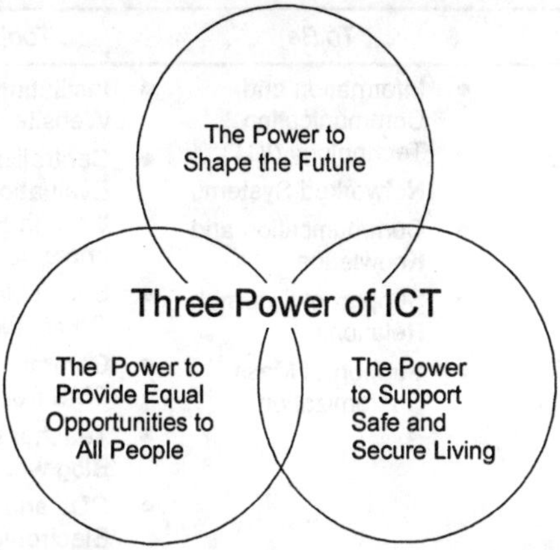

Source: http://www.fujitsu.com/global/about/csr/feature/2013/ict/

facilities is on the increase. In addition, it is catering to life-long learning aspirations and that too at affordable cost. The last two decades have witnessed the inclusion of developments in ICTs in higher education systems around the world. Even then the challenge to develop a higher education system that is flexible and dynamic so as to holistically integrate the technology in the management and delivery of learning programmes is daunting.

The first section presents briefly the present profile of higher education in India. Role of ICTs in higher education and the areas in which they can be integrated to play prominent role are discussed in the second section. The final section explores the challenges in expanding the role of ICTs for future development in higher education.

Importance of ICT in Higher Education

The importance of ICT in Higher Education can be seen in the following points:

1. Researchers can access current literature; work collaboratively with colleagues around the world; submit, edit and review journal articles, theses and conferences papers; and access web-based services and databases.
2. Instructors can create electronic and traditional course materials, including web-based resources and e-journals, communicate with students via e-mail, use e-learning tools to manage course, submit marks; and issue and receive assignments electronically.

Table 11.1: The Role of ICT in the 21st Century for Higher Education

As Is	*To Be*	*Tools of ICT*
• Information Technology • Stand-alone Systems • Data and Information • Support of Internal Organization • Support of Mass-Production	• Information and Communication Technology (ICT) • Networked Systems • Communication and Knowledge • Support of External Relations • Support of Mass-Customization	• Institution's Interactive Website • Centralization of Evaluation System through ERP Implementation • Social Media: Facebook, Orkut, Twitter etc. • Communication through SMS from Centralized • Teacher Websites and Blog writing • CDs and Other Electronic Devices • Virtual Classrooms/Video Conferencing

3. Students can use local and web course materials and resources instead of relying purely on lectures as the sole source of information and knowledge; participate in courses and programs even if not physically present on campus; and access online administrative system for course registration and mark retrieval.
4. Administrators can reduce archaic paper-based systems; can have certain level of control and knowledge about the areas they manage; and can be responsive to staff and students' needs.
5. HEIs become attractive partners for research networks and education grids.
6. Society at large has the benefit of ICT-literate graduates.
7. With their new-found ICT expertise and experience, the university ICT specialist becomes a prime resource, helping the public sector start using ICT effectively.

Technology-Based Higher Education

A global economy driven by increased trade, investment and mobility of people has forced many states to adapt their higher education to the transformed global realities. This has led to changes in the occupational structure and enhancement of skills and knowledge requirements for employment. A paradigm shift has been noticed in higher education now-a-days from 'national education' to 'global education' from 'one time education for a few' to 'life education for all' from 'teacher-centric education' to 'learner centric educations'. These changes make news

What ICT Delivers?

✓ Environmental Awareness
✓ ICT infrastructure to support 21st Century transformation of teaching & learning (e.g. industrial strength out/indoor learning)
✓ Move from industrial to knowledge economy-problem solving (key skill changes
✓ ICT as the Vth Utility (robust and working)
✓ Personalized Learning Environment (Martini) learner led-learners creating content
✓ Flexible and sustainable to adapt to future learning environments (children competing in world market for jobs)
✓ Transformation to raise standards (kit that works when needed)
✓ ICT to help break down barriers (parent classes, information screens)
✓ Ability to allow children to collaborate with each other, community, other schools and other countries
✓ Curriculum training support in conjunction with NCC Advisory Service

demands and pose fresh challenges to the established education systems and practices in India (UGC Recommendations).

Innovative Technology in Higher Education provides opportunities to identify needs among our communities and learners, envisions solutions, and identifies technology, resources, partnership and programs to make it happen. In the process, we learn that the pathway is not linear, and that as we are learning about technology along the way, we are also learning about our learners, our organizations, and ourselves (Kins, P. Kathleen & Jaon K. Griggs). Working with pioneering technologies in higher education is a vibrant and rigorous process of envisioning, determining and discovering the potential of schooling and learning. Looking at the differences sectors, most studies indicate that the use of ICT for learning is most widespread in tertiary education. The HELIOS e-Learning Observatory concludes:

1. Tertiary education is the sector where ICT usage is most diffused, and this is supported by significant public and sometimes private investment.

2. The level of ICT usage in schools and for Vocational Education and Training (VET) is still moderate and related investments are also judged to be moderate, or low, though it is increasing in majority of the countries.
3. The level of usage of ICT for learning and related investment in continuous training and lifelong learning is from low to moderate, though more investments are being made, as in the case of VET (HELIOS, 2006, Punie Dieter, Yves, & others, 2006). ICT can be used as a tool in the process of education in several ways.

Higher Education in India

Higher education is a means to social mobility and empowerment in a society, highly stratified by class and other traditional status markers. The notion about higher education is that it is a freezing and moulding process by which individuals learn to lead the "examined life". Social mobility, on the other hand, is brought about in relation to two things: The first is the role of credentials acquired at this level in "opening doors" in meritocratic societies. The second is of the individual at this level of education that entitles him/her to claim larger share of the "value created" in manufacturing and service sectors of the economy (Chandrasekharan, Sandhya, 2011).

Economic reforms in early 1990s saw a rise in entrepreneurship in India. The growing culture of entrepreneurship accelerated the expansion of higher education, especially private higher education in the country. During this period, very few universities and colleges were set up by the Government sector and fewer were provided with Government financial support. The post 1980 period saw the emergence of new types of providers for higher education in India. At the same time, barriers to entry and operation of these institutions also became effective.

The challenges before the education system in India are of the following character:

- *Access to Higher Education*: Individual's participation in higher education is dependent on his/her religious affiliations, socio-economic status and demographic characteristics (Basant, Rakesh & Gitanjali Sen., 2010), (S. Thanuskodi, 2011).
- *Quality of Education*: Naresh Kumar has highlighted and focused on poor technology/infrastructure support in many institutions in India and observed that physical facilities are obsolete. Significant quality problems exist in less-selective colleges and universities in India. The university arrangements inherited in

the mid 20th century were not helpful for the development of an effective higher education (Altbach, Philip G, 2009).

- *Funding Allocation*: India faces significant challenges in funding its rapidly expanding higher education system (Agarwal, 2009).

To summarize, the Table 11.2 shows the main benefits of using ICT in education to the various stakeholders:

Table 11.2: Benefits of ICT in Higher Education to its Stakeholders

Sl. No.	*Construct*	*Content Categories*
1.	Student Administration	• Usage of electronic media by students to apply for admissions. • Usage of computers for student's registration/enrolment. • Availability of timetable/class schedule in electronic form. • Usage of computers for maintenance of attendance of students. • Usage of e-media for notifications regarding hostel accommodation. • Usage of e-media for notifications regarding transportation.
2.	Staff Administration	• Usage of computers for recruitment and work allotment to staff in the Institution • Automation of attendance and leave management of staff members in the Institution. • Usage of electronic media for performance appraisal. • E-circulars from the institution regarding official matters. • E-kiosks are available in the institution. • Communication with staff using e-media.
3.	General Administration	• Usage of e-media for scheduling/allocation of halls for examinations. • Dissemination of information in the institution through e-kiosks. • Usage of e-media by students to apply for university examinations. • Usage of e-media for the processing and display of results of students. • Facility for students to make fee payments electronically.

There are concerns about the quality of higher education provided in India currently. India has debatably one of the least-enabling environments in higher education and has always shied away from the elementary reforms required to make it competitive. There is an annual outflow of more than 150,000 students to institutes in the west every year, driving out nearly 2 to 3 billion dollars in foreign exchange per annum. It makes India the second largest target market globally for educational institutes in the west (Bhatia, Kareena & Manoj, Kumar Dash (2011). In 2010-11 there were 7,361 degree providing institutions that ran 10,364 programmes with an intake capacity of 19, 54,482 students. However, the engineering and technical infrastructure is not uniform and is more skewed towards South Central, South and North West region. Andhra Pradesh, Tamil Nadu, Uttar Pradesh and Maharashtra have the largest number of institutes and North East States have least number of technical institutes (Naresh Kumar).

In India, the problem of reaching world class standards, over the years, has not been as pressing as meeting the larger needs of the population, which has resulted in low standards. However, in the current Indian scenario, graduates have done well for themselves, and as industries have also flourished, they have found a gainful place in knowledge-controlled world economy. Jobs, particularly in disciplines and subjects that have link with knowledge industry, have increased (Lather, Anu Singh, & Khatri, Puja, 2011). The Indian youths now prefer those educational institutions which adhere to high standards.

In India, the students cannot move between institutions carrying credits for completed coursework with the ease with which their counterparts do in the US, Europe or China (Balakrishnan,Uday, 2009). The Indian system of technical education is passing through a transitional phase as many private players are entering the educational system. The universities need to establish links with industries and research organizations to meet the present and future challenges of rapid technological changes and industrial development in India.

Integrating Technology in Higher Education

In India, traditionally the main source of ICT and software professionals has been the public sector educational institutes such as the IITs (Indian Institute of Technology), ITIs (Industrial Training Institutes) and engineering colleges. In 1984, the Sampath Committee reviewed the training needs in the fields of electronics and software, and in 1985 a Standing Committee on Computer Education was set up to plan further actions. By 1996, new courses were introduced in about 400 institutions, under the computer manpower development program, supported by DoE, and produced some 15,000 software personnel. The DoE's support has not been restricted only to financial grants, but also involves curriculum development. These include NCST and C-DAC (offering advanced software engineering courses) and CMC Ltd., ETTDC and NIC, providing routine software application training (K J Joseph, 2002).

Notable initiatives of use of ICT in education in India include:

- *Indira Gandhi National Open University (IGNOU):* It uses radio, television, and internet technologies.
- *National Programme on Technology Enhanced Learning*: This is a concept similar to the open courseware initiative of MIT. It uses internet and television technologies (National Programme on Technology Enhanced Learning, India, 2007).
- *Eklavya Initiative*: It uses internet and television to promote distance learning (EKLAVYA Technology Channel, India, 2007).
- *IIT-Kanpur:* It has developed Brihaspati, an open source e-learning platform (Bhattacharya and Sharma, 2007).
- *IIM Calcutta:* This premier institute has entered into a strategic alliance with NIIT for providing programmes through virtual classrooms. Jadavpur University is using a mobile-learning centre (Bhattacharya and Sharma, 2007).
- *IIT-Bombay*: It has started the program of CDEEP (Centre for Distance Engineering Education Program), as emulated classroom interaction, through the use of real time interactive satellite technology (Centre for Distance Engineering Education Programme, India, 2007).
- *One Laptop per Child (OLPC):* Under this initiative, in Maharashtra, all efforts are being made to make provision for one Laptop per child (2007).
- *One Laptop per intermediate passed students scheme:* This scheme was started by Uttar Pradesh Government (2012).

India has actively promoted the use of ICTs in the education sector, ranging from radio to satellite based interactive television. The GOI has implemented several national as well as state precise schemes that run parallel to large number of privately led ICT initiatives at school and higher education levels.

The Knowledge Commission Report constituted in 2005 suggested for the creation of knowledge in science and technology laboratories. It also suggested for improving the management of institutions engaged in Intellectual Property Rights. Yashpal Committee gained a deeper understanding of the critical issues afflicting the Indian higher education (An Interim Report). The challenge that the universities and other higher educational institutions have to respond to is how to connect to the fragmented reality that has resulted from the powerful forces of modernity.

The Twelfth Five Year Plan has proposed for improved technology for education delivery at higher educational level. Technology for enhancing the teaching-learning experience will ensure better outcomes. India's higher education can be expected to be better aligned to industry and global practices, and be more transparent and inclusive by the end of

Twelfth Plan Period, provided the Government is able to create an enabling regulatory environment and put in place robust implementation, monitoring and quality assurance mechanisms. The Government intends to achieve enrolment of 35.9 million students in higher education institutions with a GER of 25.2 per cent by the end of Twelfth Five Year Plan through the co-existence of multiple types of institutions, including research-centric, teaching and vocation-focused ones (Higher Education in India, Twelfth Five Year Plan (2012-2017) and Beyond.

Conclusion

Diffusion of Technology, in Indian higher education scenario, would respond to the twenty-first century demands. The contemporary higher education systems are aiming for acquisition of technology skills as part of the core education system. Given the wide disparities in access to ICTs between different groups, there are serious concerns that the use of ICTs in education will widen existing divisions drawn along economic, social, cultural, geographic and gender lines (Tinio, Victoria, L.). The introduction of ICTs in education, when done without careful deliberation, can result in the further marginalization of those who are already disadvantaged.

Recommendations

1. The stakeholders should be convinced about the need of technology for teaching and learning. The availability of equipment and its integration into the classroom should be looked into.
2. Accountability of inspection and maintainance of quality control of classroom technologies.
3. Maintaining supplies appropriately and adopting approaches (including staff training) for speedy responses to breakdowns.
4. Offer training programs and launch particular venues wherein faculties can come together and exchange experiences with usage of softwares for instruction.
5. Universities should reorganize institutional support programs to make them as efficient as possible. To supply the finest opportunities for each student's learning, the University needs to guarantee a system than can deal with a range of problems.

12

The Islamic Philosophy of Education

Andleeb

Islam has a comprehensive philosophy in every sphere – social, political, economic, educational, etc. Islam lays greater emphasis on seeking knowledge. In addition, it always encourages education, research and improvement of the societal structures. The personality of Prophet Muhammad as a philosopher was most comprehensive and dynamic. He was the model of virtue and spirituality. He was a noble and compassionate teacher, a guide, and a reformer. He always emphasized peace and harmonious relations instead of fight. He built sacred bonds of brotherhood within the community. In his interactions with everybody, his approach was always that of an educator. His teachings address the entire life cycle (i.e., from birth to afterlife). Muslims believe that he is the last Messenger sent by God for the guidance of humankind until the Day of Judgment.

The paper discusses the principal tenets of educational philosophy of Islam as conveyed by Prophet Muhammad. These include principles and aims of education, emphasis on seeking knowledge, main bodies of knowledge prevailing at the time of the Prophet, various methods and techniques of teaching, women education, discipline, education for inculcating values and status of teacher, etc.

Islamic Philosophy

The Arabic word *falsafah* is a direct borrowing from the Greek words *philo sophia,* meaning philosophy. During Islamic history, the term was used for Islamic philosophy as well as for the debates between the philosophers and the theologians from one period to another.

Each religion has its own philosophy. Islam has a comprehensive philosophy in every sphere, socio-political, economic, educational, etc. Unfortunately, Islam has only recently begun to receive the attention it deserved in the non-Islamic world. The following statement of Ali (R.A.) displays the core philosophy of Islam, "*Have you fully realized what Islam is? It is indeed a religion founded on truth. It is such a fountain-*

head of learning that several streams of wisdom and knowledge flow from it. It is such a lamp that several lamps will be lighted from it."

Islam lays greater emphasis on seeking knowledge. Islam decrees education for all humans – men and women. In addition, Islam always encourages education, research and improvement of the societal structures. The Muslims contributed to the development of physics and chemistry, and they were the ones responsible for the creation of Algebra. We should learn from others, complying with the words of Prophet Muhammad, "*Seek knowledge from the cradle to the grave. Seek knowledge even if it is to be found in a place as distant as China.*"

Early Life of Prophet Muhammad

Prophet Muhammad (peace be upon him) was born in Mecca, the desert of Arabia, on April 20, 571 C.E. Prophet Muhammad received divine revelations -The Holy *Qur'ân*- from God via angel Gabriel. Muslims believe that he is the last Messenger sent by God for the guidance of humankind until the Day of Judgment. In addition to the instructions in the *Holy Qur'an*, over 100,000 *Hadith* (sayings of prophet and explanations of the revealed information) are attributed to him. All his teachings offer guidance in the fundamentals of Islamic education for every Muslim. His teachings address the entire life cycle (i.e., from birth to after life).

Principles Followed by Prophet Muhammad

A comprehensive review of Islamic literature reveals that many scholars (Al-ghazali, Al'asqalani, Swayyid) have investigated prophetic education. The Prophet strove to convey the key principles of Islam to his companions. Some of the principles followed by the prophet are

(1) Provide guidance to the humanity
(2) Begin from the possible
(3) See advantage in disadvantage
(4) Make a friend out of an enemy
(5) The power of peace is stronger than the power of violence
(6) Do not be a dichotomous thinker
(7) Always look for a third option, instead of focusing on two alone
(8) Gradualism instead of radicalism
(9) Be pragmatic in controversial matters

British orientalist remarked: "He faced adversity with the determination to writing success out of failure".

Aims of Education in Islamic Philosophy

In the system of Islamic Republic, there should be a purpose in every act. Moreover, the aims and purposes should be definite. The learner, who is a human, is made up of two components – spirit and body. The spiritual faculty is known as the *ruh* (soul), *aql* (mind), *qalb* (emotion), or *nafs* (self). *Aql* elevates above the rest of creation. The soul could be elevated to the noblest and it could be debased to the lowest, depending upon the knowledge and actions of the person.

Realization of truth and reality

"Truth and Reality" are most emphasized themes in Islam. Therefore, Islam believes in the possibility of obtaining knowledge of what is truth and real. Here we can see the influence of Idealism.

Maintaining purity of soul

The Prophet said, "*Fear Allah wherever you are, and follow up a bad deed with a good deed and it will wipe it out. And behave towards people with a good behavior*" (Al-Nawwi, 2000, Hadith 18). This *hadith* addresses several of the Prophet Muhammad's aims. The first statement is an acknowledgment between the human and Allah that one should maintain the purity of one's soul for Allah at all times because Allah is always watching what we do.

Being good to people

The Prophet wanted people to know that they do not exist on this planet alone, rather they live in a society. Therefore, it is imperative that they interact with each other politely, with consideration for the needs and feeling of others. Being good to all people and dealing with them justly is one of the ultimate aims of Islam. The Prophet summarized his educational vision and mission by saying, "*I have been sent only for the purpose of perfecting good morals*" (Al-Hakim, 2000).

Principal Tenets of Prophet's Islamic Philosophy of Education

Seeking Knowledge is Obligatory

There are several *Ahadith* (sayings of Prophet Muhammad) regarding seeking knowledge. Some of them are:

- "Seeking knowledge is obligatory for every Muslim"
- "Seek knowledge and impart it to the people."
- "The best form of worship is the pursuit of knowledge."
- "Scholars should endeavor to spread knowledge and provide education to people who have been deprived of it. For, where knowledge is hidden, it disappears."

- "Seek for knowledge and wisdom, whatever the vessel from which it flows, you will never be the loser."
- "To listen to the words of the learned and to instill unto others the lessons of science which is better than religious exercises."
- "Acquire knowledge; it enables its possessor to distinguish right from the wrong, it lights the way to heaven, it is our friend in the desert, our society in solitude, our companion when friendless, it guides us to happiness, it sustains us in misery, it is an Ornament among friends and an armor against enemies."

Allah says in the Quran:

- "*Read in the name of your Lord who has created man from a clot of blood... Who (Allah) has taught by the pen. He taught man what he knew not*" (96:1-5)
- Allah says: "*Are those who know equal to those who know not? It is only (persons) of understanding who will remember (get a lesson from Allah's Signs and Verses)*" (39:9).

Al-Ghazali (1997) referred to engagement in the learning process as the most sincere form of worship. Knowledge and its pursuit were of utmost importance to the Prophet. From the very beginning of the revelations from Allah through Gabriel, the messages stressed the importance of learning, particularly reading and writing. Learning by writing is one of the best ways of education. Writing once is equal to reading ten times. By writing, we engrave the topic both on the paper and in our minds and hearts. Prophet Muhammad said as follows regarding this issue: "*Bind knowledge by writing.*" Muslims are encouraged to remember and implement all of their spiritual and intellectual knowledge and skills. The Prophet Muhammad also advocated that both males and females learn to read and write. Some of his lectures were addressed specifically to women. Because he hoped to eliminate illiteracy, he sent Abd Allah ibn Said ibn Al-Asi of Mecca to Madinah to teach the people there to read and write (Bilgrami & Ashraf, 1985). The Prophet Muhammad said, "*How can some people not educate, teach, advise and admonish their (neighbors), and how can some people not learn, not be enlightened or advised by their (neighbors)...*"

Value of Scholarship

For the learners, the Prophet said, "*A believer is never satisfied with the acquisition of knowledge till he reaches Paradise*" (Tirmidhi). The function of the prophet and the scholar appears to be essentially similar in nature according to certain traditions. According to Prophet

Muhammad, "*The Lord revealed to Abraham, 'O Abraham, I am Alim (one who knows), and I love all who have knowledge.*" According to another tradition, "*The superiority of the scholar over the recluse is that of the full moon over the rest of the stars and the learned scholars are the inheritors of the Messengers of God.*"

Branches of Knowledge

(1) *Stories*: The prophet would narrate stories to his companions and taught them lessons from these stories. Story telling became popular in the early days of the caliphate and Umar bin Khattab was the first Caliph to allow Tamim-ad-Dari (a companion of prophet and great story teller) to relate stories.
(2) *Languages:* Prophet's companions learned other languages in order to communicate the Islamic philosophy and teachings to the people of those languages. Prophet himself learned words of different languages.
(3) *Arithmetic:* The prophet laid great emphasis on a sound knowledge of inheritance. One can learn law of inheritance well only when he knows arithmetic. When the prophet enjoined on the faithful the learning of the law of inheritance, he was virtually pronouncing a religious decree in favour of learning Arithmetic. There is a well known saying by Ibn Dawwam, "*Teach your child Hisab (Arithmetic), before putting him on to the kitab (Book)*".
(4) Astrology: Al-Ghazzali, the science of astronomy, deals with the relation of cause and effect, and predicts the movements of the planets. Muslims have made splendid contributions to the development of astronomy in the past. Their calendars and astronomical charts, observations and appliances, technical names etc derived from Arabic that occurs so abundantly in the terminology of modern astronomy – all prove that this science was a respectable branch of learning from the early days.

Astronomy is recognized in the Quran as a branch of knowledge which deals with the movement of the heavenly bodies:

> "*And there is a measure for the sun and the moon.*" *Again,* "*We have assigned the moon its stages until it reverts like an old sprig*" *(The Qur'an: 36:39).*
> "*It is He who appointed the sun to give radiance, and the moon to give light, assigning it phases so you could know the number of years and reckoning of time*" *(The Qur'an; 10:05).*

Methods and Techniques of Instruction

Prophet Muhammad used various methods in order to teach people. These methods are still in vogue and prove to be very helpful in teaching-learning process. Some of these methods are-

(1) *Eloquent fingers*: Most of the traditions which involved an action which could be demonstrated with the help of the movement of the fingers of the hand describe also the actual movement made by the prophet on that occasion. Thus, he made the traditions more understandable.

(2) *Encouraged by questions*: The Prophet was very approachable. He always showed interest in what people said before him, or in what they asked about him. People would interrupt him on the pulpit and ask questions, which he answered happily; he would also praise them for asking questions. The Prophet would get students' attention by eye contact and by facing them. He was sparing in what he said and would teach only a little at a time, so as not to overload them with information. Therefore, our teachers should use questions as an opportunity to elaborate upon a topic. If the question is not a good one, teacher should turn it into a more thoughtful question.

(3) *Story telling*: Prophet Muhammad would tell stories to his companions to illustrate points. For example, the woman who gave water to the dog was forgiven of her sins by Allah because of her act of kindness. These stories and analogies can be narrated to the students in the schools for their benefit. This way they will have a richer knowledge of history, culture and ancient traditions. There is need to create common experiences to help the learner understand life better in the present context.

(4) *Teaching with examples*: One of the best methods of education is to teach by giving examples of the past. Stories and examples of great personalities have a special effect on the learner. The information imparted through stories is etched in the mind of the learner and retained for much longer.

(5) *Use of cliffhangers*: Prophet Muhammad would say something, not explain it fully and give time for the listener to figure it out. Teachers must tell the outcome at the end of the lecture otherwise this strategy will not work again. This gives room for constructive learning as well. Prophet Muhammad would at times ask a trainee to answer a question to see how well he understood.

(6) *Learning by doing*: Ahadith states that "verily knowledge comes by learning," and "One learns more by experiencing than by merely hearing" (Ahmad, 2000). One of the most effective ways of teaching is demonstrating by means of practice. People do not forget what they are taught with practice. Teaching by practice is the most fruitful method of

teaching. Our Prophet showed a man who asked about how to perform ablution. Teaching by practice engages both the eyes and the ears, and thus helps the information to stick in the mind.

(7) *Use of drawings*: Another way of providing information which will stay permanently in the mind of the learners is to make use of drawings and figures. The Prophet Muhammad explained the features of the ways of Allah and Satan by drawing shapes on the ground while sitting together with Jabir (RA). Jabir told the story as follows: When he was sitting together with the Prophet, he drew a line in front of him and said, "This is the path of Allah." Then he drew two lines to the right, and two lines to the left of the same line and said, "And these are the paths of the Satan". Then he put his hand over the line in the middle and recited the following verse of Quran: "This is my (God's) straight path, so follow it, and do not follow other paths…" The Prophet used a variety of teaching methods to instruct his companions, such as telling stories and making gestures to illustrate his point.

(8) *Repetition*: Through repetition the information is transferred from the short term memory to the long term memory. For this reason, when the Prophet Muhammad introduced new information to his companions, he often used to repeat it three times and in that way he tried to get the important points to stick in the mind. Also the number of repetitions could change according to the capacity of the interlocutors. Some might get it when it was said just once and some might need more repetitions. Anas (RA) said: "When the Messenger of Allah said a sentence, he used to repeat it up to three times making sure that it was understood" (Hakim).

(9) *Arousing interest*: A frequent technique employed by the Prophet was to ask people questions, so as to make them think and provide information themselves, upon which he would comment on the answer. He once asked: "Do you know who is a bankrupt?" to which they replied: "Someone who has no dirham or dinar?" The prophet explained: 'No, the real bankrupt is the one who comes on the Day of Judgment having collected many good deeds, but having also hit or insulted someone. Some of his good deeds will have to be given to the one he hit in compensation, and some to the one he insulted, etc. until very quickly nothing is left for him." Thus he engaged them by arousing their interests and expectations in learning.

(10) *Providing knowledge according to the mental capacity of the individual*: A number of traditions deal with a number of fundamental problems of classroom instruction, viz the adaption of teaching material to the intellectual capacity of the pupil. According to a tradition, Prophet Muhammad said, "I belong to the group of prophets and I have been commanded by the lord to treat people according to their ranks and talk

to them according to their intellectual capacity." The main aim was not to parade his knowledge of these linguistic curiosities but to bring home the people he addressed and to mould learning according to the nature of the audience. It is clearly evident that the Prophet's teachings were clear enough to be understood by all – the ignorant, the learned and the sophisticated.

Language used by Prophet Muhammad in Teaching

(1) *Soft and clear speech*: Psychologists believe that the way one speaks is actually more important than what one says. Prophet Muhammad was the most effective orator of all times and was loved by his followers. He spoke in a very easy and understandable manner. Because of this, his followers were able to memorize most of his teachings. The Prophet's wife, Aishah said: "He used to speak so clearly that if somebody wanted to count the number of his words, he could do so."

(2) *Value of spoken word*: The addresses which the prophet delivered on various occasions are couched in a simple, direct and forceful language. They are pleasant combination of high idealism, universal truths and hard realities of concrete situations. His addresses were both long and short, adapted to the needs of the situations. Generally, he did not like to deliver lengthy addresses. According to Ibn Masud, "He would cut short his address in order to save us from inconvenience."

(3) *Spontaneity and brevity in speech*: The Prophet's statements were also marked by two characteristics – spontaneity and brevity. Spontaneity and brevity mark all the genres we have in the Hadith. He was an expert at retaining the attention of his audience during the sermon and the question-answer sessions.

(4) *Use of Figures of Speech*: The similes and other figures of speech which he used did not belong to the domain of rhetoric; they were an essential device for making the meaning clear and were accordingly adapted to the intellectual level of the audience. For example, he claimed to be the last of the hierarchy of Prophets and he compared himself to the capping stone of a noble edifice without which the whole plan could not be brought to completion.

Education of Women

The prophet had a soft corner in his heart for women. In his view, their indignity and endless suffering was the darkest spot in the social life of pre-Islamic Arabia. According to Abi Said al Khudri, Prophet Muhammad said, "*One who has brought up three or two daughters, educated them, married them and acted otherwise handsomely towards them has won his title to heaven.* The Holy Prophet Mohammad said, "*Searching of knowledge is incumbent for every Muslim (male and female).*" Every boy or girl, man or woman should pursue his/her education as far as it is possible. In the history of Islam, we find that there were women who were narrators of Hadith, mystics, scholars, writers, poets and teachers in their own right. For example, Aisha Abu Bakr, the wife of Prophet Muhammad (PBUH), was known for her intellect and was a scholar of jurisprudence. Shaykha Nafisa was such a great authority on Hadith that the Imaam Shaaf'ee sat in her circle. The famous mystic Rabia al-Adawiyya (Basria) was also a woman of great wisdom and knowledge.

Counselling for Young

"*If one person gets guided by your hands, it is better for you than a red she-camel* (considered precious in Arab)", said the prophet. Despite the fact that the Prophet was confident enough to act on his own, he did not disregard the advice of others, male or female. There are several occasions, where he himself sought input from his most trusted companions. Prophet stressed on consulting with others before beginning a new work.

The confidence reposed in the younger generation by the prophet found reflection in the thought and practice of his companions. Umar would send to younger people when faced with a crisis, took their counsel on important matters of state and availed himself of their innate intelligence in the affairs of administration. They were constantly reminded of the heavy responsibility which they were expected to shoulder in future and for which they were encouraged to make preparation in earnest from the very beginning. Hasan ibn Ali said to his son and nephew, "*Learn because, although you are the younger members of the community today, you will be their great ones tomorrow.*"

Inculcating Morals and Values

Prophet Muhammad urged Muslims to restrain themselves from anger. Shouting, getting angry, embarrassing students causes them to stop listening and learning. Shouting is ineffective. Speaking quietly is more effective and certainly better for classroom control. The prophetic teachings on how to conduct one's life are in the form of instruction manual. Each person must behave appropriately and treat fellow humans with respect. These rules are same for both men and women. Women are entitled to the same education and opportunities as men, and are likewise, equally responsible for conveying these principles to their children. In order to know what to do, one must take every opportunity to learn.

Application of the Knowledge

The Prophet placed a high priority on seeking knowledge and its proper application. He took the opportunity to teach the foundations of Islam, using methods that were appropriate to the situation, and likewise encouraged his followers to do the same, a process which continues even to this day.

Discipline

The Prophet was also known for tailoring specific lessons for a particular pupil. The Prophet's guidelines for determining an appropriate punishment or penalty for undesirable behavior were that the consequences should be related to the situation. The Prophet's companions commented that his method of correcting bad behavior by example helped them remember what they were taught. *He used to criticize bad behavior, not the agent.* He said good words and did good deeds. He knew that evil words blemish the heart, and evil in the heart reflects upon the soul. For this reason, he never said an evil word either to any friend or foe. He said, "*Every child is born free from sin.*" Change and personal growth come from within; behavior does not improve spontaneously. Muslims are required to persist in modifying unacceptable behaviors, and do good deeds in order to atone for transgressions.

Educationalists and psychologists say that for sustainable long-term education, a stable and uncritical relationship between teacher and learner is a must. If we want to lead people to behave positively and prevent them from acting badly, the safest way to do this is to reward and appreciate positive action. To be loved and appreciated is what people crave. In the process of learning, people conclude from the appreciation and approval of the educators. He used a style in his speeches that affected people and made them think. Thus, he achieved permanent behavior change in people by means of the best educational methods. One example in Islamic literature tells the story of a young man who came to the Prophet and requested permission to commit adultery. The Prophet asked the young man, "Would you like your own mother to be in such illicit sexual relation?" The young man said, "No, O Prophet of God." Thus the Prophet was able to demonstrate why his request was unacceptable. The Prophet replied, "Others, too, do not like their mothers and sisters associated with fornication" (Nadvi, 1988).

No Student Left Behind

In classrooms all over the world, it is a common practice for teachers to separate the strong students from the weak. The 'weak' students are delegated to less challenging classes that do nothing to nurture the mind, while the 'smarter' ones are given every opportunity to excel. Prophet Muhammad made no distinction between students based on intelligence level, social standing or any other classification that separate them in society. He also never sought to exclude or expel anyone from the religion of Islam, but rather delivered a message that was all-inclusive to the whole of mankind.

Status of the Teacher

The teacher of higher education enjoyed a unique status in the Islamic world. Mohammad presented a pattern of moral and social leadership, which remains unexampled in the social structure of the modern world. In the educational world, a teacher's quality was determined by the number of distinguished scholars who had graduated under his direction. With respect to teachers, he said "*Allah, His angels, the dwellers of the heaven and the earth, even the ant in its hole and the fish (in water) invoke blessings on him who imparts good knowledge to the people*" (Tirmidhi). According to another tradition, the teacher is the God's trustee on earth. Another set of traditions, the group nearest to the rank of apostlehood are teachers. A number of traditions place the scholar above the martyr in merit. The scholar stands one rank higher than the martyr on the Day of Judgment. One who honours a teacher earns the merit of honouring seventy prophets and one who honours a pupil earns the merit of honoring seventy martyrs.

Prophet Muhammad as a Teacher

The Prophet as a Teacher does not need justification, since all prophets are meant to be teachers in the first instance, and the Qur'an itself has talked of the function of the Prophet Muhammad as *to teach them the book and wisdom and make them grow in purity*. The leadership of Prophet Muhammad was most comprehensive and dynamic. He was the model of virtue and spirituality. He was a noble and compassionate teacher, a guide and a reformer. He always emphasized peace and harmonious relations instead of fight. He built sacred bounds of brotherhood within the community. In his interactions with everybody, his approach was always that of an educator: "*a benevolent teacher, very tolerant, and sympathetic*" (Bilgrami & Ashraf, 1985).

Implications in Education

As a model in human relationships, the methods that the Prophet Muhammad (Peace be upon him) used in spreading his cause and mission, will prove to be effective if we can apply them successfully in our own educational activities.

What is more important than what we teach in education is how we teach it. Of course, we have to teach good and useful things to people and youth, but this must be done in an effective way. It is a well known fact that students who do not like a teacher generally do not like the subject either. A good educator should care about and love his addressee and he should be genial and positive; in fact, he should devote himself to his profession and students. Prophet Muhammad (PBUH) devoted himself to his duty. He had more qualities that an educator is expected to have. Psychologists say that the way one speaks is more important than what one says. According to research, the words spoken contribute seven per cent of the effect; the tone of voice thirty-eight per cent; and the gestures and body language have fifty-five per cent of the effect in communication between people.

To conclude, Prophet Muhammad was the best teacher of all times. His philosophy of education was based on the inner goodness of the pupil, truth and reality, and behavior modification.

13

Value Education as an Incumbent in Learner Progression

Babitha Ann Joseph

Values remain a prime factor in the quality of life, value education should also develop students' overall aspects such as effort, diligence, and perseverance in order to promote academic learning, foster an ethic of brilliance, and build up skills desirable to proceed in leading endeavors. Research on the complementary contributions of value education towards human development and achievement, and portray the ways in which teachers and schools can become capable of enhancing the learners' progression through value education is reviewed here. In this expanded vision of value education, a school or community is one that lends a hand for "being unsurpassed" in all vicinities of life.

The current wearisome civilization is crammed with hostility, conflicts, unhealthy rivalry and de-humanization activities. Mere academic and intellectual development will not equip the students to lead a serene and peaceful life in this era. Thinkers on Education have observed that 'the failure of education in the present century is not the failure to teach humankind science, language or Mathematics, but the failure to teach humankind to live together in peace and to harness the potentials in individuals and societies for full and equitable development' (V. Ordonez, 1998). This paper sets forth an expanded view of values and value education that recognizes the worth of values (in the present era) as well as value education (as an incumbent in learner progression).

Values are defined broadly as ' the principles and fundamental convictions which act as general guides to behavior, the standards by which particular actions are judged as good or desirable' (Halstead and Taylor, 2000). They are long-standing standards or principles that are used to judge the worth of an idea or action. Current Neuroscience research advocates that concepts of cognition, or intellect, are far-flung more knotted with social and emotional growth than previous educational paradigms have allowed for. In other words, the most excellently laid strategies about the technical aspects of pedagogy are bound to fail unless the growth of the whole person – social, emotional, moral, spiritual and intellectual, is the pedagogical target. Recent research on the impact of value education has clarified its association with students' vigor and wellbeing, and the need to see productive pedagogy and positive education as the growth of the whole person: intellectual, social, moral and emotional (Wyn, 2009; Snyder, Lopez & Pedrotti, 2011).

Values education is broader and refers to any explicit and/or implicit school-based activity to promote understanding and knowledge of values among students, and to inculcate the skills and dispositions of students so they can enact particular values as individuals and as members of the wider community. Presently, the scope of value education has been expanded to education from the holistic point of view. In the traditional model of value education, prominence was given to the essence of values and not on the valuer, who chooses and acts on the values. The approach is more teacher-centered, and the learner simply adopts a more passive role, simply engrossing the content being handed down. There is a shift in the humanistic model, from content to process based, values to valuer-focused, and teacher to student-centered orientation. The greater part of the learning will now involve the valuing process where a dynamic interaction within the individual learner (and educator) and between each other occurs. Here, the educator awakens the consciousness of the learners in terms of their responsibility as valuers, the ones who determine their own value system.

The Australian Government's *National Value Education Initiative* (2002-2010) highlights the strong links and explicit nature of value education as outlined in the *Melbourne Declaration on Educational Goals for Young Australians 2008* which states that 'schools play a vital role in the oral, spiritual and aesthetic development and wellbeing of young Australians'. In particular, it notes (pp. 6-9) that schools have a responsibility to support young Australians so that they develop personal values and attributes such as honesty, resilience, empathy and respect for others; have the knowledge, skills, understanding and values to establish and maintain healthy and satisfying lives; act with moral and ethical integrity; and are committed to national values of democracy, equity and justice and participate in Australia's civic life. The process of teaching students how to clarify and analyze their own values and those of others has added a new dimension to value education.

Learner Progression

Learner progression is defined as the affirmative advance of the learner towards the goals of Education. It refers to the expedition by the learner towards personal and educational goals and aspirations. Learner progression is a significant entity in the upcoming life of the learner since it's about the development of one's own aspirations and ambitions of life. There are various characteristics for learner progression such as

- Has no binding of time and thus it can be measured at any period of time.
- Significant for personal development, since it enhances self worth and confidence of the learners.
- Can affect, change and make the goals of an individual.
- Encouragement of the learner is essential in this venture.
- The pathways and the destinations may not be clear to the learner in the initial stage.
- It is an individual-centered process.
- Involves a complex combination of learning styles and strategies.
- Variety of modes like self study, blended learning, distance education, technology etc can be used which aid in the empowerment of the learner.
- It may not be concentrated in a specific place and can be taken up in a wide range of situations.

Aim Higher West Area Partnership (2010) put forward a concept of learner progression which points out that progression to higher levels of education requires more than just attainment of qualifications. Based upon this idea that learner progression is a product of three interrelated factors, we can derive a simple equation for progression from the point of view of the learner:

Aspiration + Awareness + Attainment = Progression

The notion of learner progression in the educational endeavour has a large impact on the holistic development of the learner. As the most influential aspects of learner Progression is related to the realm of affect, the value structure of the individual needs becomes a major concern. The self impetus, personality traits, internal value system, decision making power etc of the learner affects the progression. It was found out that confidence in one's ability to master academic work is a strong predictor of school achievement among academically struggling students (NRC, 2004).

The deterioration of values has been in existence throughout the history of mankind and is shared by all cultures, but the present-day degeneration of values has become a subject of big concern in our nation. Children are surrogates of the upcoming generation. As per the population projection, India will have one of the youngest populations in the world by 2020. The kind of education we provide to them will have bearing on the value foundation of the society. So the educators and curriculum framers should be vigilant in setting up a fruitful frame work of value education in the school curriculum.

Value Education as an Incumbent in Learner Progression

Value education acts as an incumbent in the learner progression. Three main facets of value education that are needed to promote learner progression, as illustrated in Figure 13.1. given below are focussed here. First, to construct secure and caring learning milieu; second, to promote a culture that encourages feedback; and finally to strengthen mastery learning strategies. Taken together, these three components of value education will mutually reinforce each other in the enrichment of learner progression.

Figure 13.1 Enrichment of Learner Progression

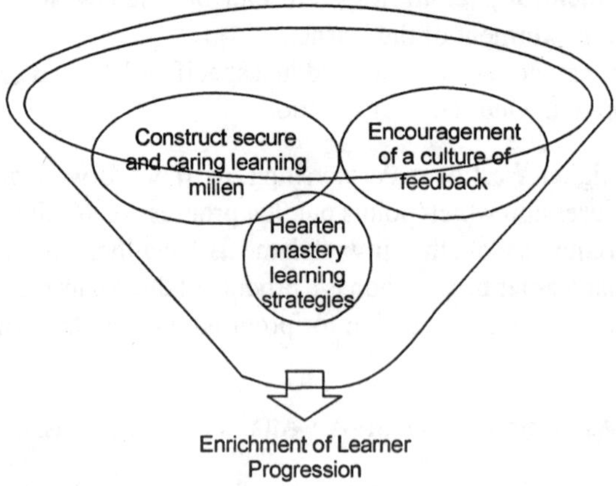

Construct Secure and Caring Learning Milieu

A safe and supportive learning environment is a prime factor for the conducive development of the learner. The relationship between the teachers and students, democratic atmosphere in and out of the classroom and tolerance among the students will have an impact on the learner progression. The teachers should train the students how to handle their behaviour and resolve conflicts; and how to use opportunities to acknowledge and reinforce appropriate behaviour. If the students receive a greater sense of love, support, care, connectedness and belongingness, they will achieve a greater competence for self reflection and self appraisal. So a secure and caring learning milieu is a nurturing factor for the enrichment of learner progression.

Promotion of a Culture that Encourages Feedback

Individual and Group feedback sessions can serve as a vital approach for budding the learner progression. Students need to develop a culture of showing their efforts to the peers, seek explanations and ideas from their peers and the teacher, and use that feedback to improve and progress their work. The educator can use the feedback gathering as the best possible situation for teaching students indispensable academic concepts and skills. Through this course of action of encouraging group critique, guided by norms of reverence and concern, students function as an ethical learning community where they not only follow their own best work but also make every effort to bring into focus each other's best work. This will encourage students to develop a better capability for regulating their own and their peers' behavior. It will also help the teachers to re- examine the students' practices and roles which in turn will facilitate in the enhancement of learner progression.

Strengthen Mastery Learning Strategies

Mastery learning was put forward by Benjamin.S. Bloom (1968) as an approach to teaching that has much potential to develop performance character. Mastery learning requires all students to achieve a certain level of mastery of a given concept or skill. If they do not achieve it on the first try, they keep trying. The students have to ponder in the process of construction of knowledge and learning occurs through making mistakes and tackling them. The attitude of self help, motivation, decision making power, ability to handle different skills in unison etc will be fostered in the students. The inculcation of mastery learning strategies will develop the confidence level of the learners. In total the usage of mastery learning strategies aids in the advancement of learner's progression.

Conclusion

Education is an inevitable procedure of inculcating values to endow the learner to lead a gratifying life in accordance with the cherished values and morals of the society. Since the current mode of education focuses primarily on the cognitive aspects, the alienation between head and heart is not properly taken care. The ultimate goal of education is for the enhancement of learner progression. The learner progression takes place successfully through the three main facets of value education viz, construct secure and caring learning milieu, promotion of a culture that encourage feedback and finally to hearten mastery learning strategies. In this expanded vision of value education, a school or community is one that lends a hand for "being unsurpassed" in all vicinities of our lives.

14

Women Empowerment in India

A Case Study

Ashok Mittal, Qamar Alam and *Arifa Saleem*

> "There is no tool for development more effective than the empowerment of woman" –*Kofi Annan* (Former UN Gen. Secretary)

Empowerment is the most frequently used term in development dialogue today. Empowerment literally means "to enable". It refers to accessibility and control over the existing resources that include material, human and intellectual aspects. The term "women empowerment" refers to the process of strengthening the hands of women who have been suffering from various disabilities, inequalities and gender discrimination. Women empowerment means self-esteem and self-reliance.

Intellectuals have long taken the socio-economic development of Indian Muslims for granted. This is evident from the scarcity of systematic studies on their socio-economic conditions. Two official reports, the *Gopal Singh Committee Report* (1982) and the *Sachhar Committee Report* (2006) have addressed socio-economic conditions of Muslims to some extent. After the submission of the Sachar Committee Report, several studies have undertaken data-based analysis of the socio-economic and educational conditions of Muslims in India. Sachar Committee Report was probably the first attempt to analyse the conditions of Muslim community, using large-scale empirical data. It clearly brought out the relative deprivation of Muslims in India in various dimensions, including employment and education. After publication of the Report, researchers and social scientists tried to focus on education, elimination of gender discrimination and economic status of Muslim women in India. In this paper, we are mainly focussing on the empowerment of Muslim women in India with special reference to Aligarh city.

It is essential for women to be able to lead an independent existence and emerge from their secondary status. Mrs. Pratibha Devi Singh Patil (former President of India) rightly said, "Half the population is women's population i.e. half the talent, half the progress and half the development".

Thus, there is a need to develop and empower women in order to achieve growth and development of the country. The concept of development requires a 'relook' and it should include a focus on women.

Through empowerment, women would gain the strength to create space for themselves to grow, seek justice, have access to resources, equal opportunities and lead a life of her own towards self-fulfilment. Women today have acquired their own role in the growth and development of the economy. Under the Five Year Plans, several approaches were adopted for women in India. Welfare approach was adopted from first to fifth five year plan. There was a shift in approach from welfare to Development Approach in the seventh five year plan and continued in eighth five year plan. Further, the approach was shifted to Women Empowerment in the ninth five year plan. Women empowerment is typically discussed in relation to *political, social and economic empowerment*, but the economic empowerment of women has received particular attention and is often cited as one of the most important ways to promote gender equality, reduce poverty and improve the well-being of not only women but children and societies at large. Economic empowerment includes women's participation in economic activities as well as women's economic decision-making power. Employment, specifically paid employment, is seen as the fundamental component of economic empowerment. The assumption is that there is a link between employment and women empowerment.

Some existing literature on economic, social and political empowerment of women studied is described in Table 14.1.

Table 14.1: Brief Review of Literature

	Studies
Economic Empowerment	Blumberg (2005), Ahmad, J. (2009), OECD (2011), Muzammil (2002 and 2014)
Social Empowerment	Rao (1986), Stephan (1994), Achala (2009), Vimala (1998)
Political Empowerment	Sushila (1988), Saskia, W. (1994), Chattopadhyay and Duflo (2001), Karat, G. (2005), Desai and Thakkar (2007), Figueras (2008)

We are mainly emphasizing on economic empowerment of women in general and Muslim women in particular. Economic empowerment constitutes one of the fundamental building blocks in efforts towards the overall empowerment of women. Participation in formal economic activities on terms and conditions which reflect productive capacity of women, and their control over their own incomes, are some of the important dimensions of economic empowerment. Access to earned income improves women's position within the household substantially, gives them greater control over the distribution of such earning and household resources, and generally improves their status and strength in society as well as their own self-esteem. The ability to earn income from outside and to engage in activities other than household-oriented ones can lead to significant social change in the long run. Where women are generally denied the ownership of property and control over assets, the ability to earn outside income can become an important instrument for the transformation of gender relations and challenge many traditional modes of social and economic relations.

Demographic Size and Caste Ratio in India

Muslims are the largest minority in India and the number of Muslim women (about 60 millions) in India (in 2001) was larger than the total population of United Kingdom or France. The proportion of different communities in total population in India is shown in Table 14.2.

Table 14.2: Minorities in India: Proportion of Total Population

Category	*Ratio in Population in India 2001 (percentage)*	*Adult Sex Ratio (women per 1000 men)*	*Child Sex Ratio (girls per 1000 boys)*
Hindus	81.4	931	925
Muslims	12.4	936	950
Jains	00.4	940	870
Sikhs	01.9	893	786
Christians	02.3	1009	964
Buddhists	00.8	953	942
Others	00.7	992	976

Note: Child sex ratio is about 0-6 years of girls per 1,000 boys.
Source: Eleventh Five Year Plan, GoI, Vol. II

Muslim women are unevenly distributed in the country, concentrating mostly in Bihar, Uttar Pradesh and West Bengal, apart from Jammu and Kashmir where the Muslim population is predominant. The provision of reservation has adversely affected the employment position of the Muslim community and Muslim women. The reason is quite simple. While 22.2 per cent of Hindu population is under Schedule Caste (SC) category, only 0.8 per cent Muslims come under this head. Similarly, while 9 per cent of the Hindus are classified as Schedule Tribes (ST), only 0.5 per cent Muslims belong to this group. Even in the Other Backward Caste (OBC) category, where the ratio is substantial even in the Muslim community, it is still lower (39.2%) as compared to the ratio of OBC in the Hindu community (42.8%). Table 14.3 represents the distribution of different religions, caste-wise population. It highlights the dominance of general category among the Muslims to the order of about 60 per cent as compared to 26 per cent for Hindus.

Table 14.3: Distribution of Population by Caste Categories

Religion	*SC*	*ST*	*OBC*	*General*	*All*
Hindu	22.2	9.1	42.8	26.0	100
Muslim	0.8	0.5	39.2	59.5	100
Christian	9.0	32.8	24.8	33.3	100
Sikh	30.7	0.9	22.4	46.1	100
Jain	0.0	2.6	3.0	94.3	100
Buddhists	89.5	7.4	0.4	2.7	100
Zoroastrians	0.0	15.9	13.7	7.4	100
Others	2.6	82.5	6.2	8.7	100
Total	19.7	8.5	41.1	30.8	100

Source: Muzammil, (2014) ed. Mishra, R.

Economic Empowerment of Muslim Women

Women as such are poorest of the poor in the world. A study of the World Bank has shown that they have only 2 per cent of property ownership in their name (Muzammil, 2002). Since the Muslim community is a poor community in India, the general status of Muslim women is bound to be poor. Although, Muslim women have been given by *Islamic Sharia* equal rights in economic matters like men, in practice, they are often denied those rights and are unable to participate and receive pecuniary benefits. The ratio of Muslim women employment as regular workers in urban areas is 15.7 per cent as compared to 27.7 per cent for Hindu women, and 51.5 per cent for Christian women. This highlights their marginal presence in salaried jobs. Islam as such is a fashioner of development. It does not obstruct the educational or economic development of its womenfolk. However, the man-made *Islamic Sharia* came in the way of the socio-economic upliftment of the community. The work participation rate of Muslim women is certainly lower among the minority communities, but not the lowest as highlighted in Table 14.4.

The female work participation rate among Muslim women is almost half of the Hindu community. As a matter of fact, it is the lowest among the women of the Jain community. There are a number of reasons for low work participation rate of Muslim women in India. They mostly have to stay at home and take care of their siblings. The child population is higher in the Muslim community. Some 23 per cent of the Muslim population is under nine years of age, which force them to stay at home. Another reason is lack of entrepreneurship among Muslim women and disbursement of

Table 14.4: Work Participation Rate of Muslim Women and other Communities

Category	*Female Work Participation Rate (percentage)*
Hindus	27.5
Muslims	14.1
Jain	9.2
Sikhs	20.2
Christians	28.7
Buddhists	31.7
Others	44.2

Source: Eleventh Five Year Plan, Vol-II, GoI.

loans to Muslims has been relatively less as compared to other minorities. The average amount of the bank loan disbursed to the Muslims is 2/3rd of the amount disbursed to other minorities (Sachar Committee Report, 2006).

Educational Status

According to Gandhi if you educate a male you educate a person, but if you educate a woman, you educate the entire family. Education has continued to evolve, diversify and extend its reach since the dawn of human history. Now the time has come to give a new direction to the age-old education system. Education is essential for all and is fundamental to their all-round development, material and spiritual. Every community develops its own standard of education to express and promote its unique socio-economic identity and also to meet the growing challenges with the changing times. Muslims are at a double disadvantage with low levels of education, combined with low quality education. Their deprivation increases many-folds as the level of education rises. With a wide gender gap in literacy level, Muslim women also have a high rate of dropouts at an early stage. The female literacy rate in India for Muslims is about 50 per cent and for Hindus 53 per cent (see Table 14.5).

Economic backwardness is often the result of educational deprivation. There are several reasons responsible for the pathetic state of affairs of Muslim women. In densely populated states like Bihar and Uttar Pradesh, the condition of Muslim women is very deplorable and this is one of the reasons of their economic subordination and overall poor living conditions.

Table 14.5: Total Female Literacy of Different Communities in India

Category	*Total Literacy (percentage)*	*Female Literacy (percentage)*
Hindus	65.1	53.2
Muslims	59.1	50.1
Jains	94.1	90.6
Sikhs	69.4	63.1
Christians	80.3	76.2
Buddhists	72.7	61.7
Others	47.0	33.2

Source: Eleventh Five Year Plan, Vol-II, GoI.

A CASE STUDY OF ALIGARH CITY

Aligarh is an ancient city in the north Indian state of Uttar Pradesh. It is situated in the western part of Uttar Pradesh. Aligarh has several best educational institutions of India. It is popularly known as the 'Mecca of Education'. The present population of the city is more than 8.27 lakhs.

Let us examine and assess the factors which may be considered crucial in enhancing women empowerment and awareness of various government policies for women through a convenient sample of 300 women from two localities of Aligarh city. Data has been collected by questionnaire method. We have tried to analyse, interpret and capture the various factors at micro level like relationship between age and occupation, occupation and job satisfaction, occupation and level of education, etc. A Chi-square test is employed to test the various hypotheses

Factors Responsible for Women Empowerment

Age and Occupation

H_0: There is no relationship between age and occupation.
H_1: There is a relationship between age and occupation.

On the basis of Table 14.6 our calculated Chi-square value, i.e. 1140.25 is greater than the tabulated value, i.e. 12.592 at 6 degrees of freedom and 5 per cent significance level. Thus, we reject the null hypothesis and accept the alternative. We conclude that there is a relationship between age and occupation.

Age and Job Satisfaction

H_0: There is no association between age and job satisfaction.
H_1: There is an association between age and job satisfaction.

Table 14.6: Age and Occupation

Occupation	Age (years)				
	Upto 20	20-35	35-50	50 and above	Total
Employed	18	36	48	6	108
Self-employed	12	18	6	12	48
Unemployed	6	108	18	12	144
Total	36	162	72	30	300

Table 14.7: Age and Job Satisfaction

Job Satisfaction	Age (Years)				
	Upto 20	20-35	35-50	50 and above	Total
Satisfied	24	90	66	18	198
Dissatisfied	18	60	12	12	102
Total	42	150	78	30	300

In Table 14.7, our calculated Chi-square value is 510, which is greater than the tabulated value 7.815 at 3 degrees of freedom and 5 per cent significance level. We, therefore, reject the null hypothesis and accept the alternative and conclude that there is an association between age and job satisfaction.

Age and Motive of Job

H_0: There is no association between age and motive of the job.
H_1: There is an association between age and motive of the job.

Table 14.8: Age and Motive of Job

Motive of Job	Age (years)				
	Upto 20	20-35	35-50	50 and above	Total
Income	30	90	42	24	186
Job Satisfaction	6	72	30	6	114
Total	36	162	72	30	300

Table 14.8 reveals that the calculated value of Chi-square is 589.7 which is greater than the tabulated value, i.e. 7.815 at 3 degrees of freedom and 5 per cent significance level. Thus, we accept the alternative hypothesis and reject the null hypothesis. We conclude that there is a significant association between age and motive of the job.

Occupation and Monthly Income

H_0: Level of monthly income does not depend on occupation.
H_1: Level of monthly income depends on the occupation.

Table 14.9: Occupation and Monthly Income

Occupation	*Monthly Income (rupees)*				
	Upto 5000	*5000-15000*	*15000-25000*	*25000 and above*	*Total*
Employed	24	54	18	24	120
Self-employed	6	6	24	6	42
Unemployed	102	18	12	6	138
Total	132	78	54	36	300

Table 14.9 projects the calculated Chi-square value, i.e. 350.8 is greater than the tabulated value, i.e. 12.592 at 6 degrees of freedom and 5 per cent significance level. We, therefore, reject the null hypothesis and accept the alternative and conclude that the level of monthly income depends on the occupation.

Occupation and Levels of Education

H_0: Occupation does not depend on levels of education.
H_1: Occupation depends on levels of education.

On the basis of our calculation in Table 14.10, the calculated value of Chi-square 162.98 is greater than the tabulated value 12.692 at 6 degrees of freedom and 5 per cent significance level. Thus, we accept the alternative hypothesis and reject the null hypothesis. We conclude that occupation depends on level of education.

Occupation and Literacy

H_0: The occupation does not depend on literacy.
H_1: The occupation depends on literacy.

Table 14.10: Occupation and Levels of Education

Occupation	*Levels of Education*				
	Less than High School	*Intermediate*	*Graduate*	*PG and above*	*Total*
Employed	30	24	42	24	120
Self-employed	18	6	12	6	42
Unemployed	18	6	12	102	138
Total	66	36	66	132	300

Table 14.11: Occupation and Literacy

Occupation	Number of Literates		
	Yes	No	Total
Employed	84	24	108
Self-employed	30	18	48
Unemployed	138	6	144
Total	252	48	300

From Table 14.11, the calculated value of Chi-square, i.e. 2200.47 is greater than the tabulated value, i.e. 5.991 at 2 degrees of freedom and 5 per cent significance level. We have observed that there is a significant difference between observed and expected frequencies of occupation and literacy of women. Thus, we conclude that occupation depends on literacy.

Occupation and Share in Household Expenditure

H_0: Occupation is not associated to women share in household expenditure.

H_1: Occupation is associated to women share in household expenditure.

Table 14.12: Occupation and Share in Household Expenditure

Occupation	Share in Household Expenditure (percentage)			
	0-25	25-50	50-75	Total
Employed	30	24	54	108
Self-employed	6	30	18	54
Unemployed	102	24	12	138
Total	138	78	84	300

From Table 14.12, the calculated Chi-square value is 250.77, which is greater than the tabulated value, i.e. 9.488 at 4 degrees of freedom and 5 per cent significance level. Thus, we accept the alternative hypothesis and reject the null. On this basis we conclude that there is an association between occupation and women share in household expenditures.

Occupation and Bank Account

H_0: There is no association between Occupation and Bank Account.

H_1: There is an association between Occupation and Bank Account.

From Table 14.13, the calculated Chi-square value 1893.14 is greater than the tabulated value 5.991 at 2 degrees of freedom and 5 per cent significance level. We, therefore, accept the alternative hypothesis and

Table 14.13: Occupation and Bank Account

Occupation	*Bank Account*		
	Yes	*No*	*Total*
Employed	96	18	114
Self-employed	42	6	48
Unemployed	120	18	138
Total	258	42	300

reject the other. Thus, we conclude that there is an association between occupation and bank account.

Occupation and Consultation in Money Matters

H_0: Women occupation does not affect the consultation power of women in money matters.

H_1: Women occupation affects the consultation power of women in money matters.

Table 14.14: Occupation and Consultation in Money Matters

Occupation	*Consultation Power*			
	Never	*Sometime*	*Often*	*Total*
Employed	36	24	48	108
Self-employed	24	12	12	48
Unemployed	36	72	36	144
Total	96	108	96	300

From Table 14.14, the calculated Chi-square value, i.e. 262.2 is greater than the tabulated value 9.488 at 4 degrees of freedom and 5 per cent significance level. We, therefore, reject the null hypothesis and accept the alternative.

Occupation and Humiliation of Women in the Society

H_0: Humiliation of women in society is not associated with occupation.

H_1: Humiliation of women is society is associated with occupation.

From Table 14.15, the calculated Chi-square 1177.05 is greater than the tabulated value 9.488 at 4 degrees of freedom and 5 per cent of significance level. Thus, we accept the alternative hypothesis and conclude that humiliation of women in the society is associated with occupation.

Table 14.15: Occupation and Humiliation of Women in the Society

Occupation	*Humiliation in the Society*			
	Never	*Sometime*	*Often*	*Total*
Employed	48	30	30	108
Self-employed	24	24	6	54
Unemployed	48	84	6	138
Total	120	138	42	300

Occupation and Share of Women in Household Decision-Making

H_0: Occupation did not affect that share of women in household decision making

H_1: Occupation affects the share of women in household decision making.

Table 14.16: Occupation and Share of Women in Household Decision Making

Occupation	*Share in Household Decision Making*			
	Never	*Sometime*	*Often*	*Total*
Employed	6	54	54	114
Self-employed	6	18	24	48
Unemployed	18	72	48	138
Total	30	144	126	300

On the basis of calculation from Table 14.16, the calculated Chi-square value 823.87 is significantly greater than the tabulated value 9.488 at 4 degrees of freedom and 5 per cent significance level. We therefore reject the null hypothesis and accept the alternative hypothesis.

Occupation and Permission to Move

H_0: There is no association between occupation and permission taken by women to move.

H_1: There is an association between occupation and permission taken by women to move.

From Table 14.17, the calculated Chi-square value 984.69 is greater than the tabulated value 9.488 at 4 degrees of freedom and 5 per cent significance level. Thus, we reject the null hypothesis and accept the alternative hypothesis. We conclude that there is an association between occupation and permission taken by women to move.

Table 14.17: Occupation and Permission to Move

Occupation	*Permission to Move*			
	Never	*Sometime*	*Often*	*Total*
Employed	18	60	30	108
Self-employed	18	24	6	48
Unemployed	6	90	48	144
Total	42	174	84	300

Occupation and Women Humiliation by Family/Husband

H_0: Muslim women humiliation by family/husband does not depend on their occupations.

H_1: Muslim Women humiliation by family/husband depends on women's occupation.

Table 14.18: Occupation and Women Humiliation by Family/Husband

Occupation	*Women Humiliation by Family/Husband*			
	Never	*Sometime*	*Often*	*Total*
Employed	48	36	24	108
Self-employed	18	24	6	48
Unemployed	72	60	12	144
Total	138	120	42	300

From Table 14.18, the calculated value of Chi-square, i.e. 718.13 is greater than the tabulated value 9.488 at 4 degrees of freedom and 5 per cent significance level. We, therefore, reject the null hypothesis and accept the alternative hypothesis.

Occupation and Awareness of Women's Protection Act and Welfare Programmes

H_0: There is no association between occupation and awareness of women's protection act and welfare programmes.

H_1: There is an association between occupation and awareness of women's protection act and welfare programmes.

From Table 14.19, the calculated Chi-square value 570.84 is greater than tabulated value 5.991 at 2 degrees of freedom and 5 per cent significance level. We, therefore, reject the null hypothesis and accept the alternative.

Levels of Education and Bank Account

H_0: There is no association between levels of education and bank account.

Table 14.19: Occupation and Awareness of Women's Protection Act and Welfare Programmes

Occupation	*Awareness of Protection Act and Welfare Programmes*		
	Yes	*No*	*Total*
Employed	60	48	108
Self-employed	36	12	48
Unemployed	102	42	144
Total	198	102	300

H_1: There is an association between levels of education and bank account.

Table 14.20: Levels of Education and Bank Account

Bank Account	*Levels of Education*				
	Upto High School	*Intermediate*	*Graduate*	*PG and above*	*Total*
Yes	24	24	60	132	240
No	42	6	6	6	60
Total	66	30	66	138	300

On the basis of our calculation in Table 14.20, the calculated Chi-square value, i.e. 2846.74 is significantly greater than the tabulated value 7.815 at 3 degrees of freedom and 5 per cent significance level. Thus, we reject the null hypothesis and accept the alternative. We conclude that there is an association between levels of education and bank account.

Levels of Education and Consultation in Money Matters

H_0: Muslim Women's consultation with regard to money matters does not depend on their level of education.

H_1: Muslim Women's consultation with regard to money matters depends on their level of education.

Table 14.21: Levels of Education and Consultation in Money Matters

Consultation Level	*Levels of Education*				
	Upto high school	*Intermediate*	*Graduate*	*PG and above*	*Total*
Never	18	6	30	54	108
Sometime	12	12	18	72	114
Often	42	12	18	6	78
Total	72	30	66	132	300

From Table 14.21, the calculated Chi-square value, i.e. 389.88 is greater than tabulated value 12.592 at 6 degrees of freedom and 5 per cent significance level. Thus, we accept the alternative hypothesis and reject the null hypothesis.

Levels of Education and Humiliation by Society

H_0: Humiliation of Muslim women in the society does not depend on the level of education of women.

H_1: Humiliation of Muslim women in the society depends on the level of education of women.

Table 14.22: Levels of Education and Humiliation by Society

Humiliation	*Levels of Education*				
	Upto High school	*Intermediate*	*Graduate*	*PG and above*	*Total*
Never	12	18	24	54	108
Sometime	30	18	30	66	144
Often	24	6	6	12	48
Total	66	42	60	132	300

On the basis of our calculation from Table 14.22, the calculated Chi-square value, i.e. 313.72 is greater than the tabulated value, i.e. 12.592 at 6 degrees of freedom and 5 per cent significance level. We, therefore, reject the null hypothesis and accept the alternative hypothesis.

Levels of Education and Participation in Household Decision Making

H_0: There is no association between level of education of Muslim women and participation in household decision making.

H_1: There is an association between level of education of Muslim women and participation in household decision making.

Table 14.23: Levels of Education and Participation in Household Decision Making

Participation	*Levels of Education*				
	High school	*Intermediate*	*Graduate*	*PG and above*	*Total*
Never	6	6	6	18	36
Sometime	30	6	18	90	144
Often	24	24	42	30	120
Total	60	36	66	138	300

From Table 14.23, the calculated value of Chi-square is 235.99, which is greater than the tabulated value, i.e. 12.592 at 6 degrees of freedom and 5 per cent significance level. Thus, we accept the alternative hypothesis and reject the null. We conclude that there is an association between the level of education of Muslim women and their participation in household decision making.

Levels of Education and Permission to Go Out

H_0: The permission to move does not depend on the level of education of Muslim women.

H_1: The permission to move depends on the level of education of Muslim women.

Table 14.24: Levels of Education and Permission to Go Out

Permission	*Levels of Education*				
	High school	*Intermediate*	*Graduate*	*PG & above*	*Total*
Never	6	6	6	6	24
Sometime	24	18	54	90	186
Often	36	12	6	36	90
Total	66	36	66	132	300

On the basis of calculation from Table 14.24, the calculated Chi-square value, i.e. 726.32 is greater than the tabulated value i.e. 12.592 at 6 degrees of freedom and 5 per cent significance level. Therefore, we reject the null hypothesis and accept the alternative. We conclude that the permission taken by Muslim women to move depends on their level of education.

Levels of Education and Humiliation by Family/Husband

H_0: Humiliation of Muslim women by family/husband does not depend on their level of education.

H_1: Humiliation of Muslim women by family/husband depends on their level of education.

Table 14.25: Levels of Education and Humiliation by Family/Husband

Humiliation	*Levels of Education*				
	High School	*Intermediate*	*Graduate*	*PG and above*	*Total*
Never	6	12	30	78	126
Sometime	18	18	30	42	108
Often	42	6	6	12	66
Total	66	36	66	132	300

From Table 14.25, the calculated Chi-square 457.38 is greater than the tabulated value 12.592 at 6 degrees of freedom and 5 per cent significance level. Thus, we accept the alternative hypothesis and conclude that the humiliation of Muslim women by family/husband depends on their level of education.

Levels of Education and Awareness of Protection Act and Welfare Programmes

H_0: There is no association between level of education and awareness of women protection act.

H_1: There is an association between level of education and awareness of women protection act.

Table 14.26: Levels of Education and Awareness of Protection Act and Welfare Programmes

Awareness	*Education level*				
	Upto High school	*Intermediate*	*Graduate*	*PG and above*	*Total*
Yes	30	24	42	78	174
No	36	12	24	54	126
Total	66	36	66	132	300

On the basis of our calculation from Table 14.26, the calculated Chi-square value, i.e. 262.88 is greater than the tabulated value, i.e. 7.815 at 5 degrees of freedom and 5 per cent significance level. Thus, we reject the null hypothesis and accept the alternative. We conclude that the awareness of women's protection act has an association with the level of education of women.

Conclusion and Suggestions

India is amongst the fastest growing countries in the world today, with a GDP growth rate ranging between 5 and 9 per cent during the last one decade. This high level of growth can be sustained only when all sections of the society, especially women become equal partners in the development process. It is well recognised that societies which discriminate on the basis of gender tend to experience less rapid economic growth and poverty reduction than societies which treat men and women equally. Gender equality and empowerment need to be a core development goal if higher growth is to be achieved.

Age may play a significant role for involving in any occupation vis-à-vis women empowerment. We have observed that age and occupation are highly associated. Job satisfaction and motive of the job significantly depends on age. Therefore, we may say that age is an important factor in empowering women. From our analysis, we find that money available at their disposal is higher for employed women as compared to unemployed women. We also observe that working women are contributing higher in total household expenditure i.e. sharing the responsibilities of the family.

It is observed that the humiliation of Muslim women by the family/ husband or society is not associated with level of education and occupation. Muslim Women are humiliated, though they are working as well as educated. Therefore, we may say that humiliation of Muslim women is a social problem rather than economic. It is observed that there is an association between occupation and permission to go out. Mostly, Muslim women either employed or unemployed have to take permission to go out from husband/family. Further, occupation and education are associated with awareness of Women Protection Act among women. Most of the working Muslim women are aware of of this Act but did not get benefited by it due to various reasons.

Level of education plays a significant role in women empowerment. It makes a difference in employment in the market and the monthly income. It is observed from the survey that there is an association between level of education and bank account; most Muslim women in Aligarh are educated and have bank accounts. It is analysed that mainly highly educated women have more power or have more control over money matters and decision making in household matters. From the analysis, we can conclude that education, employment and age play an important role in women empowerment, though there are some cases of women harassment. In general, we may conclude that to empower Indian Muslim women, there is a need to educate them, offer them maximum opportunities in employment and change the social attitude of people towards them.

15

Impact of Women Education: Employment and Fertility

A Case Study of Infant Mortality in Gujarat

Shamshad

The study analyses the impact of women education and employment on the fertility and infant mortality in the state of Gujarat. The overall analysis of study reveals that the northern and north-western parts of the state had a low level of women education, while, the southern and eastern-parts witnessed medium and high level of women education. It is observed that women employment gradually increased from western to eastern parts in the state. The fertility rate is lower in the south-eastern and south-western parts, while it is medium and higher in the northern and north-eastern parts of the state. The infant mortality rate is lower in the north-eastern parts, whereas it is medium and higher in the southern, western and central parts of the state. The analysis further shows that women education and employment do have marked impact on the fertility and infant mortality in some parts of the Gujarat state.

The impact of education is considered very paramount on the geo-climatic, socio-economic, particularly demographic conditions in the developed and developing societies of the world. Moreover, educational changes depend on the starting levels of education and fertility, as well as other contextual factors of socio-economic development (Caldwell 1980; Portes, 2006 and Cohen, 2008). Despite the theoretical importance of education as a contributing factor in the fertility transition (Soares & Falcao, 2008), there have been relatively few studies on education and fertility (Sajjad & Ahn, 2014). Very little attention has been paid to the causal linkages between education and fertility; however, education obviously affects fertility (Westoff & Ryder, 1977; Rindfuss & Sweet, 1977; Cho, Grabill & Bogue, 1970 and Whelpton, Cambell & Patterson, 1966). Notwithstanding, there are numerous studies documenting a negative relationship between female education and fertility (Sander, 1992; Schultz, 1997; Lam & Duryea, 1999; Lloyd et al., 2000; Axinn &

Barber, 2001; Sathar et al., 2003; Caldwell & Caldwell, 1985; Caldwell, 1979; Jejeebhooy, 1995; Rutstein, 2002; Bongaarts, 2008 and 2010; Shapiro & Gebreselassie, 2008 and 2010; Cohen, 1998 and Garenne & Joseph, 2002)

Women education is very important because it increases the value of women's time in economic activities through labour force participation, higher labour productivity and wages (Baah-Boateng et al., 2013). It also results in higher household income and contributes towards reduction in poverty (Subbarao & Raney, 1992). Some empirical studies explain that higher female literacy not only results in better healthcare (Hobcraft, et al. 1984; Mensch, et al. 1985; Cleland & Van Ginneken 1988; Bicego & Boerma 1993; Heaton, et al. 2005; Strauss & Thomas, 1995 and Gakidou et al., 2010) but also reduces the rate of population growth (Wheeler, 1980; Sackey, 2005; Lam & Duryea, 1999; Ainsworth et al., 1996; Vavrus & Larsen, 2003; Singh, 1994; Ben-Porath, 1973; Gardner, 1973 and Schultz, 1973).

The evidence in the literature also suggests that female education creates social gains by improving women's and child health status (Becker, 1981; Schultz, 1981; Guilkey et al., 1998 and Gardner, 1973) through the reduction in fertility (Bongaarts, 2003 and Jejeebhoy, 2005) (Subbarao & Raney, 1992). Schultz (1992) describes that the structural relationship between fertility and infant mortality rates depend on certain exogenous variables which include education, better health care facilities, family planning services and socio-economic conditions (Sohler et al., 2003) which determine fertility and mortality (Jahan, 2008). In fact, female literacy can go a long in reducing infant and maternal mortality rates (Mustafa, Becker & Lewis, 1973; Bicego & Boerma, 1991 and Hobcraft, 1993), because education acts as a proxy for the socio-economic status of a family and geographic area of residence (Desai & Alva, 1998).

Schultz (1993) confirms that women's education is associated with smaller desired family size across the world. For example, educated women who desire occupational advancement wish to delay the onset of childbearing and also prefer fewer children, whereas less educated women have children at relatively young age and have a large family size (Blossfeld and Huinink 1991; Brewster and Rindfuss 2000; Martin Garcia and Baizan 2006; McCall 2000; Rindfuss, Bumpass, and St. John 1980; Rindfuss, Morgan, and Offut 1996 and Spain & Bianchi 1996).

The empirical literature addresses the causes of fertility restraint and the impact of employment opportunities for women (Becker 1960 and 1965; Mincer 1962 and Willis 1973), the effect of the female relative wage and the child quantity-quality trade-off (Galloway, Lee, & Hammel, 1998; Brown & Guinnane, 2002; Dribe, 2009 and Becker, Cinnirella, &

Woessmann, 2010). In fact, employment opportunities for women and cultural factors might have shaped the demographic transition at the end of the nineteenth century (Crafts, 1989; Galloway, Hammel & Lee, 1994).

Thus, women's employment is recognized to play an important role in the variation in fertility levels within and between countries (Becker, 1993; Rindfuss & Brewster, 1996; Shockaert, 2005 and Standing, 1983). A negative relationship is generally expected between the female labour force participation and fertility (Kishor 1993; Murthi, Guio, & Dreze 1995; Rosenzweig & Schultz 1982; Killingsworth & Heckman 1986; Angrist & Evans 1998; Kalwij 2000 and Lehr 2009), at the micro level, although there is a controversy about the causal direction of the inverse relationship between the two phenomena (Cramer, 1980; Felmlee, 1993; Stolzenberg & Waite; 1977; Basu & Basu 1991 and Kishor 1992). While a consistent negative relationship between women's paid work and fertility has been found at the micro level in developed countries (Budig, 2003 and Lloyd, 1991), however, no clear pattern has emerged in developing countries upto now.

The present study has been undertaken with the following objectives:

i. to analyse the geographical patterns of woman education in the state of Gujarat,
ii. to examine the regional variations of woman employment in the state,
iii. to inspect the spatial patterns of fertility and infant mortality in the state, and
iv. to find out the relationship between woman's education-employment with fertility and infant mortality.

The work is based on the secondary sources of data collected from Census of India publications 2011, New Delhi and vital health statistics from Gujarat State Govt. Publications 2010-11, Gandhinagar. In the present analysis, woman education-employment, and fertility and infant mortality, and the relationship of fertility and infant mortality with woman education and employment have been taken into account to depict the spatial patterns in the 26 districts of the state.

The raw data of these variables have been computed into standard score. It is generally known as Z value or Z score. The scores quantify the departure of individual observations, expressed in a comparable form that is a linear transformation of the original data (Smith, 1973: 85). It may be expressed as:

$$Z_{ij} = \frac{X_{ij} - \overline{X_i}}{\sigma_i}$$

Where,

Z_{ij} = Standardised value of the variable *i* in district *j*,
X_{ij} = Actual value of variable *i* in district *j*,
$\bar{X}_i$ = Mean value of variable *i* in all districts, and
σ_i = Standard deviation of variable *i* in all districts.

The positive values relating to the districts Z score show high level of woman education-employment, fertility and infant mortality, while negative values exhibit the low level of these variables in the study area.

Besides, this statistical technique, GIS Arc-view (version 3.2) programme has been applied to show the spatial variations of woman education-employment, fertility and infant mortality among the districts of the Gujarat state through maps.

The Results and Discussion

Table 15.1 visualizes the district wise z-core of women education-employment, and fertility infant mortality in Gujarat. The whole ranges of spatial variations of these variables among the districts of Gujarat from maximum to minimum or highest to lowest, may be arranged into three categories such as high (above 0.500 score), medium (0.500 to -0.500 score) and low (below 0.500 score) as given in Table 15.2.

Women Education

Table 15.2 indicates that the eleven districts of the state have a high score of (above 0.500 score) women education. These are Mahesana, Gandhinagar, Ahmedabad, Rajkot, Kheda, Anand, Vadodara, Navsari, Valsad, Surat and Tapi, in which the districts of Mahesana, Gandhinagar, Ahmadabad, Kheda, Anand and Vadodara in the central-east, the districts of Valsad, Navsari, Surat and Tapi in the south-east, and Rajkot district in the south-western parts make three remarkable regions in the state. The seven districts of the state come under the medium grade of (0.500 to -0.500 score) woman education, wherein, the districts of Jamnagar, Porbandar, Junagarh, Amreli and Bhavnagar constitute a big contiguous region in the crescent shape along the shore line of Arabian Sea in the south-western part, whereas, the Dangs district in the south-east and Sabar Kanthado district in the north-east do not share the boundary with adjacent districts of the same grade from any region in the state.

The eight districts of the state fall under the low level of (below -0.500 score) women education and form three distinct regions in the state. The first region is constituted by the districts of Kutch, Banas Kantha,

Table 15.1: District Wise Distribution of Women Education-Employment, and Fertility and Infant Mortality in Gujarat, 2011

Districts	*Woman Education*	*Woman Employment*	*Fertility*	*Infant Mortality*
Kachchh	-0.856	-1.155	0.455	0.289
Banas Kantha	-1.925	0.055	1.343	-1.001
Patan	-0.810	-0.025	1.068	-0.743
Mahesana	0.858	-0.395	-0.010	-0.485
Sabar Kantha	-0.422	0.735	0.878	-1.517
Gandhinagar	1.006	-0.775	-0.856	0.031
Ahmadabad	1.351	-1.315	-0.940	2.095
Surendranagar	-0.788	-0.085	-0.179	-0.227
Rajkot	0.756	-0.925	-0.200	1.579
Jamnagar	-0.342	-0.755	-0.792	1.321
Porbandar	-0.064	-0.675	-0.581	-1.001
Junagadh	-0.151	-0.275	-0.285	-0.227
Amreli	-0.224	0.065	0.244	-0.227
Bhavnagar	-0.230	-0.435	0.561	-0.743
Anand	1.052	-0.515	-0.179	0.031
Kheda	0.687	-0.345	-0.222	-0.485
Panch Mahals	-1.054	0.965	1.977	-1.001
Dohad	-2.346	1.654	1.343	-1.001
Vadodara	0.655	-0.385	-1.025	1.063
Narmada	-0.620	1.494	0.180	-0.485
Bharuch	-0.848	-0.555	-0.771	-0.227
The Dangs	-0.013	2.294	1.977	0.289
Navsari	1.234	0.145	-1.553	-0.485
Valsad	0.721	0.095	-0.877	1.063
Surat	0.937	-1.145	-1.553	2.095
Tapi	1.437	2.264	NA	NA

Source: Calculation is based on District level Published data, Census of India, 2011 and Vital Health Statistical, Govt. of Gujarat, 2010-11.

Patan and Surendranagar in the north and north-western parts of the state, the second region by Panch Mahals and Dohad districts in the eastern part and the third region comprises Bharuch and Narmada districts in the south-eastern part of the state. The spatial analysis of the Figure 15.1 reveals that the high level of women education is witnessed in the central and south-eastern districts of plain area and medium level of women education is observed in the south-western parts of Saurashtra region while low level of women education is found in the north-western parts among the districts of Kutch region.

Women Employment

Table 15.2 shows that the six districts come under high level of (above 0.500 score) women employment, wherein, the three districts in the

Table 15.2: Women Education-Employment and Fertility and Infant Mortality in Gujarat, 2011

Category	*Z-Score*	*No. of Districts*	*Districts*
Woman Education			
High	Above 0.500	11	Mahesana, Gandhinagar, Ahmedabad, Rajkot, Anand, Kheda, Vadodara, Navsari, Valsad, Surat and Tapi
Medium	-0.500 to 0.500	7	Sabar Kantha, Jamnagar, Porbandar, Junagadh, Amreli, Bhavnagar and The Dangs
Low	Below -0.500	8	Kachchh, Banas Kantha, Patan, Surendranagar, Panch Mahals, Dohad, Narmada and Bharuch
Woman Employment			
High	Above 0.500	6	Sabar Kantha, Panch Mahals, Dohad, Narmada, The Dangs and Tapi
Medium	-0.500 to 0.500	11	Banas Kantha, Patan, Mahesana, Surendranagar, Junagadh, Amreli, Bhavnagar, Kheda, Vadodara, Navsari and Valsad
Low	Below -0.500	9	Kachchh, Gandhinagar, Ahmadabad, Rajkot, Jamnagar, Porbandar, Anand, Bharuch and Surat
Fertility			
High	Above 0.500	7	Banas Kantha, Patan, Sabar Kantha, Bhavnagar, Panch Mahals, Dohad and The Dangs.
Medium	-0.500 to 0.500	9	Kachchh, Mahesana, Surendranagar, Rajkot, Junagadh, Amreli, Anand, Kheda, Narmada
Low	Below -0.500	9	Gandhinagar, Ahmadabad, Jamnagar, Porbandar, Vadodara, Bharuch, Navsari, Valsad and Surat
Infant Mortality			
High	Above 0.500	6	Ahmadabad, Rajkot, Jamnagar, Vadodara, Valsad and Surat
Medium	-0.500 to 0.500	12	Kachchh, Mahesana, Gandhinagar, Surendranagar, Junagadh, Amreli, Anand, Kheda, Narmada, Bharuch, The Dangs and Navsari
Low	Below -0.500	7	Banas Kantha, Patan, Sabar Kantha, Porbandar, Bhavnagar, Panch Mahals and Dohad

Source: Based on Table 14.1.

Figure 15.1: Gujarat: Woman Education, 2011

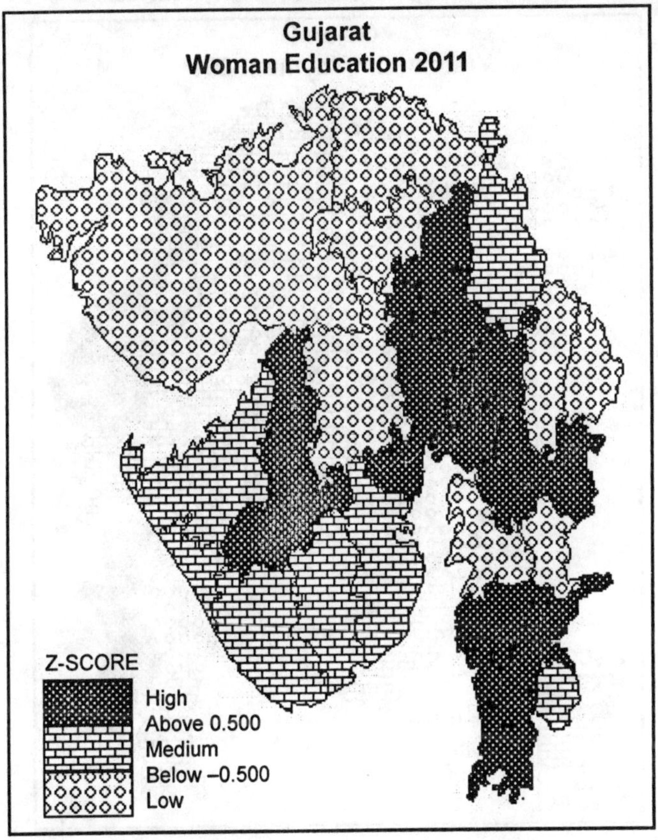

northern side namely Sabar Kantha, Panch Mahals and Dohad and three districts in the southern side namely Narmada, The Dangs and Tapi created two notable regions on the eastern margin of the state.

The eleven districts of the state fall under medium grade of (0.500 to -0.500 score) woman employment. Among them, the seven districts i.e. Banas Kantha, Patan, Mahesana, Surendranagar, Junagadh, Amreli and Bhavnagar constitute an extensive long linear region in the mid of the state extending from Banas Kantha in north to Bhavnagar in south. While remaining districts viz., Kheda and Vadodara in the eastern part, and Navsari and Valsad in the south-eastern part make two small regions in the study area.

Remaining nine districts of the state witnessed low level of (below – 0.500 score) woman employment. Further, the districts of Kutch, Rajkot, Jamnagar and Porbandar in the western and south-western parts and Gandhinagar, Ahmedabad, Anand, Bharuch and Surat in the central and

Figure 15.2: Gujarat: Woman Employment, 2011

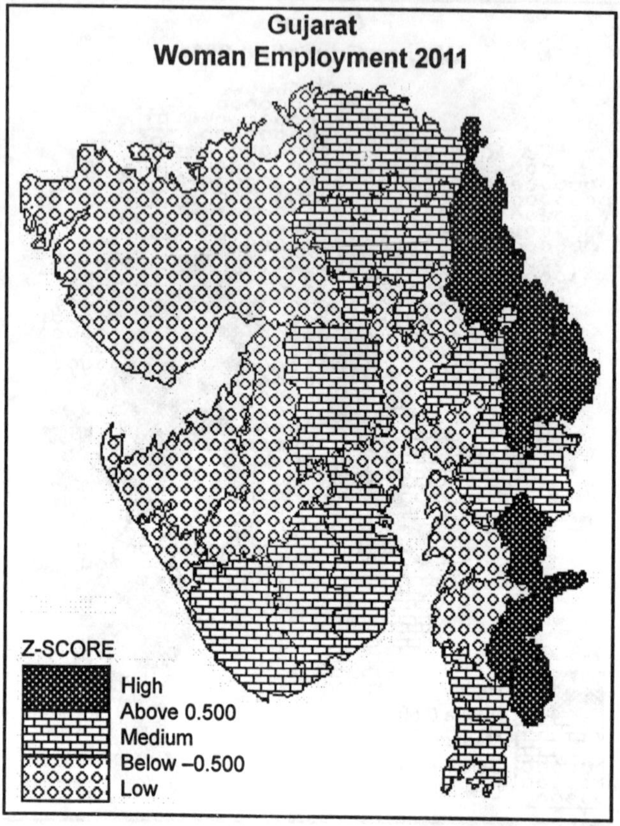

southern parts make two separate distinguished contiguous regions in the state of Gujarat.

The regional analysis of the Figure 15.2 depicts that the women employment is gradually increases from low to medium level and then medium to high level from western parts to eastern parts in the state of Gujarat.

Fertility

Table 15.2 exhibits that there are seven districts having the high rate of (above 0.500 score) fertility form an identifiable region in the north-eastern part of the state (Patan, Banas Kantha, Sabar Kantha, Panch Mahals and Dohad), excluding Bhavnagar and the Dangs districts. The nine districts that have the medium rate of (0.500 to -0.500 score) fertility are Kutch, Mahesana, Surendranagar, Rajkot, Junagadh, Amreli, Anand,

Kheda and Narmada, wherein, five districts namely Kutch, Surendranagar, Rajkot, Junagadh and Amreli constitute a big long linear shape region, propelling from north to south direction in the western part of Gujarat, while, the districts of Anand and Kheda make a small region in the east-central part of the state. Mahesana and Narmada districts are widely scattered in the study area.

At last, the nine districts recorded a low level of (below 0.500 score) fertility and these districts created three small distinct separate regions in the state. The first region in the south-western part constituted the districts of Jamnagar and Porbandar, the second region in the central part comprises the districts of Ahmedabad and Gandhinagar, and the last third region in the south-eastern part involves the districts of Vadodara, Bharuch, Surat Navsari and Valsad. The geographical examination of the Figure 15.3 shows that north-eastern and north-western parts recorded the high and medium rate of fertility respectively whereas south-western and south-

Figure 15.3: Gujarat: Fertility, 2011

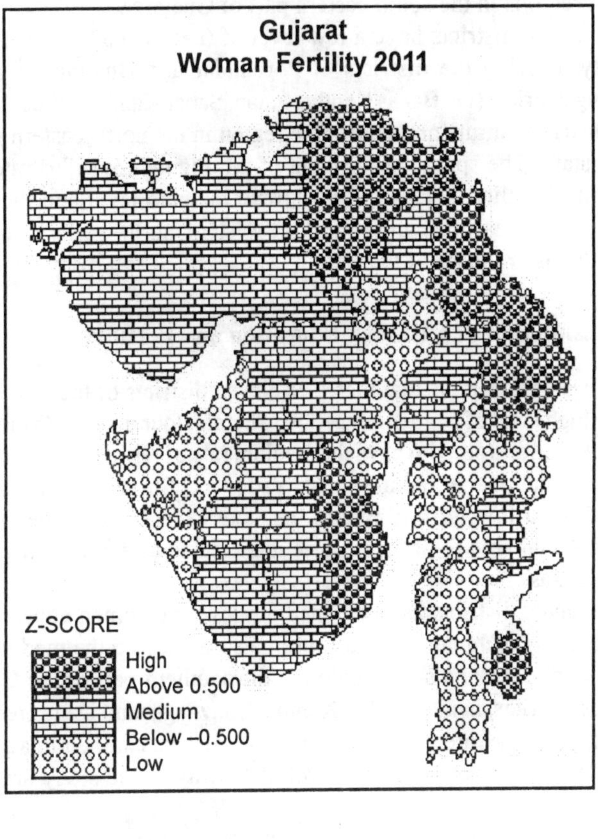

eastern parts accounted respectively medium and low level of fertility in the state of Gujarat.

Infant Mortality

Table 15.2 depicts that six districts experienced a high rate of (above 0.500 score) infant mortality, namely Ahmedabad, Rajkot, Jamnagar, Vadodara, Valsad and Surat. Among them, only Rajkot and Jamnagar districts composed a small region in the western part of the state, whereas remaing districts were widely scattered in the study area. The twelve districts having medium rate of (0.500 to – 0.500 score), infant mortality formed four distinguished regions in the study area. The districts of Kutch, Surendranagar, Mahesana, Gandhinagar, Kheda and Anand constitute an extensive interconnected region in the western and central parts of the state. The Junagadh and Amreli districts make a notable region in the south-western part of the state. However, the districts of Narmada and Bharuch, and then The Dangs and Navsari districts created two separate different regions in the south-eastern part of Guajarat.

The seven districts have a low level of (below 0.500 score) infant mortality. Barring the districts of Porbandar and Bhavnagar, all the remaining districts (i.e. Banas Kantha, Patan, Sabar Kantha, Panch Mahals and Dohad) constitute an identifiable region in the north-eastern part of Gujarat state. The spatial assessment of the Figure 15.4 illustrates that the infant mortality increases from low to medium level and then high level from north-eastern part towards the western, north-western, southern and south-eastern parts of the state.

Relationship between Women Education and Fertility

The Figure 15.6 depicts that there are eleven districts of the state which have the high level of women education, wherein, four districts (Mahesana, Rajkot, Anand and Kheda) have the medium rate of fertility and remaining districts (Gandhinagar, Ahmedabad, Vadodara, Surat Navsari, Valsad) recorded the a low fertility rate in the state except Tapi (The Fertility data is not available for Tapi because it is created as a new district 2011 Indian Census).

The seven districts have the medium level of women education, in which districts of Junagadh and Amreli also witnessed the medium rate of fertility and make a small region in the southern part of the Gujarat. The three districts, namely Sabar Kantha, Bhavnagar and Dangs recorded the high fertility rate while the last two districts i.e. Jamnagar and Porbandar experienced the low level of fertility in the study area. The

Figure 15.4: Gujarat: Infant Mortality, 2011

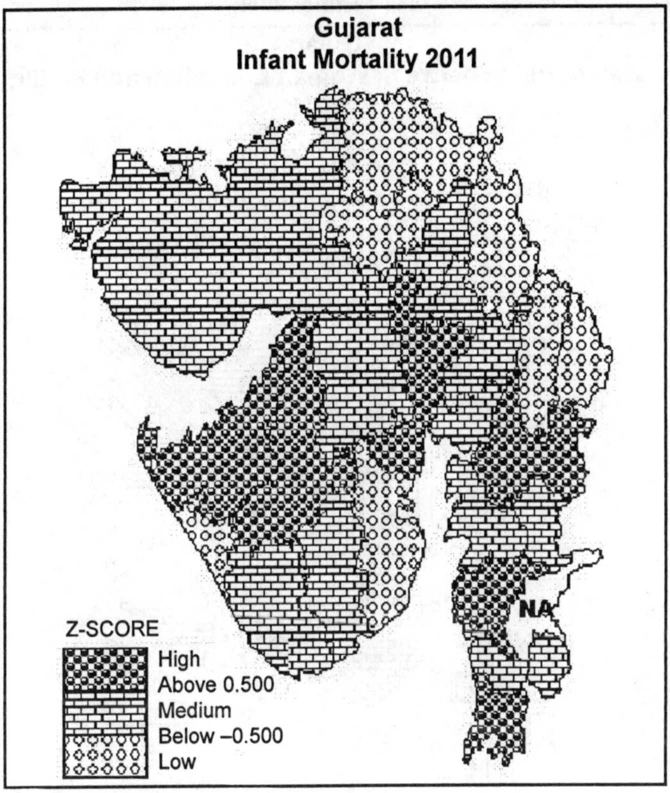

eight districts registered the low level of women education, in which only one district (Bharuch) witnessed low rate of fertility. The districts of Kachchh, Surendranagar and Narmada accounted the medium rate of fertility wherein Kutch and Surendranagar constituted a remarkable region in the north-western part of the state, while remaining four districts viz., Banas Kantha and Patan in the northern part, and Panch Mahals and Dohad in the eastern part having the high fertility rate created two distinct regions in the state of Gujarat.

The spatial analysis of the Figure 15.5 shows that women education in the fifty percent districts (13 districts) had no marked impact on the fertility by registering low or medium level of women education, as five districts having the medium level of women education observed the high and medium level of fertility, and seven districts accounting low level of women education registered the high and medium rate of fertility while one district had both low level of women education and fertility.

Figure 15.5: Gujarat:Relationship between Women Education and Fertility, 2011

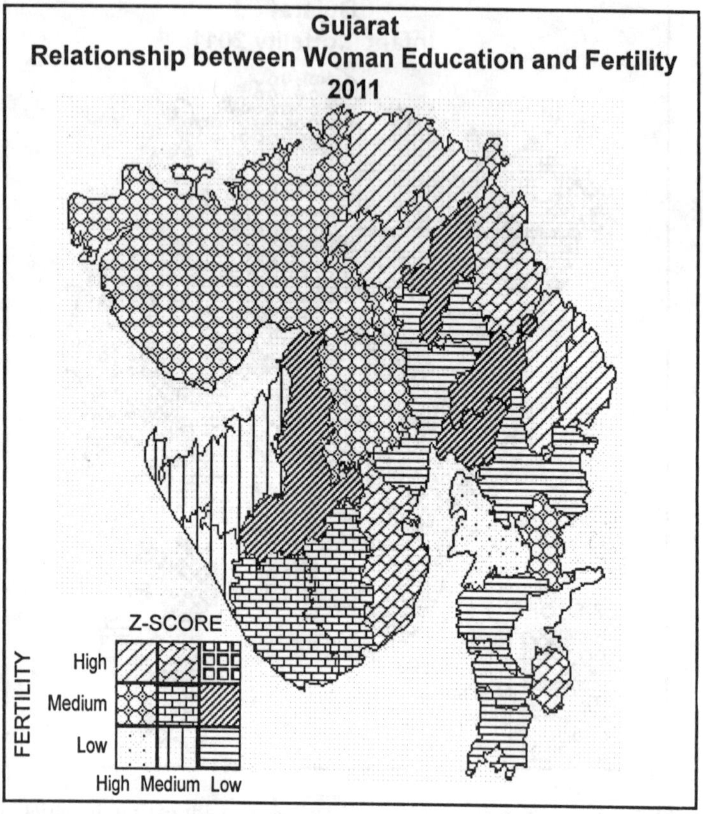

However, in the remaining 12 districts, women education had an impact on the fertility because the ten districts having a high level of women education observed medium and low rate of fertility, and two districts recording medium level of women education witnessed low fertility rate in the study area.

Relationship between Women Education and Infant Mortality

The Figure 15.6 indicates that the eleven districts of the state namely Mahesana, Gandhinagar, Ahmadabad, Rajkot, Anand, Kheda, Vadodara, Navsari, Valsad, Surat and Tapi which have high level of women education, among them nearly fifty percent districts (Ahmadabad, Rajkot, Vadodara, Surat and Valsad) also have the high infant mortality rate and they are widely scattered in the state, while five districts (Mahesana,

Gandhinagar, Kheda, Anand and Navsari) witnessed medium level of infant mortality and all of them form a region in the central part of the state, excluding the district of Navsari. The data of infant mortality rate of Tapi district is not available I nthe census due to its creation as a new district..

The seven districts have a medium level of women education wherein three districts namely Junagadh, Amreli and the Dangs experienced medium level of infant mortality, and three districts viz., Sabar Kantha, Porbandar and Bhavnagar recorded low level of infant mortality, but Jamnagar district had the high level of infant mortality rate in the study area. The low level of women education was observed in the eight districts of the state, in which, four districts i.e. Banas Kantha and Patan in the north, and Panch Mahals and Dohad in the east also accounted low rate of infant mortality and the two small different regions in the state, and remaining four districts i.e. Kutch and Surendranagar in the north-western part and Narmada and Bharuch in the south-eastern part recorded medium level of infant mortality rate.

Regional analysis of the Figure 15.6 reveals that about fifty percent districts of the state lie in the same grades i.e. high women education and high infant mortality, medium education and infant mortality, and low women education and low infant mortality. Moreover, four districts having low level of women education registered the medium rate of infant mortality and one district having medium level of education recorded high rate of infant mortality. However, the five districts witnessed high level of women education but they had medium rate of infant mortality. Likewise, three districts experienced medium level of women education but these districts recorded low infant mortality rate in the state. Hence, women education has had moderate impact on the infant mortality rate in the majority of the districts.

Relationship between Women Employment and Fertility

The Figure 15.7 shows that the six districts namely Sabar Kantha, Panch Mahals, Dohad, Narmada, The Dangs and Tapi having high level of women employment rate also have high fertility excluding the Narmada and Tapi districts because Narmada district experienced medium rate of fertility while fertility data is not available for Tapi district. The districts Sabar Kantha, Panch Mahals and Dohad also constitute an outstanding region in the north-eastern part of the state. The eleven districts accounted the medium level of women employment in the state of Gujarat, among them the five districts also observed the medium fertility rate. These are Mahesana, Surendranagar, Junagadh, Amreli and Kheda, wherein

Figure 15.6: Gujarat: Relationship between Women Education and Infant Mortality, 2011

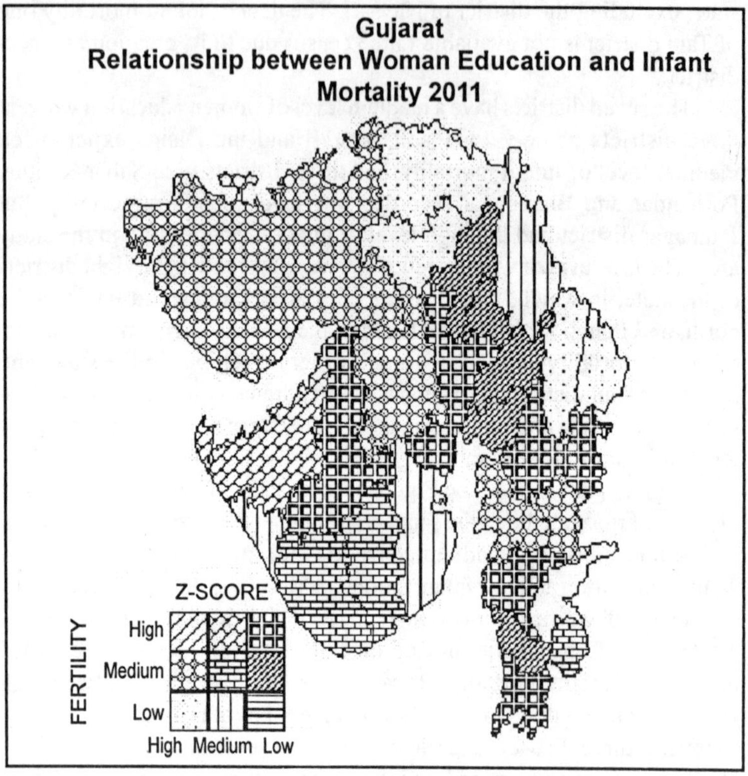

Junagadh and Amreli in the southern part and Mahesana and Surendranagar in the central part make two small regions while Kheda district does not share boundary with adjacent district to form any region in the study area. The three districts, namely Banas Kantha, Patan and Bhavnagar having high rate of fertility form a small region in the northern part of the state, except Bhavnagar district. The remaining three districts viz., Vadodara in the east, and Navsari and Valsad in the south-east created two distinguished regions in Gujarat.

The nine districts which registered a low level of women employment rate are Kachchh, Gandhinagar, Ahmedabad, Rajkot, Jamnagar, Porbandar, Anand, Bharuch and Surat. Among them, the six districts, namely Jamnagar and Porbandar in the south-western part, Gandhinagar and Ahmadabad in the central part, and Bharuch and Surat in the eastern part having low fertility rate also constituted three identifiable regions in the study area. The last three districts i.e. Kutch, Rajkot and Anand recorded the medium level of fertility, in which, the districts of Kutch

Figure 15.7: Gujarat: Relationship between Women Employment and Fertility, 2011

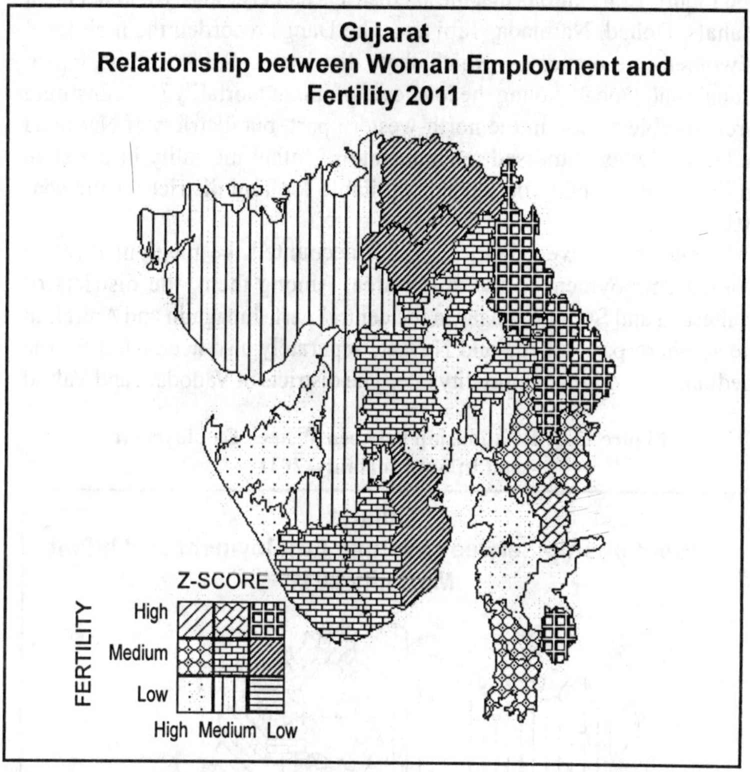

and Rajkot formed a big remarkable region in the western and north-western parts of the Gujarat state.

The geographical analysis of the Figure 15.7 depicts that women employment had its direct impact on the fertility in the four districts in which one district (Narmada) having high level of women employment recorded medium rate of fertility, and three districts recording medium level of women employmen, experienced low level of fertility in the state. Moreover, women employment had its indirect impact on fertility having medium and/or low level of employment accounted high/medium/low rate of fertility, e.g. the seven districts accounting the medium rate of women employment witnessed the high and medium level of fertility. The remaining nine districts having low level of women employment registered a medium and low rate of fertility in the study area. However, women employment, in some districts, had no discernible impact on fertility, because four districts having high level of women employment also observed high fertility.

Relationship between Women Employment and Infant Mortality

The Figure 15.8 exhibits that the six districts namely Sabar Kantha, Panch Mahals, Dohad, Narmada, Tapi and The Dangs recorded the high level of women employment, in which, three districts i.e. Sabar Kantha, Panch Mahals and Dohad having the low level of infant mortality rate constitute a remarkable region in the north-western part, but districts of Narmada and The Dangs witnessed medium rate of infant mortality in the state while infant mortality data is not available for Tapi district for the year 2011.

There are eleven districts which accounted the medium level of women employment in the study area. Among them, the districts of Mahesana and Surendranagar in the central part, Junagadh and Amreli in the southern part, Kheda and Navsari separately also accounted for the medium level of infant mortality rate. The districts of Vadodara and Valsad

Figure 15.8: Relationship between Women Employment and Infant Mortality, 2011

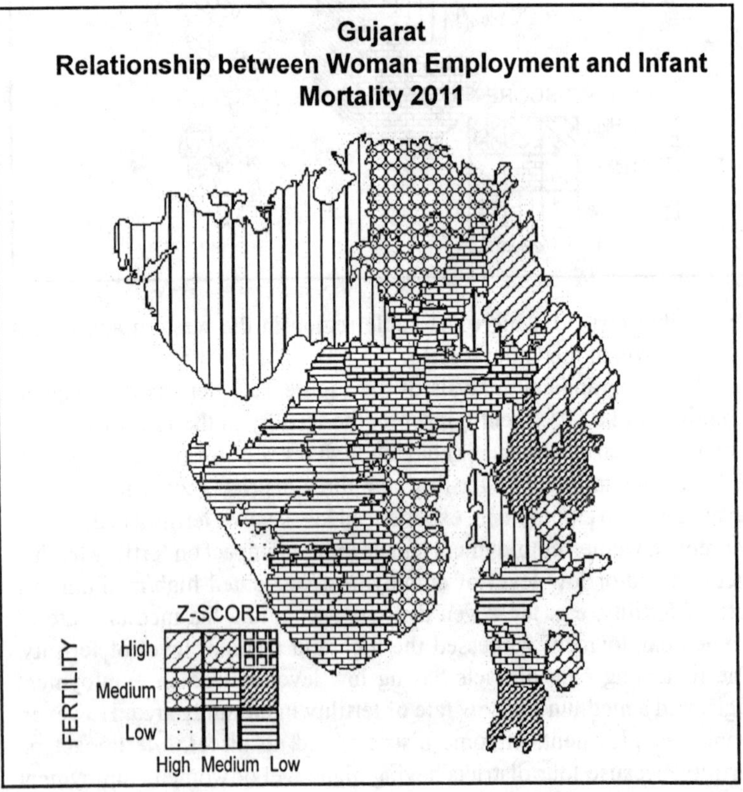

in the south-eastern part witnessed high rate of infant mortality. The remaining three districts i.e. Bhavnagar in the south and Banas Kantha and Patan in the north having low rate of infant mortality make two small regions in the study area.

The remaining nine districts which have low level of women employment are Kutch, Gandhinagar, Ahmadabad, Rajkot, Porbandar Jamnagar, Anand, Bharuch and Surat. The only one district (Porbandar) also has low rate of infant mortality, the four districts namely Kutch, Gandhinagar, Anand and Bharuch recorded a medium level of infant mortality rate and they failed to form any region by sharing the boundary with adjoining states of same category. The districts Jamnagar and Ahmedabad in the south-western part, Rajkot in the central part and Surat in the south-eastern part having high level of infant mortality formed three different regions in the state of Gujarat.

Analysis of Figure 15.8 clears the fact that women employment does have its significant direct impact on the infant mortality rate in the one-third districts of the state. For example, five districts having high women employment, experienced low and medium infant mortality rate; and three districts accounting for medium level of women employment had low infant mortality rate. Moreover, women employment in the remaining districts had influence on the infant mortality indirectly, e.g. the eight districts having medium level of women employment experienced high and medium level of infant mortality rate, while eight districts registering low level of women employment accounted for high and medium level of infant mortality rate in the state.

Conclusion

The present study reveals that the high level of women education is witnessed in the central and south-eastern parts; the medium level of women education is observed in the south-western parts; and low level of women education is found in the north-western parts of the state of Gujarat. Women employment gradually increases from the low to medium level and thereafter from medium to high level from western to eastern parts in the state. The north-eastern and north-western parts of the state recorded high and medium rate of fertility respectively, whereas south-western and south-eastern parts had medium and low level of fertility. The infant mortality rate increased from the low to medium level and then to high level from north-eastern part towards the western, north-western, southern and south-eastern parts of the state.

Women education had a lot impact on the fertility rate in the state of Gujarat, as ten districts having the high level of women education observed medium and low fertility rate and two districts recording medium level of women education witnessed low level of fertility in the study area. Moreover, women education in the half of the total districts had marked impact on fertility by recording low or medium level of women education, e.g. five districts having medium level of women education observed high and medium level of fertility and seven districts accounting for low level of women education registered high and medium fertility rate.

This means that districts of high level of women education observed low and/or medium fertility rate, on the contrary, districts of medium and low level of women education registered high and/or low fertility rate. About fifty percent districts of the state followed the same categories in both the aspects women education and infant mortality. Moreover, four districts having low level of women education registered the medium rate of infant mortality and one district having medium level of education recorded high rate of infant mortality. However, the five districts having high level of women education experienced medium rate of infant mortality; likewise, three districts experienced medium level of women education, but these districts recorded a low level of infant mortality rate in the state. This implies that women education has moderate impact on the infant mortality rate in the majority of the districts.

Women employment had a direct impact on fertility in the four districts, e.g. Narmada district having high level of women employment recorded medium rate of fertility, and three districts recording medium level of women employment experienced low level of fertility in the state. Moreover, women employment had indirect impact on fertility having medium and/or low level of employment. It recorded high or medium and/or low level of fertility. However, women employment, in some districts, had no discernible impact on the fertility because four districts having high level of women employment also observed high fertility. Women employment had its direct important impact on the infant mortality rate in the one-third districts of the state. Moreover, women employment in the remaining districts had its influence on the infant mortality indirectly, e.g. the districts having medium and low level of women employment experienced high and medium level of infant mortality rate.

16

Teacher in the Digital Age

Issues and Challenges

Deepshikha Saxena

Present century is the age of technology, also called as digital age. The world around us is experiencing a digital revolution. Technology has fundamentally altered how we live and work as well as how we learn. We as a part of society have accessibility to new technological resources. Change is coming in educational system as well, which is driven by many factors and facilitated by technology. This change is inevitable as it is no longer possible to do things the way we used to do them. Computing and communication are challenging traditional methods of knowledge collection and dissemination. Students are addressed today as "digital age learners" reflecting on their techno- savvy and free-agent approach to learning. With their modern day gadgets like tablets, phones, computer games, social media and text messaging, these students have access to resources and knowledge beyond traditional school structures and practices. These students are less dependent upon traditional educational institutions for knowledge acquisition and are much self reliant, exercising their internet-based skills to aggregate data and information.

These evolving students' characteristics and the increased presence of technology and digital resources certainly provide challenges for schools as they work to adapt and embrace this rapidly changing environment. Issues like access and resources, teacher training and professional development along with structures and delivery methods must be addressed. However the digital learning era also provides great opportunity to help schools advance student learning and acquire 21st Century skills.

Challenges in the current workplace are far more complex than they ever were. The skills required to face these challenges go far beyond mere thinking skills and conceptual knowledge. It is increasingly becoming an independent and connected world. Technology is taking giant strides, creating new innovations and making the impossible possible. Thus 21st century living requires a diverse array of skills specially designed to enable an individual to navigate this ever changing and challenging world and create successful, well adjusted lives for themselves.

The list of 21st Century skills and competencies is given below:

1. Information Processing Skills
2. Communication Skills
3. Media Literacy and ICT Literacy
4. Thinking and Problem Solving skills
   (a) Inventive Thinking
   (b) Creative Thinking
   (c) Problem Analysis and Solving
   (d) Decision Making
   (e) Logical Thinking
   (f) Critical Thinking
   (g) Systems Thinking

Interpersonal and Intrapersonal Skills

(a) Flexibility and Adaptability
(b) Initiative and Intrinsic motivation
(c) Social and Multicultural Adaptability and Co-existence
(d) High Efficiency and Accountability
(e) Leadership and responsibility

As Alvin Toffler says, "The illiterate of the 21st Century will not be those who cannot read and write, but those who cannot learn, unlearn and relearn". This is one aspect of change. The second paradigm shift in education system is moving to learner-centered pedagogy from teacher-centered pedagogy. The main focus of a 21st century classroom is to create inspiring, meaningful, challenging and engaging learning experiences for students. The demands of system have also changed. The main goal of education system has undergone a transition. Main focus is on the development of new age skills. Three fundamental dimensions of digital technologies are interactivity, symbolic flexibility and the vast array of available information. All these resources are to be harnessed in meaningful fashion in order to outline an effective teaching learning system.

Opportunities of Modern Age Classroom

(1) *Increasing student enrichment*: This deals with the classroom interaction. In the traditional classroom teacher plays a role of information owner and students are regarded as knowledge seekers. But in the modern age classroom these roles have become meaningless. The students have greater access to knowledge and they show advanced level of skills to

gather and comprehend information. It is a challenge in the present context to design meaningful, challenging and engaging classroom experiences. New pedagogy where students and teachers are the learning partners is needed to be designed. Constructivist pedagogies and democratic practices are the cornerstones for engaging students in interactions that are meaningful as well as for promoting diversity and mutual understanding. They focus on integrating learning goals, new pedagogies and technology. Methods like presentations, panel discussions, seminars, group discussions, project based learning which focus on collaborative and peer based learning are the need of the day. This shall provide students with a platform to showcase their talent as well as develop right set of social values and attitudes.

(2) *Addressing Teacher Effectiveness*: In the new age the traditional teaching learning method which has become obsolete, needs to be addressed. Teacher as a facilitator of learning should focus on problem based learning, web based teaching learning systems. System should be designed to measure frequent checks on effects of teaching, obtaining feedback, reciprocal teaching and assessment of learning based on technologies like portfolio assessment.

(3) *Mitigating Inequality*: The modern age classroom also provides arrangement for differential teaching and learning. With the advent of computer aided instructions, we can promote self paced learning which shall help slow learners. Secondly, need of those students who lack basic skills or have poor background knowledge can be addressed with the help of technology. This helps to make the classroom self engaging experience.

(4) *Preparing Students for Success*: Choosing an appropriate teaching learning design shall help students to become self reliant and indoctrination of positive values among them.

This means a holistic program needs to be undertaken for teacher education which focuses on preparing humane and professional teachers. Along with content and methodology, there is a need to integrate emotional competencies such as self awareness and self management, social sensitivity and social management. There is need to integrate life skills such as self awareness, empathy, interpersonal relationship, effective communication, critical thinking, decision making, problem solving and coping up with emotions and stress. There is need to integrate information processing skills such as asking, accessing, analyzing, applying and assessing (Goel & Goel, 2013). There is a need to integrate technology based skills along with spiritual intelligence dimensions (Goel, 2013).

Challenges Ahead

Shift to more powerful learning paradigms: There is a need to shift to more powerful learning paradigms, such as linear to hypermedia learning, instruction to discovery and construction, teacher-centered to learner-centered education, learning how to navigate and learn, teacher as transmitter to teacher as facilitator.

ICT Illiteracy: It is an age of Information and Technology but a large number of teachers at all levels are ICT Illiterate. The students being latest generation are excelling the teachers in ICT.

Information Explosion and Knowledge Poverty: There is information explosion and media implosion in all facets of life and living, but still we teachers have knowledge poverty. It is because we have more of a media crowd than media culture. Most of us do not know where from and how to access information.

Technology Alienated Education: We do not have technology integrated education. On one side we have International Standard Digital Network, on the other we do not have interconnected networks.

Thin population of Techno savvy, Net savvy and Info savvy: We have very thin population of techno-savvy, info-savvy and net-savvy teachers. It is because the education system as a whole has been relatively indifferent towards techno-culture. Our educational radio, educational television, educational computers, EDUSAT, SIET, etc have lost their educational identities.

Rare expression of ICT Aided Constructivist Approaches in Education: The latest phenomenon in education is constructivism which is applied to both learning theory and epistemology. Here the role of a teacher is that of a facilitator who encourages learners to reflect, analyze, design and develop the process of knowledge construction and the learners are active agents who engage in own knowledge construction by integrating new information into their scheme.

Hence it is important that the teachers' role has to be revitalized and the teacher education system has to inculcate the culture of germination of new ideas, innovation, creation and construction.

Constraints in Integration of ICT in Education

Certain constraints in integration of ICT in education are (UNESCO, 2002):

- High cost of internet connection
- Redesigning of curriculum for integrating ICT
- Training of teachers in ICT
- Lack of professionalism on part of teachers and inescapable, indifferent attitude

- Lack of leadership roles on part of school
- Lack of proper budget planning
- Maintenance of ICT resources and lack of technical staff
- Sustainability
- Limited availability of educational software and courseware

What to Do?

(1) Professional Development of Teachers

Information, communication and media technologies are the high octane fuel that drive global connections, exchange of knowledge and resources; create the platform and provide tools to collaborate and connect. To face the challenges of the present century, it is very essential to enhance the soft skills of teachers. Majority of teachers in India are lacking computer skills and that places a barrier so it is imperative that the teacher should be made computer literate. A national program has been initiated by the Ministry of Human Resource Development to develop computer literacy through National Mission on Education through ICT. Under this mission, a proper balance between content generation, research in critical areas relating to imparting of education and connectivity for integrating our knowledge with the advancements in other countries is to be attempted. There were three guiding principles of this mission viz, human resource development, E-content development and building connectivity and knowledge network.

The Indian government approved the establishment of National Knowledge Network in 2010. It is a major step towards building a knowledge society without boundary. It is a multi gigabit, unified, high speed network that aims to connect over 1500 institutions like universities, research institutions, libraries, laboratories, healthcare and agricultural institutions, nuclear, space and defence research agencies in the country.

These insights are useful for establishing the ICT learning environment to excel in the higher education. It will increase flexibility so that learners can have access to education, regardless of time and geographical barriers. It can influence the way students are taught and how they learn. It would enable development of collaborative skills as well as knowledge creation skills.

It is imperative that such training is also a part of in-service and pre-service teacher education programs. Efforts are being made in this direction. The new NCTE curriculum also mentions ICT as an integral component of all teacher education programs. Now its implementation is to be ensured with sincerity and objectivity. So a teacher training program should include the following:

(a) *Providing technical Expertise:* Teachers will need to be comfortable with navigating technology and digital resources to support the learning of students.
(b) *Leverage technology to Individualistic Instruction:* The facilitation of learning includes the use of technology to guide students and customize activities to meet individual needs.
(c) *Use technology to transform assessment and foster data driven instruction:* Technology and digital learning offers teachers the ability to collect and interpret various points of student assessment data. Teachers will need to be trained in how to use these data effectively to inform instruction and increase student learning.

Thus, with the expansion of digital learning and technology in the classroom, the training and professional development of teachers must transition to fully realize the potential of these resources to foster student learning. Preparing teachers to take full advantage of technology for learning will require new professional learning content centered on several key ideas and skills, including, designing relevant, rigorous learning tasks that leverage the power of technologies and the internet; developing facilitation and collaboration strategies; creating classroom systems and routines that support collaborative and independent learning; establishing guidelines for ethical and appropriate use of digital media and content; using various technologies and the Internet in instructional planning and decision-making; and, using digital technologies in evaluation of learning (assessment, data-driven decision making, portfolios, etc.).

To support the development of these skills and build teachers' comfort with technology will require a strong commitment to professional development. But the reality of creating and implementing professional development systems to move towards the goal of all students becoming technologically literate and all teachers leveraging the power of technology in their classrooms will require an approach that goes beyond policy requirements and the establishment of standards. Effectively scaling up professional development for teachers on the use of technology to guide instruction will involve broad access, ongoing support and accountability. Specifically, policymakers, districts and schools need to ensure that teachers are provided multiple opportunities to attain professional development. If professional development should be designed for face-to-face delivery, with several dates to accommodate teachers' schedules.

(2) Enhancing Skill

In the present age, a proper balance between content creation, research in critical areas relating to imparting of education and connectivity, for integrating our knowledge with the advancements in other countries, is to be attempted. The digital age demands a changed mindset about schooling, learning, teaching and assessment. Presently, a number of our schools suffer from a low quality education delivery, primarily due to inefficient infrastructure, tiny classrooms and lack of teachers. Teacher Education courses should equip teachers not just with basic ICT skills, but should encourage the evolution towards integrating technologies into teaching subjects and practices. The point is not that how to use technologies but also about why and when to use them in transforming teaching practices. The integration of ICT in teacher professional development according to Perraton *et al.* (2001, cited in Anderson and Glen 2003) involves two sets of activities or roles: one is training teachers to learn about ICT and its use in teaching as computers are introduced to schools. The other role of ICT is as a means of providing teacher education, either as a core or main component of a programme or playing a supplementary role within it.

The teacher's role shifts from instructional owner to instructional designer – the facilitator who creates and guides learning experiences. Teachers are needed to be comfortable with navigating technology and digital resources to support the learning of students.

Thus with the expansion of digital learning and technology in the classroom, the training and professional development of teachers must transition to fully realize the potential of these resources to foster student learning. This encompasses using technology, to guide instruction and to measure, evaluate and understand student learning through data driven instructional methods. In addition to this shift in role, many teachers lack proficiency with technology. These gaps – the teacher's role in digital learning environments and teacher technology skills – prevent digital learning and technologies from being used effectively.

Efforts are required in the direction to improve infrastructural facilities. As we are aware, our schools located in villages, small towns lack basic amenities. Thus, discussion about ICT mediated learning appears obsolete. But higher learning institutions are capable of bridging this gap. Some training programs should be implemented for the students to develop their competencies in the use of computers and internet. Secondly, we should set a minimum level of learning for the students. Recently governments have launched such programs where students are being given this training free of cost. These facilities are to be communicated to the students with the right mindset and positive thinking.

Ensuring equitable access to quality higher education for students coming from poor families is a major challenge. Students from poor background are put to further disadvantage since they are not academically prepared to crack highly competitive entrance examinations that have bias towards urban elite and rich students having access to private tuitions and coaching. This also requires providing facilities at institutions to create conducive environment in classrooms.

Lack of resources also limits the teacher. If proper facilities are not available to the teacher then new pedagogy cannot be implemented. Proper facilities like computers, projectors, internet, CDs and DVDs, online modules are necessary. Teachers are to be motivated for undertaking extra efforts to generate interest and motivation in students.

(3) Creating Conducive Learning Environment

Technology, which is a boon in making learning an engaging experience, also may hamper the classroom environment. Excess use of technology and easy access to these resources may pose a challenge in the classroom in the form of students using social networking media in the classroom. So, proper care and vigil is to be exercised in the classroom. Ethical use of these resources is to be promoted. We observe wrong use of technology among adolescents and young adults which is a challenge for the society. For this, judicious use of technology is to be promoted, including value education among others to be made a part of the curriculum. Teachers should teach and practice moral, ethical and right social values which include respect, truth, modesty, honesty, equality, self reliance among others.

Conclusion

ICT has fundamentally changed the way we live now. We find a world of difference in the practices and procedures of various fields such as medicine, travel, tourism, business, banking, engineering, in how they operate now in comparison to how they operated two decades ago. In contrast, the impact of ICT on education however has been far and slow. The most fundamental cause seems to have been the deep seated belief that teaching is an art with no role of technology in the design and delivery of instruction. This belief system has been largely responsible for the restricted access to higher education, quality of in class experience being limited to chalk and talk and marked by absence of opportunities for stimulating and evaluating learner engagement and higher order learning. But now times have changed and the paradigm of education and learning has changed from art and science to technology mediated instruction and learning. ICT can therefore be perceived as a big change agent for education and the realization seems to have dawned on the teaching community that ICT is primarily meant to empower them and not to replace them.

17

Concept Mapping: An Effective Teaching Practice

Approach in School

Rasheed Ahmad

The present age is based on rapidly increasing and changing information; the goal of education is no longer to train students to store and retrieve information received in the classroom. The ability to recall and explain a concept does not necessarily reflect understanding, nor does it guarantee that students can apply and use the concept in a meaningful way (Chen, 2003). The goal of education in this new age is to prepare students to use their skills to solve real-world problems on the basis of their previous experiences, to develop the potentials to make life purposeful.

National Curriculum Frameworks (NCF-2005) addresses these educational goals and emphasises on the children's creativity. NCF-2005 also highlights the significance of contextualisation of education and situated learning in context of students' prior learning experiences. Once a teacher develops the faith in students abilities, he/she will be able to design challenging tasks for their learning and wil be able to engage them in the process of knowledge construction on the basis of prior experiences.

The construction of knowledge and understanding by involvement of students' active participation and their prior experiences is an integral part of constructivism. Constructivism emphasises that students can construct their own knowledge and understanding of the world by connecting new ideas to existing ones (NCF-2005). Constructivism is a major approach in NCF-2005.

There are several approaches of learning in constructivism and concept mapping is one of the most important approaches. It was developed by Novak and his research group in Cornell University in the early 1970's as an approach to identifying knowledge structures of an individual. It is now used as a vehicle to represent and assess changes in students' understanding of science (Novak, 1990). Concept mapping is a technique to representing knowledge in graphs. Thus, whole concepts/

information are presented by graphs in concept mapping approach. This tool will prevent memorizing, which is very common method of our education system and will promote sensible learning. Sensible learning creates a logical meaning by an individual between the new information that has learned by previous education (Karakuyu, 2010).

Concept Mapping

A concept map typically represents ideas and information as boxes or circles, which it connects with labelled arrows in a downward-branching hierarchical structure. The relationship between concepts can be articulated in linking phrases (Novak, 1995). Concept maps have been defined as two-dimensional, hierarchical, node-linked diagrams that depict verbal, conceptual, or declarative knowledge in succinct, visual or graphic forms (Horton et al., 1993). Novak's work is based on the cognitive theories of David Ausubel (assimilation theory), which stressed the importance of prior knowledge in learning of new concepts, and advocated that 'the most important single factor influencing learning is what the learner already knows'. Novak concluded that meaningful learning involves assimilation of new concepts and propositions into existing cognitive structures. Novak taught various class, ages, students with the help of concept map. Students as young as six years old were taught by Novak by concept mapping approach to represent their response to focus on questions such as, "What is water?", "What causes the seasons?"

Thus the concept mapping is a visual representation of an individual's knowledge structure on a particular topic. The maps contain several components, representing students' knowledge. They include concepts, which are defined here as "perceived regularities in objects or events that are designated by a sign or symbol" (Novak, 1991). Concepts are usually enclosed in circles or boxes, and relationships between concepts are indicated by connecting lines that link them together. Words on the linking line specify the relationship between the concepts.The smallest units of meaning of a concept map is a proposition which includes two concepts linked together using a linking phrase. The Figure 17.1 represents the concept of concept map and it is developed by the Ruiz-Primo School of Education, Stanford University.

Concept mapping delineates individual differences in learning; different students construct different types of concept map, even in the same subject area. Besides this concept mapping can be used to stimulate the generation of ideas, to aid creativity and some time for brain-storming.

Figure 17.1: A Concept Map Showing the Key Concepts Involved in Concept Mapping

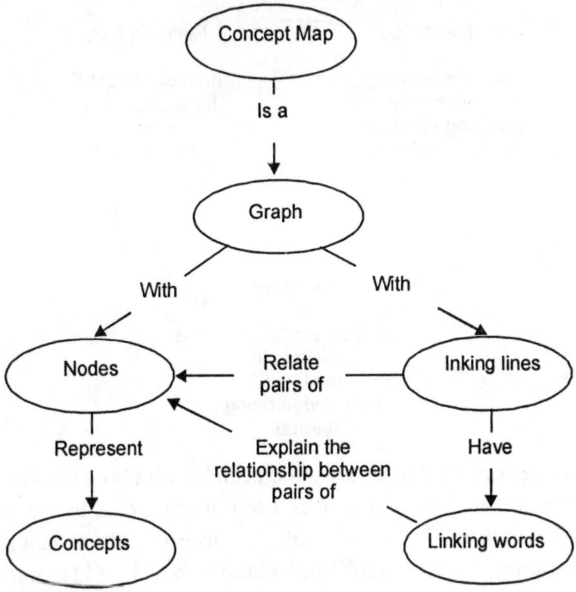

Concept Mapping – Why Use them?

Novak's work is based on the cognitive theories of David Ausubel (assimilation theory), who emphasized that prior knowledge is important for learning new concepts. Thus the most important factor influencing learning is what the learner's prior knowledge is. Ausubel believed that the mind is organised in a top-down fashion and that students relate new information to previous knowledge contained in their cognitive structures. These new concepts are sorted, related, and added to the existing hierarchies to create meaning.

Hence, meaningful learning takes place when a learner is able to organise, relate and include concepts into his or her cognitive structures. Concept mapping in its pure form treats teaching and learning as a student-centred process. This makes concept mapping process as a powerful learning strategy that forces the learner to actively think about the relationship between the terms. Therefore, Concept Mapping is especially suited for studying science as the learners often perceive, incorrectly, that studying science means simply memorizing facts (Dorough and Rye, 1997).

Figure 17.2: Concept Mapping Classroom Triangle

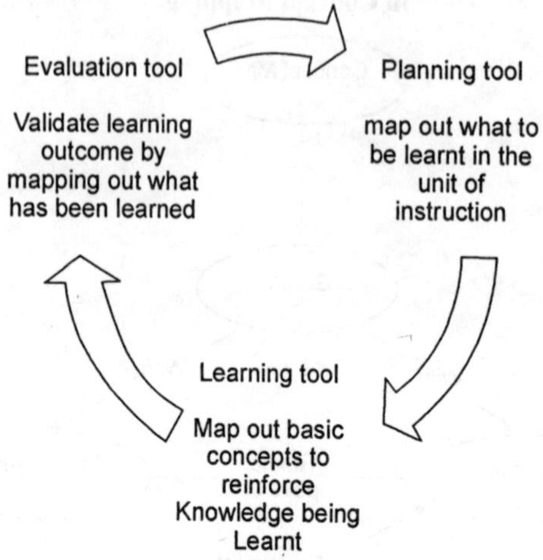

This tool is versatile in nature which can be used both for instruction and for assessment. The tool can be used at any point in the learning process. The Figure 17.2 points out the three important tasks where concept mapping is useful in fulfilling classroom tasks: (1) as a planning tool (to plan instruction and provide students with a visualization of what is to be learned and how it connects), (2) as a learning tool (to reinforce concepts learned in a unit of instruction), (3) as an evaluation tool (to validate learning by mapping out a perception of what has been learned).

Components of Concept Map

- Nodes represent concepts.
- Lines represent relations between concepts, arrowheads indicate direction.
- Labels on the lines describe the nature of the relationship.
- Combined, these three components create propositions or meaningful statements.

Kinds of Concept Mapping

There are four major categories of concept maps. These are distinguished by their different format for representing information. Examples of the various types of concept maps are presented on the following pages. Click over each in order to open a special window that contains several images. After viewing them, click over the upper left corner of the special window to close it.

Spider Concept Mapping

The "spider" concept map is organized by placing the central theme or unifying factor in the center of the map. Outwardly radiating sub-themes surround the center of the map.

Figure 17.3: Spider Concept Map

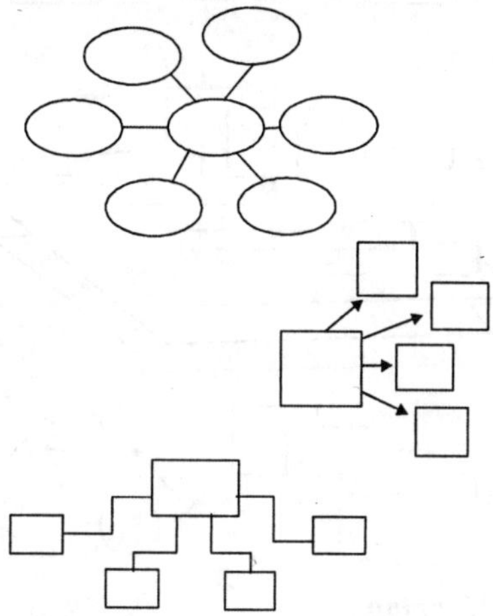

Hierarchy Concept Mapping

The hierarchy concept map presents information in a descending order of importance. The most important information is placed on the top. Distinguishing factors determine the placement of the information.

Figure 17.4: Hierarchy Concept Map

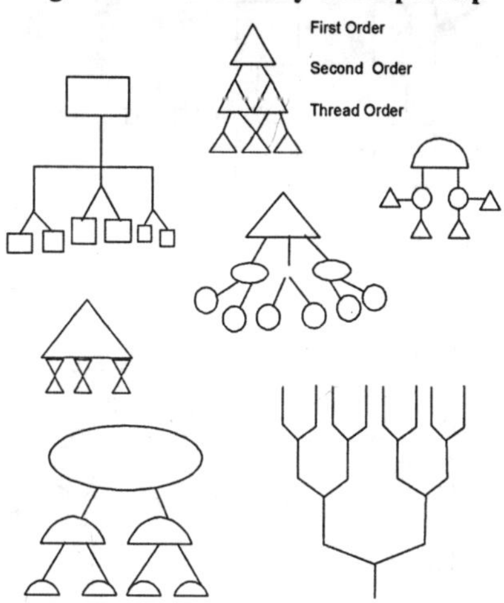

Flowchart Concept Map

The flowchart concept map organizes information in a linear format.

Figure 17.5: Flowchart Concept Map

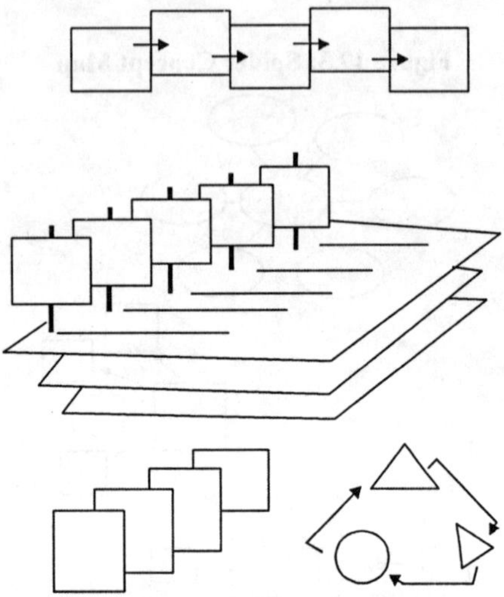

Systems Concept Mapping

The systems concept map organizes information in a format which is similar to a flowchart with the addition of 'INPUTS' and 'OUTPUTS'.

Figure 17.6: Systems Concept Map

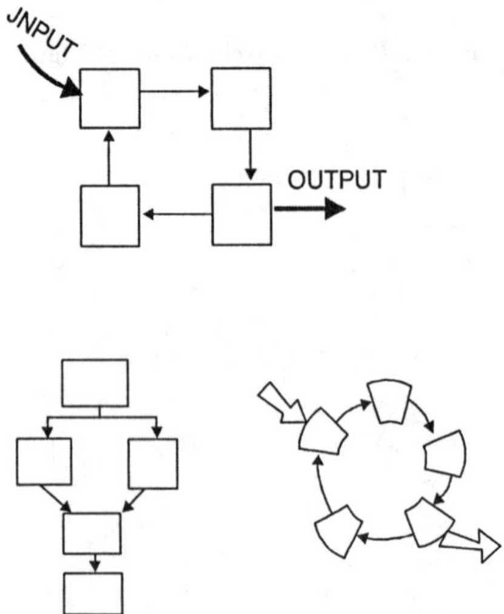

Constructing Concept Map

There are several key steps that, when followed, result in a 'good' concept map that represent students' understanding of a domain. As mentioned previously, the initial step is the identification of the focus questions/ concepts. A good teacher brainstorms the students by presenting a good question. Once the question is identified, the student must then construct their map to answer the question. This can be carried out by adhering to the following steps:

Step 1 – Identify the major concepts

The students' list the most important concepts that come to mind when they read the concerned question. For example, while constructing a map to answer the question "What is light?", the key concepts will include, straight line, reflection, refraction, spectrum, white light, sun and dispersion. These concepts are referred to the "seed" concept in the map. While constructing the concept map, it is important to include concepts that answer the focus question; students will tend to deviate from the focus question and include concepts that relate to the domain but do not specifically answer the question.

Step 2 – Arrange the concepts on paper

The students must organise the concepts in a hierarchy, from general to more specific. In the case of light, the students will begin with concepts such as the sun and branch down to the different colours of white light (Figure 17.7)

Figure 17.7: Concepts arranged in a Hierarchical Structure

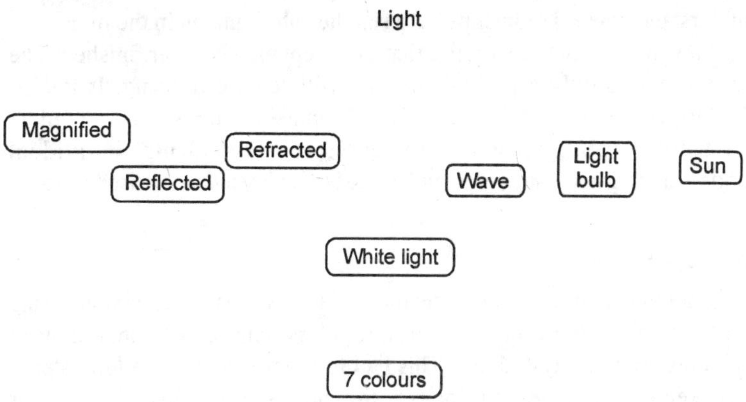

Step 3 – Link the concepts, including the linking phrases

Once the concepts are represented in a hierarchy, the next step is to connect the concepts to form propositions (Figure 17.8). The purpose of the linking phrase is to show the relationship between two concepts.

Figure 17.8: Concepts Connected with Linking Phrases representing the Relationships between Concepts

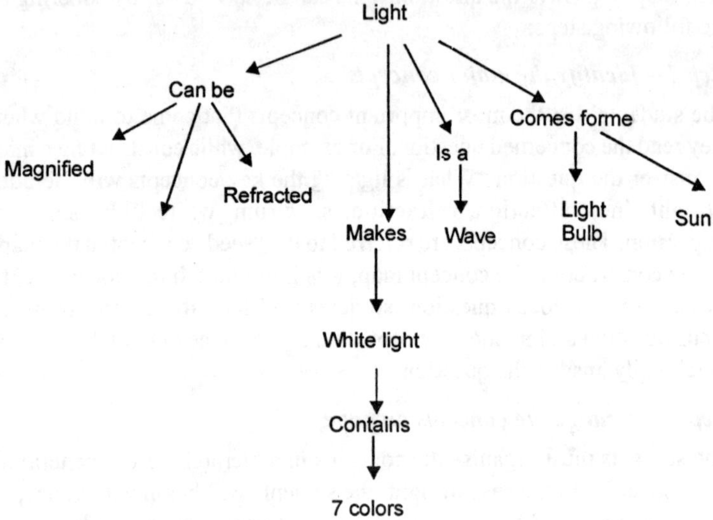

Step 4 – Make Cross links

A crosslink is a relationship that "exists between two concepts in different vertical segments of the map" (Dorough & Rye 1997, p. 37). Cross-links are a critical measure of map complexity and represent that the student understands the relationships between the sub-domains in the map.

It is important to recognise that a concept map is never finished. The initial map is only a preliminary and will require revising. It is also important to notc that these steps are intended to only serve as a guide. Concept Mapping is a tool to represent the students' individual understanding and knowledge and hence is a highly individualised process.

Step 5 – Results

In order to examine and evaluate the students' views of concept mapping and the use of the tool in the physics classroom, questionnaires were administered to the students. This had four pages and was administered at the end stage of the study, prior to the end-of-term exams. The students were questioned on several aspects of the concept mapping tool and its use in the classroom, including personal information, the Concept Mapping tool itself, and finally the impact it had on their learning. Statistical analysis carried out on the student responses concerning the effect of the tool on the students' learning has been reported in previous papers, (Broggy and McClelland, 2008a; Broggy and McClelland, 2008b). As the results in this paper focuses mainly on the students' views of the tool, the results below focus on the qualitative data generated from the questionnaires.

Uses of Concept Mapping in Education

Concept mapping can also be seen as a first step in ontology-building, and can also be used flexibly to represent formal argument.

- Note taking and summarizing gleaning key concepts, their relationships and hierarchy form documents and source materials
- New knowledge creation: e.g., transforming tacit knowledge into an organizational resource, mapping team knowledge
- Collaborative knowledge modeling and the transfer of expert knowledge
- Facilitating the creation of shared vision and shared understanding among the learners
- Instructional design: concept maps used as Ausubelian "advance organizers", which provide an initial conceptual frame for subsequent information and learning.
- Training: concept maps used as Ausubelian "advanced organizers" to represent the training context and its relationship to their jobs, to the organization's strategic objectives, to training goals.
- Increasing meaningful learning, for example through writing activities where concept maps automatically generated from an essay are shown to the writer.
- Communicating complex ideas and arguments
- Detailing the entire structure of an idea, train of thought, or line of argument (with the specific goal of exposing faults, errors, or gaps in one's own reasoning) for the scrutiny of others.
- Enhancing metacognition (learning to learn, and thinking about knowledge)
- Improving language ability
- Assessing learner understanding of learning objectives, concepts, and the relationship among those concepts
- To generate ideas (Brainstorming, etc)

- To design complex structure (long text, hyper media, and large website)
- To assess the understanding and also misunderstanding

Advantages

- Concept mapping represents ideas or views from a large group of participants or stakeholders in an easy-to-interpret format.
- It generates data that can be interpreted qualitatively or quantitatively.
- It clearly defines the central idea, by positioning it in the centre of page
- It allows to indicate clearly the relative importance of each idea
- It allows to see all the basic information on the pages
- It identifies complex relationships between issues, factors, etc in a tangible, graphic format.
- It is participant focused and everybody can have his or her ideas represented.
- It shows at glance specific performance areas, their interrelationship, and their strategic priority.
- It is simple to implement and understand for both you and the participant(s).
- Concept mapping uses a structured process that can be replicated easily and reliably.
- It enables the organization to create a shared vision of performance areas and goals.
- It promotes active participation and, therefore, ensures that participant(s) stay on task.

Disadvantages

- In the absence of a structured approach for creating concept maps, this approach can become messy and hard to read.
- Concept mapping includes only a high level representation of the performance area, which is the subject of the concept. This method does not easily allow for the inclusion of detailed information.
- In concept mapping, it may be hard to identify all the relationships between the concepts or ideas.
- Interpretation of the concept map data can be involved.
- The use of this method may require an experienced facilitator.

Conclusion

Major concern of our education system is its rigidness and inflexibility which suppresses the students' creativity, curiosity and originality. Our examination system which does not provide ample opportunities to students to express their ideas and authoritative role of teachers are two big reasons for this suppression. These problems forced NCERT to bring out a new curriculum framework called NCF-2005 which emphasises upon concept mapping as a visual representation of knowledge, facilitating the nurturing of creativity among students. It can also be used to create brainstorming web and task specific organizer, in addition to thinking process map.

Concept mapping inculcates creativity by enabling the students to use novel concepts for drawing a concept map, incorporates relevant propositions and links one example with more than one relevant concept (Ahuja, 2013). Concept maps created by students can be used as powerful assessment tools to assess the their understanding of the topic in a manner that could be considered much more authentic than various traditional types of assessment tools. Thus, concept mapping can be used to assess or describe a variety of constructs and outcomes as well as in instruction. Concept mapping helps in the organization and representation of knowledge which ultimately raises the quality of learning and leads to meaningful learning. Therefore, concept mapping can be practiced as a versatile and promising tool in the area of science education.

18

Anchored Instructional Approach

Critical Pedagogy to Enhance Critical Consciousness among Students

P.K. Aruna and *Muhammed Haris C.*

Critical pedagogy is an approach to enhance critical consciousness among students. Anchored instructional approach is a powerful means to enhance critical consciousness among students. It is a technology based approach designed specifically to help students acquire the skill and knowledge necessary to become independent thinkers and learners. It has been developed by the Cognition and Technology Group (CTG) (1990). It aims to create "problem-solving environments" based on the use of video disc and computer technologies that provide a framework for sustained exploration of authentic task.

Here we bring out the fact that state anchored instructional approach is helping students to achieve skills to solve emerging problems in different situations. It is based on interaction and student-centered teaching learning process.

Paulo Freire contributed a philosophy of education that came not only from the more classical approaches stemming from Plato, but also from modern Maxist and anti-colonialist thinkers. In *Pedagogy of the Oppressed* (1990), Freire, reprising the oppressor-oppressed distinction, differentiates between the positions in an unjust society: the oppressor and the oppressed.

Freire states that education should facilitate the oppressed to regain his self respect and dignity. He acknowledges that for this to occur, the oppressed individual must play an important role in his liberation. He states:

No pedagogy which is truly liberating can remain distant from the oppressed by treating them as unfortunates and by presenting for their emulation models from among the oppressors. The oppressed must be their own example in the struggle for their redemption (Freire, 1970, p. 54).

Likewise, the oppressors must be willing to rethink their way of life and to examine their own role in the oppression if true liberation is to occur: "…those who authentically commit themselves to the people must re-examine themselves constantly" (Freire, 1970, p. 60).

Freire believed education to be a political act that could not be divorced from pedagogy. Freire defined this as a main tenet of critical pedagogy. Teachers and students must be made aware of the "politics" that surround education. The way students are taught and what they are taught serves a political agenda. Teachers, themselves, have political notions they bring into the classroom (Kincheloe, 2008).

Freire believed that "education makes sense because women and men learn that through learning they can make and remake themselves, because women and men are able to take responsibility for themselves as beings capable of knowing—of knowing that they know and knowing that they don't" (Freire, 2004, p. 15).

Freire put forward many concept for enhancing oppressed through pedagogy of oppressed. Following are the two significant concepts:

Banking Concept of Education: In terms of pedagogy, Freire is best known for his attack on what he called the "banking" concept of education, in which the student was viewed as an empty account to be filled by the teacher. He notes that "it transforms students into receiving objects. It attempts to control thinking and action, leads men and women to adjust to the world, and inhibits their creative power" (Freire, 1970, p. 77). The basic critique was not new — Rousseau's conception of the child as an active learner was already a step away from tabula rasa (which is basically the same as the "banking concept"). In addition, thinkers like John Dewey were strongly critical of the transmission of mere facts as the goal of education. Dewey often described education as a mechanism for social change, explaining that "education is a regulation of the process of coming to share in the social consciousness; and that the adjustment of individual activity on the basis of this social consciousness is the only sure method of social reconstruction. Freire's work, however, updated the concept and placed it in context with current theories and practices of education, laying the foundation for what is now called critical pedagogy.

Culture of Silence: According to Freire, the system of dominant social relations creates a 'culture of silence' that instills a negative, silenced and suppressed self-image into the oppressed. The learner must develop a critical consciousness in order to recognize that this culture of silence is created to oppress.A culture of silence can also cause the "dominated individuals lose the means by which to critically respond to the culture that is forced on them by a dominant culture."

Social domination of race and class are interlaced into the conventional education system, through which the "culture of silence" eliminates the "paths of thought that lead to a language of critique.

Anchored Instruction as a Critical Pedagogy

Paulo Freire proposed dialogic approach to free the oppressed through the use of cooperation, unity and organization and cultural synthesis. Dialogue is the way to overcome problems in society to liberate human beings. Dialogue should not become a teacher centered process. It should be democratic. Teacher should respect the students. It is a form of cultural exchange. Dialogue is not from the teacher to student but it is mutual. Educators take the stand that they are empowering students through their attempt. Empowerment does not come from the educator to the learner. They should have critical reflection through dialogue. This dialogic cultural action leads to praxis, a step to critical consciousness through critical reflection and action.

Freire's model of dialogic must be rooted within social praxis, informed reflection and political action. Dialogic and social praxis are working together to break down oppression. According to him, freedom will be the result of praxis when a balance between theory and practice is achieved. Praxis means informed action. It is a step to critical consciousness through critical reflection and action. Learner has to move from object to subject. For this, learner is needed to be involved in dialogical action with the teacher.

Anchored instructional approach is a powerful means to enhance the critical consciousness among students. Anchored Instruction approach is a technology based approach designed specifically to help students acquire the skill and knowledge necessary to become independent thinkers and learners. It is developed by the Cognition and Technology Group (CTG) (1990). It aims to create "problem-solving environments" based on the use of video disc and computer technologies that provide a framework for sustained exploration of authentic task.

For several years the concept of anchored instruction was experimented with to discover ways to structure learning experiences for students. Helping students to solve problems and to become independent thinkers and learners by developing their confidence, skills and knowledge was the main goal. To achieve it, the use of computer and video disc technologies was examined. Situating instruction in video disc based, problem solving environments resulted in the development of anchored instructional approach.

The work of several theorists was looked at and became instrumental in the development of the anchored instruction concept. Insights were incorporated from John Dewey about using theme based learning, Charles Gragg on the use of case based instruction and the advantages derived from it. Both Dewey and Nonwood Russell Hanson emphasized upon the differences between expert and novice knowledge (CTG, 1990).

Anchored instructional approach is helpful for active learning by creating a student-centered learning environment. Anchored instruction's goal is to overcome the problem of inert knowledge by providing opportunity for exploration. Anchored instruction is intended to enable students and teachers to understand not only the problems and opportunities that experts encounter in different areas but also how experts use knowledge as a tool. According to the anchored instruction researchers, experts have been immersed in educational situations and are familiar with thinking about them. When a new theory, concept or principle is introduced, which is relevant to their situation, experts are able to acknowledge how these new ideas affect their own thinking. A novice views the introduction of concept, principles, and theories as additional facts or procedures to be memorized. He has not had the immersion in educational situations to allow him to understand how new additional information may affect his thinking (Cognition and Technology Group at Vanderbilt, 1990).

Anchored instruction creates an environment that is rich in content and shared by students. It generates interest by enabling students to identify problems while examining the content from multiple perspectives through involvement in complex problem spaces called macro contexts. Being able to explore a problem space over time from multiple perspectives is enabled through the macro contexts, which act as environment allowing for cooperative learning and instructor intervention (Cognition and Technology Group at Vanderbilt, 1990, Shyu, 1999).

Guiding Principles of Anchored Instruction

Development and implementation of an anchored instruction curriculum are guided by seven key design principles: Choosing an appropriate anchor, developing shared expertise around the anchor, expanding the anchor, using knowledge as a tool for problem solving, teaching with the anchor, merging the anchor with literacy experiences, and allowing student exploration (McLarty et al.1989). According to these guiding principles using anchor videos for instruction is a meaning making activity that provides opportunities for students to use oral language, reading, writing and other literacy related skills.

Their design makes anchor videos different from the ones typically used previously in education. Prior to anchors, educational videos were a series of visual examples supplementing a traditional lecture. The videos reinforced the transmission view of instruction where knowledge is transmitted from an expert (the teacher) to novice (the student). From the anchored instruction perspective, the goal was to create realistic, yet interesting, contexts to encourage active knowledge construction by students. The macro contexts of the anchor videos were stories designed for exploration by students and teachers. Using realistic macro context stories allowed students to re-create some of the experiential learning advantages available to those participating in apprenticeships.

Conclusion

Anchored instruction provides ample chance for free thinking. Learning process takes place in a realistic situation. Paulo Freire thought that oppressed people have their own role in their liberation. It needs their response against exploitation. Anchored instructional approach provides a better chance to experience problem situation. By using knowledge as a tool, students find their own solution. The method of teaching of anchored instruction is dialogical that is the best method according to Paulo Freire. The approach of anchored instruction is also against the banking concept. Banking concept is based on teacher centered monologue but in anchored instruction it is a method of teaching through interaction. Students construct knowledge by using their cognitive abilities. This will train them to overcome the culture of silence. So, anchored instructional approach is successful in developing critical consciousness among students.

19

Right to Education Act 2009

Implementing Issues and Challenges

A. Suneera

Education is the most powerful tool for the progress of the country and social change. Education helps an individual in making rational choice and protects them from exploitation. Therefore opportunity of education must be given to everyone. In this regard, Article 26 of the 1948 Universal Declaration of Human Rights states that 'Everyone has the right to education. Education shall be free, at least in the elementary and fundamental stages. Elementary education shall be compulsory." In the year 2000, the world's governments adopted the six Education for All (EFA) goals and the eight Millennium Development Goals (MDGs), the two most important frameworks in the field of education.

The report of the International Commission on Education for the twenty-first century, UNESCO promotes a holistic view of education consisting of four pillars, namely learning to know, learning to do, learning to be and learning to live together. The education priorities of UNESCO are shaped by these objectives. The global Education for All (EFA) movement aimed to meet the learning needs of all children, youth and adults by 2015.

The text was widely adopted by India and several other countries. In accordance with the Constitutional commitment to ensure free and compulsory education for all children up to the age of 14 years, provision of universal elementary education has become a salient feature of national policy. There is a special provision of compulsory education in the Indian constitution under article 45 and 21A. The various articles of the Indian Constitution provide for education as a fundamental right. According to the constitutional provision of education, Central and State Governments need to make serious efforts to expand the education in the country. These include the scheme of Operation Blackboard (OB); Non Formal Education (NFE); Teacher Education (TE); Mahila Samakhya (MS); Lok Jumbish Project (LJP); Shiksha Karmi Project (SKP); National Programme of

Nutritional Support to Primary Education (MDM); District Primary Education Programme (DPEP) and Sarva Shiksha Abhiyan (SSA). Besides, the RTE Act of 2009 provides free and compulsory education to Indian children up to the age of 14.

Right to Education Act 2009

> "Every child of the age of six to 14 years shall have a right to free and compulsory education in a neighbourhood school till the completion of elementary education".

The Right to Education Act is an Act of the Parliament of India enacted on 4 August 2009, which describes the modalities of the importance of free and compulsory education for children in India under Article 21A of the Indian Constitution. India became one of the 135 countries to make education a fundamental right of every child, after the Act came into force on 1 April 2010.

RTE Act guarantees free and compulsory education to all children between the ages of 6-14 years, completing the elementary cycle of education in a neighbourhood school. Further, it guarantees education of a specified standard, subscribing to norms of school infrastructure, hours of instructional time and days of school functioning, pupil-teacher ratio and teacher quality. The Act does not specifically cover children below the age of 6. However, it says that the "local authorities" may provide free and compulsory education at the pre-primary stage.

According to the Act, "free" education refers to any fees or charges that may prevent a child from pursuing and completing the elementary cycle of education. It implies that any kind of tuition or other fees (sports, development, examination, etc.,) cannot be charged from any child. Further, any expenses that may prevent a child from participating in the education process from transport facilities and other physical aides such as spectacles, crutches or hearing aids, are included in the entitlement of free education for a children.

In India free education is an essential factor because majority of the Indian parents are poor and are not able to carry the cost of education to their children. By "compulsory" it means that the Government is committed to provide free elementary education to every child in the 6-14 years of age group and ensure not just admission, but attendance and completion of the elementary cycle of schooling as well. Indian parents from the backward category are not even aware about the importance and value of education. So education should be compulsory.

Under RTE Act, no child in the age group 6-14 years can be refused admission in school. If the child is 9 years old, he will be admitted to class 3. The Act makes it the responsibility of the school to provide children special training in the school location to enable him to come up to his age appropriate class. In other words, a 9 year old has the right to be enrolled in class 3 while he attends remedial classes provided by the school in the same locations till he is able to be mainstreamed. Moreover, The Act guarantees the completion of elementary education. It means therefore that the child can continue to study till he has completed class 8 irrespective of his age at that time and even if it exceeds 14 years. This provision of the act ensures that there is no dropout in the school.

The law makes it clear that the compulsion is on the state and not on the parents to ensure completion of the elementary stage of schooling. It says that to admit their children in a neighbourhood school it is the duty of every parent, but it is the responsibility of the government to ensure quality education and retention of students in school for completion of elementary education.

Historical Perspective

The Right to Education legislation has a long history. In 1950, the Constitution of India included Article 45, as one of the Directive Principles of State policy, which states: "The State shall endeavor to provide within a period of ten years from the commencement of this Constitution, for free and compulsory education for all children until they complete the age of fourteen years."

During 1964-1968, the Indian Education Commission (Kothari Commission) reviewed the status of education in India and made several recommendations. The most important recommendation of the Commission was the common school system with a view to eliminate inequality in educational opportunities. Immediately thereafter, the National Policy on Education (NPE), 1968 was framed. This policy was the first official document of the Indian Government for providing school education. The policy also required special schools to provide freeship to certain category of students to prevent social separation in schools. Nevertheless, it retained all these provisions under the 'directive principles'.

In 1976, a constitutional amendment was approved, making education a concurrent subject. This made both the Central and the State Governments responsible for education of children. By enacting a legislation to provide Right to Education, the Central Government has fulfilling its constitutional duties. In 1986, the National policy on

Education (NPE) re-affirmed the goal of Universalisation of school education and promised to take measures to achieve a common school system.

The first official recommendation for the inclusion of a fundamental right to education was made in 1990 by the Acharya Ramamurti Committee. Thereafter, several political as well as policy level changes influenced the course of FCE (Free and Compulsory education). The country witnessed an increased international focus on its initiatives regarding FCE after its participation in the World Conference on Education for All in 1990. India also ratified the UNCRC (UN Convention on the Rights of the Child) in 1992.

A great legal breakthrough was achieved in 1992 when the Supreme Court of India held in Mohini Jain Case, that "the Right to Education is concomitant to fundamental Rights, enshrined under Part III of the Constitution" and that "every citizen has a right to education under the Constitution". 1993,The Supreme court in the case of 'Unnikrishnan vs State of Andhra Pradesh', ruled that the right to education is a fundamental right that flows from the Right to life in Article 21 of the Constitution. The Unnikrishnan Judgment strengthened people with legal claim to free and compulsory education. This is evidenced by a spate of litigations that relied upon the principle of law laid down in the Unnikrishnan Judgment.

A combination of forces from different quarters, support from the judiciary, greater international attention and increased civil society and grass-root level campaigns exerted remarkable pressure on the Government to introduce a Fundamental Right to education in 1997. A Constitutional Amendment bill for the inclusion of a fundamental right to education was moved in the Parliament amidst much criticism and debate regarding the contents of the Act.

The said Amendment proposed that Article 21A be introduced, former Article 45 be deleted and Article 51A (K) be introduced. In November 2001 the bill was re-numbered as the 93rd Bill, and the 83rd Bill was withdrawn. The 93rd Bill proposed that former Article 45 be amended to provide for early childhood care and education instead of being deleted altogether. Despite continued criticism against the altered version, the Bill was passed in 2002 as the 86th Constitutional Amendment Act. In bringing this into action, the 'Right of Children to Free and Compulsory Education Bill' was drafted in 2005. This was revised and became an Act in August 2009, but was enforced on 1st April 2010.

Salient Features of the RTE Act, 2009

The salient features of the Right of Children for Free and Compulsory Education act are

- Free and compulsory education to all children of India in the six to 14 age groups.
- No child shall be held back, expelled, or required to pass a board examination until completion of elementary education.
- A child above six years of age who has not been admitted in any school or even admitted, but could not complete his or her elementary education, he or she shall be admitted in a class appropriate to his or her age. If a child is directly admitted in a class appropriate to his or her age, he or she shall, in order to be at par with others, have the right to receive special training, in such manner, and within such time limits, as may be prescribed. A child so admitted to elementary education shall be entitled to free education till completion of elementary education, even after fourteen years.
- Proof of age for admission: For the purposes of admission to elementary education, the age of a child shall be determined on the basis of the birth certificate. No child shall be denied admission in a school for lack of age proof.
- A child who completes elementary education shall be awarded a certificate.
- Calls for a fixed student-teacher ratio.
- Will apply to all of India except Jammu and Kashmir.
- Provides for 25 percent reservation for economically disadvantaged communities in admission to Class One in all private schools.
- Mandates improvement in quality of education.
- School teachers will need adequate professional degree within five years or else will lose job.
- School infrastructure (where there is problem) to be improved in three years, else recognition cancelled.
- Financial burden will be shared between state and central government.

Implementing Issues and Challenges

Out of School Children

According to the 2001 census, 8.5 core children were out of school in

India. However, latest figure from the Human Resource Development Ministry put the number at 80 lacs. These children can be classified in to 3 categories.

According to the National Crime Records Bureau, every year around 65,000 children fall victim to trafficking. Only 10 per cent of such cases are registered with the police. Trafficking in female children is for the purpose of begging and prostitution and male children used for begging as well as labourers.

Children have never been enrolled in school for several reasons like religion, poverty, social and gender discrimination. The parents also did not show much interest in enrolling the children.

Even though children are enrolled in schools, they may not complete their free and compulsory education level. After completing primary level education, they may be able to read and write. Due to this small achievement, parents may engage them in some kind of work for money, instead of allowing them to pursue their studies further.

Lack of Awareness

There should be promptness or commitment on the part of the Government to implement these laws. The poor uneducated parents may not know the importance of education. So it is the duty of the Government departments, NGO's and other social organizations to conduct various programmes and activities through which they can educate the people and parents about the importance of education.

Lack of Basic Infrastructure Facilities

Infrastructural development is the key driver for providing universal elementary education to India's children. One of the major reasons for children staying out of school or being pushed out is inadequate infrastructure. Although infrastructure has developed significantly over the last few years, there is still a considerable gap that needs to be filled to meet RTE norms.

According to the RTE Act, infrastructure facilities have to be made available to students by schools within a time frame of three years from the period of notification of the Act. Establishment of primary schools within one kilometer and upper primary schools within three kilometer distance by the Government is compulsory. All-weather school buildings should consist of well equipped classrooms, including one-teacher classrooms and a head teacher-cum-office room with barrier-free access, library, laboratory, play ground, safe and adequate drinking water facilities for all children, and separate toilets for boys and girls.

Lack of Required Pupil-Teacher Ratio

Five lakh new teachers are to be recruited and 5 lakh new classrooms are to be constructed to meet the required 30:1 pupil teacher ratio. There are seven lakh teachers in the recognized 13 lakh primary schools. Out of these, three lakh teachers are either untrained or under training. In many states large numbers of teachers are para-teachers and many of them are untrained. As per a recent report by NUEPA, Bihar tops amongst the states having poor pupil-teacher ratio and Uttar Pradesh comes at second place. In about 35 percent primary schools in Uttar Pradesh, pupil teacher ratio is 60:1. Fifty one percent primary schools in Uttar Pradesh are having three or less number of teachers. Out of these, 38 percent are para-teachers. In the present circumstances, to maintain pupil-teacher ratio as per the Act, appears a distant dream.

Quality of Education and Teachers

Section 23 gives power to the Central Government to prescribe qualifications for the teachers to various levels of education. In pursuance of this power, Department of School Education and Literacy, Ministry of Human Resources Development, Government of India issued a notification dated 23rd August 2010 which prescribes minimum qualification for a person to be eligible for appointment as a teacher in class I to VIII in all the schools to which this Act applies. But the Act or Notification is not clear about the implementation of these provisions. If the qualification of a teacher is good, then better education can be provided. Even though qualified teachers are appointed they may not be ready to work in the rural area. In some of the schools in the rural area, there is provision of just one single teacher for all the classes. The primary reason for the teachers' reluctance to go to rural areas is lack of proper infrastructural facilities.

Recognition of Schools

Section 19 of the Act requires all schools, except Government schools, to meet certain norms and standards relating to infrastructure, pupil-teacher ratio, and teacher salaries on the basis of which they are required to get recognition within three years. This clause penalizes private unrecognized schools, although they provide similar, if not better, teaching services compared to Government schools, while spending a much smaller amount. They are vulnerable to extinction in three years.

School Management Committee (SMC)

The Act requires every Government aided school to form a School Management Committee (SMC), which would include parents also. They will be responsible for planning and managing the operations of the school. School management Committee members are required to volunteer their time and effort. This can be a burden for the poor parents. And for the aided schools, the SMC rule will lead to a breakdown of their existing management structures. So this provision has been creating problems in some states.

Twenty Five per cent Reservations of Seats in Private Schools

According to RTE, it is compulsory for every private unaided school to admit at least 25 per cent at the entry level class from children belonging to weaker and disadvantaged groups. For this category of students the state government shall repay schools an amount equal to either the fees charged by the school or the per child expenditure in state schools, whichever is lower. The per-child expenditure for the purpose of reimbursement with respect to the 25 per cent quota has been defined as the total annual recurring expenditure of the government on its own schools divided by the number of students enrolled in such schools. This amount may not be enough to cover the cost that the private schools actually incur. Apart from this, a higher reimbursement amount would probably engender less resistance to the 25 per cent quota from the private unaided schools. In the current scenario, schools may have to raise their fees to cover the increased expenses. This in turn would impose an unequal burden on the parents of the non-quota students.

Conclusion

Education enables an individual to proceed from darkness to light and from morality to immorality (Tam soma Jothirgamaya, Mrutuorma Amurtogamaya). Education is the means for self realization and self expression. It helps to bring out the best in a person. In brief, it promotes physical, intellectual, social, emotional and spiritual development of children. Right to Education Act 2009 is a milestone in the history of Indian education. This act guarantees free and compulsory education to all children between the ages of 6-14 years, completing the elementary cycle of education in a neighbourhood school. But unfortunately, this act is facing some issues and challenges. Students, teachers, administrators, government personnel, legislators, members of the judiciary and all other stakeholders should join hands and work together to build a movement to ensure that every child of this country is in school and enabled to get at least 8 years of quality education.

20

Problems of Tribal Education in India

Sumana Paul

Tribals in India have come to be conceptualised primarily in relation to their geographical and social isolation from the larger Indian society and not in relation to their social formation. This is why a wide range of groups and communities at different levels of the social formation have all come to be categorised as tribes.

As distinct from the so-called mainstream population, the British used the term 'Scheduled Tribes' (ST), with respect to groups living in forests and hills, etc. It was also used with the prefix like indigenous people, etc. The term ST stands for people belonging to the tribal groups, who do not have much contact with the main culture.

The Constitution of India has made several provisions to safeguard the interests of STs in Articles 15(4), 16(4), 46, 243 M, 243Ze, 244, 334, 335, 338A, 339(1), in the fifth as well as in the sixth schedules. Besides these, the Central Government has enacted several laws. These are protection of Civil Rights Act, 1955, the Scheduled Castes and Scheduled Tribes (Prevention of Atrocities) Act, 1989; the provision of the Panchayats (Extension to Scheduled Areas) Act, 1996; the Scheduled Tribes and other Traditional Forest Dwellers (Recognition of Forest Rights) Act, 2006 etc. Despite these elaborate provisions in the Constitution and other laws, it is an unfortunate reality that social injustice and exploitation of scheduled tribes and other weaker section continue to persist.

Among the scheduled tribes or adivasis of India, mortality, morbidity and malnutrition rates remain particularly high when compared to the Indian population at large.

Traditional Characteristics of the Tribals

1. Live in rather inaccessible parts of the country.
2. Are untouched by the civilised world.
3. Belong to particular races like Australoid, Mongoloids or Negrito.

4. Speak tribal dialect.
5. Believe in ghosts and spirits and worship them.
6. Profess primitive religion known as 'Animism'.
7. Chief occupations are gathering forest products, hunting, etc.
8. Mostly meat eaters.

Total Tribal Population

The population of tribal people according to 2011 census was estimated to have reached ten crore forty two lakhs eighty one thousand and thirty four (104,281,034: Rural – 9.38 crores and urban 1.04 crores). This represented 8.6 percent of country's total population as against 8.2 percent in 2001.The population of Scheduled tribes has been found increasing (Table 20.2).

Table 20.1: All India Population and Total ST Population

(in crores)

Census Year	*Total Population*	*Male*	*Female*	*ST Total*	*M*	*F*
2011	121.05	62.31	58.74	10.43	5.24	5.18

Table 20.2: Percentage of ST in Total Population

Census Year	*Total*	*Rural*	*Urban*
2001	8.2	10.4	2.4
2011	8.6	11.3	2.8

Tribal Development Policies

Suggestion of Kothari Commission (1964-66)

Kothari Commission gave welcoming suggestions for various levels of education for ST children.

1. *Primary Education* – Primary education for the scheduled tribe children should be better organised. More schools should be opened in the densely populated areas of ST people.
2. *Secondary Education* – More secondary schools should be opened with facilities for hostels and stipends.
3. *Higher Education* – More scholarships should be instituted for higher education. Those engaged in the service of ST should be assigned a separate cadre. In the beginning, non- tribal people may be appointed in the cadre, but later on suitable persons from the tribal groups should be appointed.

Promotion of education among the STs in accordance with the provisions of the NPE (1986) and Programme of Action (1992)

The following measures are being taken urgently to bring the STs at par with others:

i. Opening schools in tribal areas is being priortised. The construction of school buildings are to be undertaken in these areas on a priority basis under the normal funds for education, as well as under the Jawahar Rozgar Yojna, Tribal Welfare Schemes, etc.

ii. As per the socio-cultural milieu of the scheduled tribes, they have their distinctive characteristics and different spoken languages. This underlines the need to develop the curricula and devise institutional materials in tribal languages at the initial stages, with arrangements for switching over to the regional languages. This task is being taken seriously and also expedited.

iii. Educated and promising ST youths are being encouraged and trained to take up teaching in tribal areas.

iv. Residential schools, including Ashram Schools, are being been established on a large scale.

v. Incentive schemes are being formulated for the scheduled tribes, keeping in view their special needs and life styles. Scholarships are being instituted with special emphasis on technical, professional and para-professional courses. Special remedial courses and other programmes to remove psycho-social impediments are also being provided to improve their performance in various courses.

vi. Anganwadis, non-formal and adult education centres are being opened on a priority basis in areas predominantly inhabited by the scheduled tribes.

vii. The curriculum in all states of education is being gradually designed to create an awareness of the rich cultural identity of the tribal people and also their enormous creative talent.

Education of Scheduled Tribe

It is ironical that despite well meaning constitutional provisions and strong laws for protecting and safeguarding the welfare and interests of the tribal communities, they continue to be marginalised.

The cultural norms and values of the tribals, which have led to the present discrimination against them, can be changed through serious and meaningful education. Therefore, education can play an increasingly powerful role in shaping the perception about difference and diversity within a society by breaking down some of the barriers that separate them from the rest of the world. As education imparts knowledge, it can be of great help in identification of self and the environment, and in instilling confidence and courage among the tribals to overcome their problems associated with exploitation and deprivation, and thereby paves the way for availing socio-economic, political and educational opportunities provided to them.

Profile of Tribal Literacy in India

Since independence, there is an increase in the tribal literacy but not as per national average. Total literacy rate of the tribals in India is 58.96 percent whereas it is 74.04 at the national level (2011 Census).

Table 20.3: Tribal Literacy in India

Census Year	All Categories			Scheduled Tribes		
	Male	Female	Total	Male	Female	Total
2001	75.3	53.7	64.8	59.2	34.8	47.1
2011	82.14	65.46	74.04	68.53	49.35	58.96

The all India literacy rates of scheduled Tribes is 58.96 per cent (Male 68.53% and Female 49.35%) as against 74.04 per cent of all category (Male 82.14% and Female 65.46%) according to 2011 census. When compared to 2001 census, it is seen that there is an increase in the literacy rate. However, compare to the male percentage women showed a lower rate. 2011 census witnessed that dropout rate continues to be very high at all levels of education. The problem is more severe in case of girls of ST communities. This situation calls for systematic efforts directed towards the educational development of ST children. There is wide variation of tribal education at the state and union territory level. For example Mizoram tops followed by Lakshadeep. The most poor performing states are Andhra Pradesh and Madhya Pradesh. ST literacy rate varies across states and union territories, from 49.21 (Andhra Pradesh) to 91.51(Mizoram).

Below given Tables (20.5 and 20.6) gives a comparative picture of the drop out rate of boys and girls at various level of education. Table 20.5 shows that in case of ST girls, the drop out rate is quite alarming. Table 20.6 shows that when the enrolment rate is 100 per cent in class I, only 26.7 per cent could reach class X and only 13.9 per cent could reach class XII.

Major Problems of the Tribal Education

Though a huge amount has been spent for the propagation of education

Table 20.4: State-wise Scheduled Tribe Literacy Rate by Residence and Sex in India (As per 2011 Census)

States/UTs	*Person*			*Male*			*Female*		
	Total	Rural	Urban	Total	Rural	Urban	Total	Rural	Urban
Andaman and Nicobar Islands	75.58	74.21	95.21	80.87	79.75	97.96	69.92	68.23	92.61
Andhra Pradesh	49.21	46.88	66.82	58.35	56.15	74.72	40.09	37.66	58.72
Arunachal Pradesh	64.58	60.37	84.59	71.48	67.65	90.34	57.96	53.3	79.38
Assam	72.06	70.95	90.04	78.96	78.04	93.75	65.1	63.77	86.35
Bihar	51.08	50.32	65.33	61.31	60.7	72.5	40.38	39.47	57.62
Chhattisgarh	59.09	57.57	76.94	69.67	68.36	84.92	48.76	47.06	68.97
Dadra and Nagar Haveli	61.85	58.46	79.53	73.62	70.84	88.03	50.27	46.3	71.1
Daman and Diu	78.79	79.65	77.96	86.23	87.47	85.03	71.23	71.74	70.73
Goa	79.14	78.39	80.19	87.16	86.36	88.32	71.53	70.68	72.71
Gujarat	62.48	61.29	72.71	71.68	70.7	79.96	53.16	51.79	65.13
Himachal Pradesh	73.64	72.96	87.39	83.17	82.69	92.48	64.2	63.36	81.94
Jammu and Kashmir	50.56	49.14	71.68	60.58	59.27	79.57	39.73	38.27	62.57
Jharkhand	57.13	55.22	75.44	68.17	66.6	83.22	46.2	43.94	67.78
Karnataka	62.08	58.99	74.82	71.14	68.54	81.88	52.98	49.39	67.75
Kerala	75.81	74.05	90.35	80.76	79.35	92.67	71.08	68.96	88.21
Lakshadweep	91.7	91.5	91.75	95.69	94.69	95.97	87.76	88.33	87.61
Madhya Pradesh	50.55	49.32	66.73	59.55	58.43	73.99	41.47	40.15	59.16
Maharashtra	65.73	63.21	80.28	74.27	72.18	86.1	57.02	54.13	74.13
Manipur	77.36	75.89	87.67	82.08	80.75	91.64	72.71	71.05	83.94
Meghalaya	74.53	70.98	91.26	75.54	72.19	92.31	73.55	69.77	90.33
Mizoram	91.51	84.48	97.92	93.59	88.57	98.37	89.47	80.25	97.5
Nagaland	80.04	76.04	92.59	83.11	79.54	94.57	76.91	72.43	90.64
Odisha	52.24	51.08	69.08	63.7	62.72	77.67	41.2	39.91	60.46
Rajasthan	52.8	51.73	68.99	67.62	66.7	81.03	37.27	36.1	55.57
Sikkim	79.74	77.48	89.15	85.01	83.21	92.9	74.27	71.39	85.58
Tamil Nadu	54.34	51.32	69.1	61.81	59.02	75.4	46.8	43.55	62.7
Tripura	79.05	78.44	92.22	86.43	86.05	94.8	71.59	70.73	89.7
Uttar Pradesh	55.68	54.48	66.97	67.08	66.23	74.81	43.72	42.28	58.02
Uttarakhand	73.88	72.39	88.33	83.56	82.49	93.73	63.89	61.97	82.63
West Bengal	57.93	56.68	71.22	68.17	67.21	78.4	47.71	46.19	64.01
India	**58.96**	**56.89**	**76.78**	**68.53**	**66.82**	**83.16**	**49.35**	**46.93**	**70.32**

Source: Office of the Registrar General and Census Commissioner, India

Table 20.5: Drop-out rate according to 2011 census

Boys			Girls		
Classes	ST	All Categories	Classes	ST	All Categories
I-V	37.2	28.7	I-V	33.9	25.1
I-VIII	54.7	40.3	I-VIII	55.4	41.0
I-X	70.6	50.4	I-X	71.3	47.9

Table 20.6: Percentage of ST students who entered class I and studied upto class XII

I	100.00
II	84.9
III	78.3
IV	72.0
V	66.6
VI	55.6
VII	49.3
VIII	41.9
IX	32.1
X	26.7
XI	15.7
XII	13.9

amongst the ST people, still there is a lot to be done. Among the STs, there is no environment of education. Most of the parents do not think that it is necessary for them to send their children to schools. Following are some of the hurdles in the field.

1. Indequate availability of schools
2. Poor physical infrastructure of schools
3. Apathy and poverty of parents
4. Lack of proper identification
5. Superstition and prejudice
6. Problems of suitable teachers
7. Poor quality teaching learning material
8. Wastage and stagnation
9. Problems of language

Some Probable Solutions of the Problems

(1) Geographical location continues to be a significant predictor to determine whether a child will attend school or for how long they will continue in school. To overcome this problem more schools should be set up within the easy access of ST children. Priority should be given for opening more primary schools in tribal areas.

(2) School buildings in the tribal areas are without basic infrastructural facilities. In order to attract students, physical facilities of the schools should be improved.

(3) The economic condition of the people of scheduled tribe is very pathetic and therefore they do not understand the importance or the need of education. Therefore, incentives should be given to indigent families to send their children regularly to school, at least till they reach the age of 14.

(4) Pre-metric scholarship schemes for children of families engaged in occupations such as scavenging, flaying and tanning should be given.

(5) Proper hostel facilities should be given. It has been observed that even in the Ashram schools which are residential in nature; there is no space for children to sleep. As a result, classrooms turn into dormitory and vice-versa. Again most of the schools in the tribal areas are single teacher schools. In such a situation the teacher can not do justice to the children. Again when the teacher is absent or goes on leave, the school has to be closed during that period. Government should take initiative to recruit adequate number of teachers for the tribal schools. In addition to this, inadequate teaching-learning materials, such as blackboard and chalk causes problems for the teacher and students in teaching and understanding the content. Therefore, residential schools need to be established on a large scale with adequate number of teachers, at least from middle school onwards.

(6) Proper Book Bank facilities should be provided.

(7) Mid-day meal scheme should be implemented in all the schools.

(8) In order to bring the tribal poor students at par with the others, proper free coaching at all levels of school education should be given to the tribal children.

(9) Attitude of the parents towards education of their children is not positive. Adult literacy programmes through non formal education centres for the parents of the tribal students should be organised so that they may be encouraged to send their children to school. So far non-formal education introduces tribal group to the letters of the alphabet and teaches them to sign their names and possibly to count up to one hundred. But this is not enough. Non-formal education should at least make the tribals aware of their basic rights; teach them about health and nutrition etc. This will help tribal parents to decide and know about the employment opportunities for their children. Women play a significant role in tribal society; therefore, the issue of their empowerment with upgradation of their skills should be addressed under non-formal education programme.

(10) Several Communities in India have not been identified as STs or SCs. For example, tea-garden labourers of Assam are not accorded

any status due to which they do not have access to any of the facilities given to SC/ST Community.

(11) Superstitions, blind belief and prejudices play negative role in imparting education in the tribal areas and tribal schools. Except tribal communities in north eastern region, there is widespread feeling in the tribal community that education makes their children defiant and impertinent and alienates them from the rest of their society. Some tribal groups believe that their God shall be angry if they send their children to schools run by outsiders. Here outsiders include formal curriculum for education, non-tribal teachers and teachers outside their locality. Counselling programmes need to be organised for the parents to convince them to send their children to school.Teachers must understand the basic cultural patterns in which children are socialised.

(12) The competency and interest of the teachers is of prime importance in generating interest of the students towards education. The non-tribal teachers cannot appreciate fully the tribal values and ways of life. The relationship between teachers and students is not very good. Apart from non-tribal teachers, some tribal teachers who consider themselves better educated and progressive, have a biased attitude towards the parents of other communities. Teachers are reluctant to reside in less developed tribal areas and therefore stay in near by towns. Non-tribal teachers have hardly any knowledge about the tribal way of life.They treat such postings in tribal areas as punishment. So there comes the problems of insincerity and non-commitment of interaction of the teachers with the guardians.

To deal with this problem and to attract teachers in tribal areas, their service condition must be improved. High pay scale and residence facility should be given to the teachers willing to serve the tribal community.

(13) Another most significant problem is the problem of wastage and stagnation. A data revealed by the Eleventh five years plan indicated the high drop-out of the STs at different levels of study. 2011 census report also witnessed this. This is happening particularly because of the clash of class hours with the working hours. Apart from this, other reasons responsible are – poverty, lack of academic atmosphere, unwillingness of the teachers to convince the parents and parental apathy towards education. To overcome this situation, balanced diet, proper medical aid, mid-day meal, adjustment of class after the working hours, especially during the harvesting period, suitable employment opportunities to the parents should be provided. In many states, tribal schools are following the same curriculum as followed by other schools. However, a tribal child who lives in a remote area can hardly be interested in a curriculum taught in non-tribal areas. Subjects like history, geography, economics, etc are

important but the tribal students have no interest in these subjects. Their knowledge is very limited and therefore do not understand or relate to what they are taught. In fact, subjects like forestry, processing of forest produce, horticulture, rural industries and their management should be made a part of the curriculum of the tribal children.

(14) Devotion and capability of teachers is of prime importance in generating the interest of tribal students towards education. The teacher education programme must emphasize on the special needs and problems of the tribal learners who are mostly first generation learners. This will sensitise and create interest in the teachers to teach the tribal students. Teachers should be trained to use ICT to provide education to tribal areas. Use of ICT will definitely make teaching interesting and may prove as a boon.

(15) Language provides social, psychological and emotional expression to an individual in a society. But in the absence of knowledge of tribal dialect, both students and teachers face the problem of communication, creating hurdle in teaching and learning process. It is observed that tribal students are often humiliated, reprimanded and even punished for speaking in their local language (Nambissan 1994).

It is the regional and national language that reduces tribals to minorities in their own home. Tribal students should be familiarized with their own language first and thereafter taught/educated in mainstream language. It's only then they can develop interest in formal education.

There is a need for introduction of tribal dialect in the curriculum and teaching learning process. There is paucity of literature and text books in tribal dialects.

Home language must be made the medium of instruction at least in the early years of school education. As far as possible teaching learning material for early years of school education should also be prepared in tribal dialects.

Only those teachers should be appointed in primary schools who have passed an examination in tribal dialect of the area.

Conclusion

The education of scheduled tribes is a very fascinating and challenging field. It needs to be explored and developed fully. Education is the most effective instrument for ensuring equality of opportunity. The problems associated with the education of the tribal children in India are manifold, complex and inter-related. We should be very careful about the progress of these pupils. Their performance should not be below that of pupils of other castes.

Factors like poverty, apathy of the parents, superstitions and prejudices, lack of suitable teachers and teaching-learning material, language problem, wastage and stagnation causes major hindrances in the process of education of scheduled tribes.

Education for the scheduled tribe requires careful planning, dynamic and variable strategies, innovative pedagogy and constant evaluation. Education should become a powerful movement of mass mobilization, taking into its stride the more pressing tribal needs.

In this context, concerned effort of the government and officials, dedication and sincerity of teachers, awareness and willingness of the tribals and their involvement is very much required.

We want persons working for the cause of humanity. Voluntary organisations must come forward to spread the light of education among the tribals. Government may consider the desirability of appointing atleast one Education Officer in each block to bring children to school from their house. We need to make the community aware that school is an instrument for change in their socio-economic development. Let us join hands to give quality education to the tribals as per the requirements of their community.

As rightly pointed out by Swami Vivekananda—

> "*We want that education by which Character is formed, strength of mind is increased, the intellect is expanded and by which one can stand on ones's own feet.*"

21

Vocationalisation of Education

Naseerali M.K.

Education is an endless process needed for the development of any nation. The main purpose of education in any society is to provide such experiences to the child, as it would enable him to live individually satisfying and socially useful life. Today India being one of the developing countries is seriously faced with the problem of unemployment among the youth and those passed out of schools. The present day need of Indian society is not simply to acquire general education but to increase productivity. Therefore, education should come to closer relationship with productivity. This function of education can be achieved by vocationalisation of education at all levels of knowledge acquisition.

Vocationalisation of education refers not only to the development of specialized skills but also to the development of a positive attitude to work and the dignity of labour. In the report 'Learning : the Treasure within' (UNESCO 1996) of International Commission on Education for the 21st century (Delores Commission), emphasis is given on four pillars on which the education throughout life is based. These pillars are *learning to know, learning to do, learning to live together,* and *learning to be.* One of the pillars, 'learning to do' is essentially related to vocationalisation of education. 'Learning to do' implies acquiring not only an occupational skill but also more broadly, the competence to deal with many situations and work in teams. Thus vocationalisation of education has a crucial role to play in this new era as affective tool to realize the objectives of a culture of peace, environmentally sound sustainable development, social cohesion and international citizenship.

Meaning of Vocationalisation of Education

The phrase 'vocationalisation of education', in its broad sense encompasses education and skill development at all levels from post primary to tertiary education, both through formal and non-formal programs. The UNESCO in its recommendation of 1974 on technical and vocational education defined it as a "comprehensive term embracing those aspects of the education process involving, in addition to general education, the study of technologies and related sciences and the acquisition of practical skills, attitudes, understanding and knowledge relating to occupations in various sectors of economic and social life".

The aim of vocationalisation of education is to give one the skills and confidence that he can make and build things, that he can act on his ideas and that he can acquire many more abilities through his own effort. Thus it means involving in physical activity in the real world which is relevant to the life of the student. Vocationalisation of education is for not just to teach him one vocation. He will not wait for someone to offer him a job; he will try to seek out the opportunities and create his own future.

Both vocational education and vocationalisation of education will involve skills developments. In the vocationalisation of education, the skill development is intended to build the capability to act in a variety of real life situations, whereas the vocational education gives skills for a specific vocation under well-defined limitations. Without the general skills development, the specific skill cannot help him to survive. Therefore vocational education can only be useful on a base of general skill development. Thus vocationalisation of education is fundamental to all education and vocational education can only build on top of it and not substitute it. This has been the main reason for the problem we are facing not only in our new vocational education programs, but also the poor quality of our general engineering and technical education.

Genesis and History of the Vocationalisation of Education

Vocationalisation of education is not new in the Indian Philosophy in general and educational process in particular. In Gita, *Lord Krishna* accorded the highest esteem to the path of *Karma* (Work) in comparison with that of *Gnan* (Knowledge) and *Bha*kti (devotion) for attainment of truth and commune with the Lord. As for educational process, the learning in the Gurukula system took place in a vocational and work environment. The knowledge was gathered on the basis of work experience as the work provides the source for knowledge and information. The system, so deep routed in a philosophy, flourished through the mode of Guru-Shishya or father-son traditions.

Education in colonial India emerged in the context of meeting the needs of alien administration rather than to those of socio-economic development. The *Wood's Despatch* of 1854, for the first time, recognized the need of giving the people an education of "such a character as may be practically useful to the people of India in their different spheres of life." But evidently this report did not make any noticeable impact until 1882. The *Hunter Commission* was set up in 1882 to examine the problems of education in general and those of technical and vocational education in particular. It recommended that at the High school stage there be two distinctive streams, first for preparing the students for entrance examinations to the university course and the second for practical occupations. The *Calcutta University Commission* (Sadler Commission) of 1917 made recommendations for the establishment of intermediate colleges with subjects of study like arts, science, medicine, and engineering. *Hartog Committee* (1929) proposed the diversion of more students towards industrial or commerce career at the end of middle stage. The *Sapru Committee* (1934) recommended the introduction of vocational courses with general education courses in the secondary schools for solving the problems of unemployment among the educated. The *Abbot-Wood Commission* (1936-37) suggested that vocational education should be on the same plane as general education. This recommendation resulted in the opening of polytechnic and technical, commercial and agricultural high schools.

Gandhiji strongly supported the vocationalisation of education and published his thoughts in *Harijan:* "Every handicraft has to be taught not merely mechanically as is done today, but scientifically. This is to say, the child, should learn the why and wher first of every process". The *Wardha Conference* (1938) had adopted resolutions based on Gandhiji's philosophy of Basic Education and stated "the process of education should centre round some form of manual productive work considering the environment of the child".

Gandhiji's view on education were given practical shape by *Zakir Hussain Committee* (1938) and chose three intrinsically inter-connected aspects – the physical environment, the social environment and the craft work – as the foci for the curriculum. The report also asked for qualified teachers to make the policy successful. The *Sargent Report* (1944) recommended two types of high schools – academic and technical. It thereby emphasized that vocational education should be organized according to the needs of various vocational areas.

After independence, the need for vocationalisation was felt more. In the reports of various successive commissions, the need and importance of vocationalisation of education has been emphasized. The *Secondary Education Commission,* also known as Mudaliar Commission (1953), recommended i) diversification of courses at the higher secondary stage, ii) establishment of multi-purpose schools, iii) opening technical schools, and iv) promotion of agricultural education. The *Indian Education Commission*, popularly known as Kothari Commission (1964-66), observed: "to bring education into closer relationship with productivity, it is necessary to give a strong vocational basis to secondary education and to increase the emphasis on agricultural and technological education at the university stage. This is of special significance in the Indian situation where the educational system has been training young persons so far mostly for Government services and the so called white-collar professions". Also the commission recommended the introduction of work experience as a major channel for vocational experience.

The Iswarbhai Patel Committee (1977), which reviewed the NCERT's document ('Higher Secondary Education and its Vocationalisation'- 1975), came forward with the concept of Socially Useful Productive Work (SUPW) as a central component of the ten year school curriculum. It defined Socially Useful Productive Work as "purposive and meaningful manual work resulting in either goods or services, which are useful to the community. The *Adiseshiah Review Committee* (1977-78) submitted the report entitled "learning to do" and recommended two board level components: i) the general education spectrum, and ii) the vocational spectrum. The National Working Group on Vocationalisation of Education (1985) considered in depth the concept and operation of Work Experience/Socially Useful Productive Work and its implementation in various states.

The *National Policy on Education 1986* made a strong case for vocationalisation of education: "vocational education will be a distinct stream, intended to prepare students for identified occupations spanning several areas of activity. These courses will ordinarily be provided after the secondary stage, but keeping the scheme flexible, these may also be made available after class eighth."

The *Ramamurthi Review Committee* (1990) suggested that for work experience, socially useful and productive work should be integrally linked with various subjects both at the level of content as well as pedagogy. The *Janardhana Reddy Committee* (1992) recommended that work experience program might be systematically implemented by allocating 5.2 per cent to 20 per cent of the school time for the activities having a practical orientation in relation to various subjects. More recently the revised policy formulations of 1992 assigned a very important place to work experience in the school curriculum at all stages. The *National Knowledge Commission (NKC 2006)* considers vocational education and training as an important element of the nation's education initiatives.

Vocationalisation of Education – Indian Context

Vocationalisation is a major transformation in education and cannot be achieved without important structural and functional changes in the whole set-up. The analysis of the recommendations made by various commissions and committees and the steps taken by different governments for over a period of 150 years reveals that the present system of education contains both the approaches of vocationalising general education by incorporation of a minor component of vocational element and establishment of exclusive institutions of vocational education such as industrial training institutions and polytechnic institutions.

But these changes in the system are not in line with the requirement of our economies and thus vocationalisation of education has not achieved the desired target and objectives set for it. Gandhi made it clear that education and vocation are to be integrated but we have excluded the vocation from education. Thus, we have created a situation wherein vocational education is looked down upon and considered useful only for socio-economically and academically inferior student population. Tagore emphatically stated that the focus may be on art but at the same time art should also facilitate the individual to earn his livelihood. With such a strong cultural and philosophical basis for vocationalisation of education, the question that arises is as to how to popularise vocational courses among all sections of the society.

Major constraints in vocationalisation of education are:

1. Inadequate management system at different levels – central, state, districts and school.
2. Low priority accorded to vocational education by the states in comparison to the other educational programs.
3. Ad hoc selection of vocational courses without assessing local needs by conducting vocational surveys.
4. Dearth of full time qualified and trained vocational teachers.
5. Non availability of quality instructional materials.
6. Limited teacher preparation facilities.
7. Insufficient infrastructural facilities in schools.
8. Insufficient collaborative arrangements with industries and other institutions.
9. Inadequate skill development in schools, on-the-job training and apprenticeship training in industries.
10. Lack of employment opportunities, guidance and counselling and bank loans for starting an enterprise.
11. Non involvement of the experts from industry and trade in planning curriculum designs resulting in a mismatch between what is taught in school and what is required in industries.
12. Mismatch between demand and supply.

Vocationalisation of Education: Need and Objectives

Education does not produce jobs, but vocationalisation of education make it more likely for an individual to get a job, or to be his own master by either starting a new productive activity or a service that may satisfy a felt need of the community. Thus vocationalisation of education reduces unemployment and leads to productivity which in turn results in economic development.

In the developmental dimension, vocationalisation of education is the need of the hour. It is the answer for solving man's problems, to increase earth's carrying capacity, to make individual life more comfortable, to provide better healthcare, to make life more pleasant and to increase our global competitiveness in production and trade.

The advantages or needs for vocationalisation of education are:

- It prepares an individual for life, for better economic and civic amenities.
- It makes education practical and useful. It can fulfil the need of life in a better way.
- It promotes economic growth of the country.
- It helps in the best and full utilization of the human and natural resources of the country.
- It enhances the competency or efficiency of an individual in a particular vocation.
- It facilitates the supply of more skilled manpower or technical personnel at the grassroot level which in turn benefits the whole society with an increased supply of technical leadership of middle grade.
- It improves the general education attainments of the students.
- It is helpful in earning a decent livelihood.
- It is also psychologically sound because it is based on the principle of diversification of human energy and talent. It provides ample scope and opportunity to the students to select the type of education suited to them on the basis of their interest, ability and aptitude.
- It opens more avenues or channels for self employment.

The major objectives of vocationalisation of education are:

1. To fulfill the national goals of development and the removal of unemployment and poverty.
2. To impart education relevant to increased productivity, economic development and individual prosperity.
3. To meet the need for skilled and middle-level manpower for the growing sectors of economy, both organized and unorganized.
4. To prepare students for self-reliance and gainful self-employment.

Re-Defining Vocationalisation of Education

The ideology behind vocationalisation of education can be translated into a reality only when we redefine the concept. Earlier, the term 'vocational education' broadly meant education in some low level manual skills; something for which graduate or post-graduate degrees were not required. Today, it has been given a wider meaning; it stands for "vocationalization of education". It aims to improve the quality of education provided to the customer (student) which will improve his chances of employability. In this context, vocationalization of education should cover all stages of education, from school to post graduate level, as it can have impact on the quality of life of people at large.

The major suggestions for the acceleration of vocationalisation of education in India are

1. Prioritisation for vocationalisation of education by the Central and State Governments must be clearly reflected in its policies, planning, decision making, allocation of funds and implementation at different levels – central, state, district and institution.
2. Enhancing status of vocational education in the country through various modalities to make it socially acceptable as a means to fulfil human resource requirements for sustainable development.
3. A comprehensive vocational education and training system should be developed to implement relevant, integrative, flexible and diversified vocational curriculum framework for the development of skilled, competent and trainable human resource.
4. An effective teacher preparation system (pre-service and in-service) for vocational teachers should be in place.
5. The NGOs/ Voluntary Organizations should be encouraged for conducting the locally need based non formal vocational programs.
6. Vocational guidance and counselling, and student support systems need to be strengthened.
7. Correlating vocational courses with the academic courses – a concept of practicing education is to be introduced.

The vocationalisation of education should be expanded speedily at all levels, from school to university level, as well as for other target groups (neo literates, special groups, disabled etc.). It is in fact a national requirement. Only vocationally competent manpower can increase productivity in all sectors of economy, create wealth, ensure socio-economic stability and bring prosperity to the nation. Thus by adopting an integrative and inclusive approach, vocationalisation of education in India can be improved to a great extent which will meet the present and future needs.

22

Community Colleges in India

An Initiative to Reach the Needs of Community

Naziya Hasan

Education always aims for the all round development of the child who may help in the development of the nation. But groups that cover larger population area still remain untouched by the opportunities and are unaware of the advantages and importance of education. Community college system is one of the alternative systems of education which works for the empowerment of the underprivileged and disadvantaged groups, including women and poor population of urban, rural as well as tribal India. It is a non-profit-making, non-commercial and community based organization which aims for the development of skills as life skill, work skill for preparation of employment. The present article is an attempt to throw light on the development and evolution of community colleges in India along with its roles in community development.

Educated and literate population of a country is considered as its asset which helps in its development and advancement in various probable but dynamic ways. It is desired to develop the population into completely advanced human capitals in multiple dynamic ways which is possible by the powerful weapon called 'Education'. A person can be developed sociologically, psychologically, intellectually as well as morally with the help of education which plays a vital role in the overall development and enrichment of the child. As education plays a catalytic role in this dynamic process of growth and development, it is necessary to plan it more methodically and work on its execution with great sensitivity. India, a country with 2nd largest population, needs an education system which will have high quality, affordability, flexibility and relevance to individual as well as to the larger society.

India now has a population of 121 crores. It is a challenging task for government and policy makers to provide employment to such a large number of people. The unemployment rate was 9.40 per cent in 2010 which shrank to 3.5 per cent in 2011. But now it is increasing with the passage of time as 3.6 per cent in 2012, 3.7 per cent in 2013 and according to Global Employment Trends (2014), it is expected to be 3.8 per cent in 2014.

Keeping in mind this situation, it can be said that there is a need for serious investment in development of skills amongst youth of the nation to bridge the gap between demands of industries and products coming from higher education professional institutions. So there is a big question mark on the quality of products. Main reason can be the disconnection or the mismatch of higher learning institutions with the requirement of the workplace. Country like India faces a mismatch between demand and supply, as the economy needs more skilled workforce than produced annually.

Problems of Higher Education in India

While general education of the government sector is affordable to a large number of population in India, professional education is gradually becoming more expensive and private professional education is almost unaffordable and inaccessible for the common masses. There are various reasons for not getting admission in the skill development courses, such as financial problems faced by common citizens of India, rigid admission procedure which focuses on qualification and background, lack of flexibility in the light of time, duration and place of study, etc. Though elementary education has been made free in India with the spreading impact of Universalization of Elementary Education and Right to Education Act, it is still very difficult for the poor population to succeed in the current competitive system and advanced higher professional education.

Community Colleges

While discussing about the growth of any nation, one cannot neglect the larger population. Education is not only meant for selected area or population but it is the fundamental right of each and every child irrespective of caste, creed, race, gender, socio-economic status, etc. We should think of those modes and techniques which can be accessible and affordable for the larger concerned population.

Community college system is one of the alternative systems of education which works for the empowerment of the underprivileged and disadvantaged groups, including women and poor population of urban, rural as well as tribal India. It is a non-profit-making, non-commercial and community based organization which aims at the development of life skill and work skill for employment. This system originated in the early years of 20th century in America which is considered as an important landmark in the history of education. According to Community College Research Center (CCRC), "Community Colleges serve multiple missions – from workforce training, to remediating students in preparation for higher education, to community enrichment."

It has a very positive role in incorporating the real needs of the community for employment and development of vocational skills. It does not require students to leave their homes because it is an open access institution. These colleges are often called as 'Second Chance' institutions as they provide a second crack at higher education for students whose motivation and earlier performance in schooling were not adequate to get them admission to four-year colleges. Its status of 'Second Chance' rests on its importance. It provides opportunity to those who have missed the chance or encountered failure. It also provides opportunity to women who decide to join the workforce after marriage or divorce or after their children have grown up.

Community colleges function with the motto: by the community, of the community and for the community. They best exemplify the notion of life-long learning and flexibility in enrollment. These colleges impart relatively job-specific occupational and vocational education. They include: academic preparation, occupational instruction, remedial education, geographical convenience, flexible enrollment capacity, equity and access, degree and training, multiple educational options, etc. These colleges are most useful in challenging some significant problems of the nation such as economic or financial vulnerability, instability of the middle class, demographic change, and those emanating from schools and communities. The Community College is developed with the purpose to promote job oriented, work related, skill-based and life coping education, which are the current requirements of the ever moving and developing society in general and vocational job market in particular.

The key words of the Community College system are easy access, flexibility in curriculum and teaching methodology, cost effectiveness and equal opportunity in collaboration with industrial, commercial and service sectors of the local area and responding to the social needs and issues of the local community, internship and job placement within the local area, promotion of self employment and small business development, declaration of competence and eligibility for employment. It also supplies the requirements of the community-based life-long learning needs as it has a strong relationship between the community, community college and job market.

It includes curriculum consisting of four distinct parts: life skills, work skills, internship and preparation for employment. It also has different kind of evaluation system, which includes four dimensions – self assessment, assessment by life skill teachers, assessment by work skill teachers and assessment by internship supervisor at the workplace. It enhances and enriches the skills among the learners. Though it provides low cost affordable vocational education and training, it never compromises its quality.

Objectives of Community Colleges in India

According to the Royal IGNOU Community College, "The objective of community college is formation of a knowledge society, promoting job oriented holistic education and employment opportunity to the disadvantaged. These institutions are to offer convenient and challenging academic experiences with appropriate skill development in collaboration with local industries, thus leading to gainful employment." IGNOU community college scheme was launched on July, 04, 2009. Under this scheme, a community college can get registered for offering academic programmes like certificate, diploma and associate degree. It also offers the advantage of tailoring programs according to local needs and state based requirements by adopting approaches that would be most acceptable to workers in the given community.

According to Indira Gandhi National Open University (IGNOU), there are various objectives behind establishment of community colleges in India:

- India has largest share of youth population which needs to be channelized into diverse and multi-level occupational areas.
- Development of the local talent and skills for community specific trades and occupations.
- In India, only 25 lac vocational training seats are available, whereas 1.28 crore people are entering labour market every year.
- Community college system is an alternative education system in India. Skill development is the only innovative alternative which would add value to the huge population of potentially employable age group of Indians, thereby establishing India as the world capital of rich human resource.
- To fulfil the needs of the school drop-outs and enable them to acquire necessary skills for livelihood and formal qualifications for social status and societal recognition.

According to the UGC's guidelines for Community Colleges, "The 12th Five Year Plan Document of the Planning Commission has laid special emphasis on expansion of skill-based programmes in higher education. It recommends setting up of Community Colleges (CC) to serve multiple needs, including

(i) Career oriented education and skills to students interested in directly entering the workforce;
(ii) Contracted training and education programmes for local employers;
(iii) High-touch remedial education for secondary school graduates not ready to enroll in traditional colleges, giving them a path to transfer to three or four year institutions; and
(iv) General interest courses to the community for personal development and interest."

Development of Community Colleges in India

Community College movement was started in South India in October, 1995 with the beginning of the Pondicherry University Community College. It was taken forward with the inauguration of the Madras Community College by the Archbishop of Mylapore in August 1996. Later, it was strengthened by the Manonmanion Sundarnar University, Tirunerveli by giving approval to 5 community colleges in September, 1998. It started spreading its wings to Andhra Pradesh with the starting of JMJ Community College in Tenali in July 1999. It also spread to the states of Gujarat, Maharashtra, Kerala, Karnataka and Uttarakhand. They were distributed in numbers: Tamilnadu – 75, Pondicherry – 01, Andhra Pradesh – 03, Delhi – 01, Karnataka – 02, Chhattisgarh – 03, Kerala – 05, Maharashtra – 01, Gujarat –02, Jharkhand –01, Uttarakhand –01 (As given in MCRDCE, 2003).

History of Community College Movement

As per the Table 22.1, community colleges are being established and developed every year in almost 17 states of the country. There are 343 community colleges in India.

According to the Preamble of UGC's Scheme of Community Colleges for Universities and Colleges (2012-17), "the idea of establishing such colleges in the country was endorsed in the Conference of State Education Ministers held on 22nd February, 2012 and a Committee of Education Ministers of nine States was constituted to finalize the concept and

Table 22.1 : Showing History of Community Colleges in India

Pondicherry University Community College	*1995*
Madras Community College	1996
Madurai Community College	1997
M.S. University Community Colleges and CCs** started by NGOs	1998
Chennai Corporation Community College, Tenali and Nallapadu JMJ CC, Andhra Pradesh	1999
RUHSA Community College, Vellore	2000
Vivekanand Pratishthan Community College, Maharashtra, SDA, Roorkee Community College, Uttaranchal AID CC, Auxilium CC, Kottiyam	2001
Chrompet CC, Rural CC, Adaikala Annai Rural CC, Tabitha CC, Dr. Chandra Devansan Rural CC, Church Park CC.	2002
St. Teresa's Community College, Eluru and Tarbes CC, Bangalore, Teresian CC, Tamil Nadu, St. Xavier's CC, Goa.	2003
Pravaham Community College, Bhopal Community College	2004
M.S. Panwar CC, Himanchal Pradesh, Unversity Community College, Hyderabad, Deepanjali CC, Jharkhand.	2005
KRUPA Community College, BWDA Community College, SVD Community college, Bethany CC, Noida and Ludhiana	2006
Govt. Polytechnic CC, Manesar, New Hopes CC, Porur	2007
Shishu Mandir CC, Bangalore, Don Bosco CC, Keela Eral, Bethel CC, Coimbatore	2008
Paul Antony CC, Sivakasi, Seva Rral CC, Chennai, Symbiosis CC, Pune, St. Joseph CC, Jamshedpur	2009
Fatima CC, Jayakondam, Vasantham CC, Dharapuram	2010
SWATE CC, Karur, Dr. Gupta CC, Chennai, Amala Annai CC, Daltennganj	2011
Sriram CC, Thiruvallur	2012
Patna Women's CC, Patna, Bihar, MCC Community College, Chennai	2013
Swame Vivekanand CC, Chennai, Mariyam Nilayam CC, Honnavar, Fatima Matha CC, Trivundrum.	2014

*Taken from 'Community College as an alternative system of education in India' taken from www.icrdcc.com/communitycolleges.pdf

**CC is used for Community Colleges

framework of the Community College scheme. The Committee after wide consultations with all concerned, presented its report to the Government which received the concurrence of the State Education Ministers in the conference held on 6th June, 2012.The Government of India has accepted this report and decided to introduce this scheme during the 12th Five Year Plan (2012-17)."

"The main objectives of the scheme are:

(i) To make higher education relevant to the learner and the community;

(ii) To integrate relevant skills into the higher education system;

(iii) To provide skill based education to students currently pursuing higher education but actually interested in entering the workforce at the earliest opportunity;

(iv) To provide employable and certifiable skills with necessary general education to Senior Secondary School pass-outs not willing to join existing higher education system;

(v) To provide for up-gradation and certification of traditional / acquired skills of the learners irrespective of their age;

(vi) To provide opportunities for community–based life-long learning by offering courses of general interest to the community for personal development and interest;

(vii) To provide opportunity to move to higher education in future; and

(viii) To offer bridge courses to certificate holders of general / vocational education, so as to bring them at par with appropriate National Vocational Educational Qualifications Framework (NVEQF)" level prepared by MHRD.

Standardization of Skills and Competency

Development of these colleges will provide the mixture of knowledge with dynamic vocational skill components. Skill components will be drawn from the credit framework prepared under the National Occupational Standards (NOS) and vocational learning outcomes will conform to the NVEQF framework. NOS specify the standard of performance an individual must achieve when carrying out a function in the work market, together with knowledge and understanding. NOS are benchmarks of good practice. With a view to make the skill acquired by the learners acceptable nationally, the curricula and system of certification has to be done as per the national standards. In order to facilitate offering of nationally standardized skill related programmes, the Government of India (Ministry of Human Resource Development) has already notified the National Vocational Education Qualifications Framework (NVEQF) on 3rd September 2012 (F.No. 1-4/2011- VE).

NVEQF is a framework which descriptively organizes qualifications according to a series of levels of knowledge along with skills. These levels of knowledge are defined in terms of learning outcomes, i.e. the competencies which the learners must possess without taking into consideration whether they were acquired through formal, non-formal or informal education and training. This would provide the stakeholders such as the learners, education and skill training providers and employers to gain information about the broad equivalence of qualifications across specific skill sectors. It is a nationally integrated education and competency-based skill framework which provides for multiple pathways, both within vocational education and between general and vocational education, to link one level of learning to another higher level and enable learners to progress to higher levels from any starting point in the education and / or skill system. Community Colleges are working towards these goals besides providing opportunities for vertical mobility and life-long learning.

Governance of Community Colleges

According to the framework set by UGC for its effective management, each community college will have a separate Board of Management which will include representatives of the affiliating university, relevant industry, their association, local bodies, state government and UGC nominee. The Board of Studies (BoS) would have representatives from the college, university to which the college is affiliated, partner industries and their associations / professional guilds. The Principal of the CC shall be the Chairperson, while the local head of one of the partner industries shall be the Co-Chairperson. The BoS shall decide the programmes to be offered by the Community Colleges, depending upon the industry needs, and develop the curriculum in modular form in consultation with the partner industry.

Recently Government of India (MHRD) and the Government of UK have signed a Memorandum of understanding on a framework for developing Community Colleges under UK India Education and Research Initiatives (UKIERI). Its duration is w.e.f. 20-01-2013 to 31-03-2016. According to this Memorandum of Understanding, Community Colleges will be developed and facilitate the link between selected community colleges of India and those in the UK. The commitment of the government of India to integrate skill development in the higher education system with flexible learning formats is reflected in its initiative to prepare a National Vocational Educational Qualifications Framework (NVEQF) for standardization and thus, wider acceptance of the skill oriented courses amongst the employers.

A delegation of government officials from India visited American Association of Community Colleges' (AACC) annual convention to learn the way in which the U.S. community colleges are so successful and how this model can be adapted in India. The visit was coordinated by the Wadhwani Foundation, which works with national and state governments in India, private industry and other partners to increase higher education opportunities for Indian students.

Once a community college model is defined for India, the committee will recommend a plan for pilot-testing at 100 colleges. To establish 100 colleges on pilot basis on the pattern of Community Colleges of the world was put in the State Education Ministers' Conference held on 22nd February, 2012. In the same conference, S. Ramadorai, advisor to the Prime Minister on skill development, said, "For better results from community colleges, they must be modeled on local requirements."

The Indian Government sees an expansion of community colleges as one of the key strategies to provide a skilled workforce to propel the nation's economic development. The foundation launched the Skills Colleges Initiatives to support government initiatives to integrate relevant skills training into mainstream education to create knowledge workers. The initiative aims to provide accessible, affordable and employability-driven, short-term programs which may lead to a vibrant, upwardly mobile middle class in India, thereby laying stepping stones towards the foundation's purpose of accelerating economic development. To support the Skills Colleges Initiative, the foundation is to develop curricula and courseware. subsidizing teaching training and faculty development, and creating a platform for online learning.

A research study, conducted in August 2003 on "The impact and prospects of community college system in India" conducted by Madras Centre for Research and Development of Community Education (MCRDCE), clearly shows that Community Colleges are serving the socially, economically and educationally weaker sections of society. It was basically conducted on the community colleges of Tamilnadu as majority of them are situated and run in that state. The study states that from total population of 8947 students, 6174 were female with 69.01 per cent proportion. There is no age bar and it ranges from 17 to 47. Larger population of students is coming from backward and scheduled castes. Among all, 87 per cent students are from economically weaker section in which 39.52 per cent are from families having below 1000 rupees monthly income. Religion wise result shows greater contribution of Hindus and lower contribution of Muslims.

Community colleges have been working in the development of skills keeping in view the needs of local industry and community thereby helping in employment, besides vertical and horizontal mobility. It is created for addressing the learning needs of the community at low and affordable cost without compromising the quality. These colleges give preference to the local community, particularly, the marginalized sections of the population that include minority uneducated backward areas and low-income groups.

Community Colleges in India are providing better training and education in various skills like retail management, computerized accounting programmes, tourism management, agri-business, health care, food processing, theatre and stage craft, automobile, fashion technology, mobile communication, hospitality, mining, printing technology, horticultural crops, nursery management, welding, fabrication, garment design, home science, interior decoration, computer animation networking, economics, finance, pharmaceutical technology, food preservation, hotel management, catering technology, beautician, stock market trading, paramedical, etc.

Conclusion

The Community Colleges have proved to be a good initiative in preparing students for vocational life. They have been helpful for the women community, besides the marginalized and deprived sections of the society. Further development and expansion of such colleges must be encouraged.

23

Morphological and Syntactic Errors in English Language Secondary School Students of Kerala: An Analysis

Noora Abdul Kader

Error analysis is an applied linguistics approach used to identify areas of great difficulty for second language learners by applying a system of formal distinction to differentiate between the learner's first language (L1) and target language (L2; Corder, 1967; Dulay, 1982). Such analysis is based on the understanding that both intralingual and interlingual factors determine the type of errors. Whereas the former involves difficulties faced by the learner due to distinctive linguistic features of the L2 itself, the latter involves the direct interference of negative transfer of structures and other features from the L1 to the L2. As use of error analysis has led to discovery that learners' errors reflect a gap in their competence, order of acquisition and accuracy in order of learning, it has become an important instrument in first and second language learning research.

According to Odlin (1989), L1 syntactic, phonetic and morphological features exert powerful influences on production of L2 structures and pronunciation. Selinker (1992) clarified that transfer of L1 structure to L2 performance is negative and errors are inevitable when L1 and L2 structures differ but positive when the structures are similar. A particular challenge identified by Cook (1992) is that regardless of the teacher's efforts, L1 knowledge remains present in the minds of L2 learners, who connect it with L2 knowledge. He therefore warned not to treat the L2 in isolation from the L1. In contrast, Khuwaileh and Shoumali (2000) found that most errors were related to tense due to lack of time sequence.

The Objecives of the Study are:

- To identify the type of morphological errors made by secondary school students.
- To identify the type of syntactic errors made by secondary school students.

- To trace out the causes of syntactic and morphological errors in English language among secondary school students.

Sample: The study was conducted on a random sample of 30 secondary school English teachers from the districts of Malappuram and Thrissur in the state of Kerala. Sample was selected from teachers of four Government schools from the two districts.

Tools employed for data collection

- Language acquisition test to trace out the types of syntactic errors made by secondary school students
- Language acquisition test to trace out the types of morphological errors made by secondary school students
- Questionnaire to analyse the causes of syntactic and morphological errors of English language among secondary school students

Results and Discussions

Syntac Error analysis in English language among Secondary School Students

Table 23.1: Result of Syntactic Error Analysis in English Language

Sl. No	*Areas of syntactic errors*	*Percentage*
1.	Concord in using auxiliaries	93
2.	Errors in using SVO Pattern	88
3.	Errors in using articles	88
4.	Frrors in using Preposition	94
5.	Errors in using correct form of tense	92
6.	Errors in using conjunctions	89

From the Table 23.1 it is revealed that high percentage of teachers is in the opinion that learners are making syntactic errors in English language.

Concord in using auxiliaries: Learners are making too many errors in using correct form of concord in primary auxiliaries like am, do, does, did, was, were, has, have and had. The errors are far more in using modal auxiliaries like could, would, should, shall and might compared to primary auxiliaries. Most of the students are considering does as the plural form of do. And they are always using 'am' while writing the first person pronoun 'I' whatever the tense form is. Students are not using the auxiliary had. It seems that they do not know when and where to use it. In the case of auxiliaries also there is no clear distinction of primary and modal auxiliaries of English, in Malayalam and the learners often makes the mistakes like "I has the book with me".

Errors in using SVO Pattern: Secondary school students are following the sentence pattern of mother tongue in most of the situations. They are using the SOV pattern instead of SVO. In Malayalam we could use both SVO and SOV pattern depending on the situations but in English language this is not possible. The difference the structural arrangement of the sentences between the languages produces syntactic errors. In Malayalam the sentence usually have a subject – object – verb pattern, but in English it is subject – verb – object.

Errors in using articles: Most of the students in secondary schools are inappropriately using the definite article 'The'. The investigator analysed the over use of this article in the formation of major and the subordinate clauses. Learners are finding this article as a supporting word that could be used anywhere in the sentence when they find themselves confused with the indefinite articles, prepositions or conjunctions.

Errors in using Preposition: Prepositional errors have also been potentially identified by investigator. There is no clear distinction like 'since' and 'for', 'to' and 'for' etc. of English in Malayalam and so, the students fail to observe it. Learners are either omitting prepositions or there is addition of prepositions in certain situations. But majority of students are using incorrect prepositions while constructing sentences.

Errors in using correct form of tense: A sensible look at the errors made by the learners lead the teachers to identify that almost most of the verbal errors are due to the interference of mother tongue. The major structural difference in Malayalam and English language like the use of linking verb, difference among simple past, present perfect and perfect tenses lead to major errors by the learners.

Errors in using conjunctions: Learners are making mistakes in using conjunctions, especially in coordinating conjunctions such as For, And, Nor, But, Or, Yet and So. They are omitting the use of subordinating conjunctions such as if, since, than that, because etc. wherever necessary. The investigator analysed the fact that secondary school students were completely unaware of where to use correlative conjunctions like not only but also, neither or etc. They are not omitting correlative conjunctions in sentence formation but over use of correlative conjunctions are seen in their descriptions.

Morphological Error Analysis In English Language Among Secondary School Students

From Table 23.2 it is revealed that most of the teachers are in the opinion that students of secondary schools are making morphological errors in

Table 23.2 Result of Morphological Error Analysis in English Language

Sl. No:	*Morphological Errors*	*Percentage*
1.	Affixation related errors	70
2.	Compound related errors	63
3.	Failure to use the marker (-er)	88
4.	Conversion related errors	83
5.	Using of plural in noun phrases	73

English language.

Affixation-Related Errors: Affixation-related errors arise as a result of misuse of either prefixes or suffixes. Thus, in order to present a clear picture of the errors, we group them into:

a. *Errors arising from the wrong use of prefixes*: At times, most ESL learners, especially secondary school pupils do make use of prefixes incorrectly while trying to create new words or give antonyms of particular words. Some of the errors of this nature found in the English usage of our subjects are like "You are diskind (unkind)", It is unsignificant (insignificant).
b. *Errors arising from wrong use of suffixes*: Errors of this kind are numerous in our respondents' scripts. These errors can be divided into:
   - Morphological errors arising as a result of wrong insertion of past tense marker as in the sentence "the crow putted the cake down"
   - Errors made as a result of analogous use of certain suffixes as in "the tortoise ran speedly".
   - Compound Related Errors: Compounding is a morphological process which consists in the combination of at least two free morphemes such as book + shop (bookshop).

According to Quirk, Greenbaum, Leech and Svartvik (1972), a compound word may be open when its constituent morphemes are written separately as in tear gas and fire engine, it may be hyphenated as in far-fetched and story-telling, and lastly, it may be solid when the constituents are written together as in classroom and blackboard. In addition to the orthographic conventions of writing compound words in English, there are phonological rules which deal with how compound words are pronounced in English (cf. Quirk *et al.*, 1972; Quirk and Greenbaum,

1973). However, most ESL learners do not always have a good knowledge of these rules and our subjects are no exception.

- Failure to use the marker (-er): secondary school students made mistakes in the use of the marker (-er) in the transcripts like "my mother is the cooker of the tea".
- Conversion-Related Errors: There are very few conversion-related errors in the written responses of the subjects. The errors are seen in sentences like, " the crow will feeling hungry"
- Using of plural in noun phrases: there were a lot of errors in using the noun phrases in the sentences among secondary school students. To quote an example, "the tea powders was put in the cup".

Causes of Morphological and Syntactic Errors Analyzing the Causes of Errors While Constructing Syntactic Structures Among Secondary School Students in the Perception of Teachers

Table 23.3: Results showing the Causes of Morphological Errors in the Perception of Teachers

Sl. No:	*Causes*	*Percentage*
1.	Inconsistency in language	63
2.	Over generalisation and misapplication of rules	65
3.	Lack of morphology related topics	93
4.	Mother tongue interference	97

Inconsistency in English language: The first important factor which compounds most ESL learners' problems in the acquisition of English morphology is the inconsistency inherent in the language (cf. Babalola and Akande, 2002). This inconsistency is caused by the polysystemic nature of English. For instance, if the plural of knife, calf and thief are knives, calves and thieves respectively, why shouldn't the plural of chief be *chieves? Similarly, if the plural of box is boxes, why is *oxes not the plural of ox? This also applies to the formation of past tense in English. Killed is the past of kill but *eated is not the past of eat. This inconsistency has a serious implication in the learning of English by ESL learners.

Lack Of Morphology Related Topics: Morphological-related topics are not taught at all in most schools. Unfortunately, the topics in most English textbooks normally reflect the syllabus to be covered by students. What this implies is that the teaching of morphology is not deemed important by whoever is in charge of drawing the syllabus. Perhaps, if English morphology is systematically taught in our schools, the pupils may be in a position to master most of the rules and their exceptions; and this will go a long way in minimizing the morphological errors in their English.

Over Generalisation and Misapplication of Rules: Also important causes are the overgeneralization and the misapplication of rules. In most cases, students do over generalise or misapply certain morphological rules. For instance, a student who forms *insultive based on his or her knowledge of the fact that instructive could be formed from instruct over generalises. Overgeneralization and misapplication of rules are usually the aftermath of the ignorance of certain restrictions.

Mother Tongue Interference: The last cause that we will like to discuss is the interference factor. Most errors especially the ones that have to do with suffixation, conversion and pronunciation are made as a result of the influence of the L1 of the subjects on English.

Analysing the causes of Errors while constructing syntactic structures among Secondary School students in the perception of teachers

Table 23.4: Results showing the Causes of Syntactic Errors in the Perception of Teachers

Sl. No	*Major Causes*	*Percentage*
1.	Attitude of students	97
2.	Interlingual interference	96
3.	Intra Present method of teaching	91
4.	Intralingual interference	80
5.	Inadequate exposure to English language	75
6.	Teacher factor	59
7.	Lack of planning to remediate problem	51

It is revealed from the perception of the teachers that a number of factors are contributing to the causes of errors in constructing syntactic elements of English language. According to their opinion inter lingual interference is one among the major factors. The difference in the syntactic arrangement of grammatical structures between the two languages is the major cause of errors in the perception of teachers. Attitude of students that there is no need of creating grammatically correct sentences to pass the examination is effecting negatively. Teachers also mentioned about the intra lingual interference of the language. The irregularity in spelling, exceptions in grammatical rules, and improper use of prepositions and conjunctions are some of the factors which makes the learners confused, leading to make errors while constructing sentences. Moreover, the present methods of teaching is not focussing on any of the forms or structures of English language which further makes the condition worse. Teachers are helpless as revealed from their opinions that they are not getting enough time to focus on any errors of the learners or to rectify those errors. They even do not get enough time to give exposure to the target language.

Minimising morphological and syntactic errors among Secondary School students

The morphological and syntactic errors in English subject would be reduced drastically if the following suggestions are made use of. The suggestions are:

(a) In the teaching of English in secondary schools, morphology should be given its rightful place. By this we mean that the outrageous imbalance in the English syllabi as well as in the English textbooks they use should be properly addressed. In other words, enough morphology-related topics should be incorporated into the English syllabi and textbooks.

(b) It is not enough for students to be taught English morphology, it is very important that it is done systematically and in order of complexity. This is the only way effective teaching and learning could be achieved. Thus, we agree here with Akande (2001) that "morphological processes be introduced and taught at different stages in line with the learners' acquaintance with them as revealed in our database."

(c) For ESL learners to be taught effectively and systematically, the teacher factor is crucial. There is need to make sure that those who are entrusted with the teaching of English Language in our secondary schools are specialists in English and are capable of doing the job effectively. Apart from having a minimum of Bachelor's degree in English or in a related discipline, they should always be made, with the assistance of our government, to attend seminars and conferences on the teaching of English. It is through this they can improve in their teaching.

(d) Lastly, it is important to say that the writers of English textbooks for secondary schools should make sure that they make use of a contrastive technique in the writing of the English textbooks. If this is done, the errors caused through L1 transfer will be reduced.

Conclusion

Regarding morphological errors, the results indicate that a failure to use or a tendency to misuse certain morphemes arises from lack of knowledge of English morphemes, whereas syntactic errors tend to arise from negative L1 interference on L2 structures, attitude of students, present method of teaching, lack of exposure to English language and intra language interference. The findings of this study demonstrate the utility of employing error analysis in identifying phonetic, morphological and syntactic errors among L2 learners to gain understanding of their causes.

References

Chapter 1

Coolahan, J. (2002). *Teacher Education and Teaching Career in an Era of Lifelong Learning* (OECD Education Working Paper No. 2.): Organisation for Economic Co-operation and Development (OCDE).

Day, C. (2001). Innovative Teachers: Promoting Lifelong Learning for All. In J. C. D. Aspin, M. Hatton, and Y. Sawano (Ed.) (Vol. *International Handbook of Lifelong Learning*, pp. 473-500). London: Kluwer.

Hargreaves, A. (2003). *Teaching in the Knowledge Society. Education in the Age of Insecurity.* New York: Teacher College Press.

Chapter 2

Asmus, J., Bonner, C., Esterhay, D., Lechner, A., & Rentfrow, C. (2005). *Instructional design technology trend analysis.* http://elgg.net/collinb/files/1136/2967/TrendAnalysisWeb.pdf

Cold, S.J. (2006). Using Really Simple Syndication (RSS) to enhance student research. *SIGITE Newsletter, 3*(1), 6-9.

D'Souza, Q. (2006). *RSS ideas for educators.*
http://www.teachinghacks.com/wpcontent/uploads/2006/01/RSS%20Ideas%20for%20Educators111.pdf

Gahran, Amy. What are Web Feeds (RSS) and Why Should You Care?
http://blog.contentious.com/archives/2004/05/04/what-are-webfeeds-rss-andwhy-should-youcare

Harrsch, M. (2006). *RSS: The next killer app for education.*
http://ts.mivu.org/default.asp?show=article&id=2010
http://www.thecanadianteacher.com/

Joly, K. (2006). *RSS: The next big thing in university web communications.*
http://www.universitybusiness.com/viewarticle.aspx?articleid=44

Levine, A., Lamb, B., Norman, D. *Syndicating Learning Objects with RSS and Trackback.*
http://www.mcli.dist.maricopa.edu/show/merlot0 3/merlot_lo_rss_paper.pdf.

Resources for Educators, http://www.TeachingHacks.com

Richardson, W. (2005). RSS: A Quick Start Guide for Educators, Ver. 1.5. http://www.weblogg-ed.com.

Richardson, W. (2006). *Blogs, wikis, podcasts, and other powerful web tools for classrooms.* Thousand Oaks, CA: Corwin Press.

West, R.E., Wright, G, Gabbitas, B., & Graham, C.R. (2006). Reflections from the introduction of blogs and RSS Feeds into a preservice instructional technology course. *TechTrends, 50*(4), 54-60

Wikipedia (2005). http://en.wikipedia.org/wiki/RSS_%28file_format%29

Will Richardson. RSS: A Quick Start Guide for Educators. http://www.weblogged.com

Chapter 3

Adams, F.H. (2013).Using jigsaw technique as an effective way of promoting co-operative learning among primary six pupils in Fijai. *International Journal of Education and Practice, 1(6)*, 64-74

Aronson, E., & Patnoe, S. (1997). The jigsaw classroom: Building cooperation in the classroom. New York, NY: Addison Wesley Longman, Inc.

Artut, P.D., & Tarim, K. (2007).The Effectiveness of Jigsaw II on Prospective Elementary School Teachers. *Asia-Pacific Journal of Teacher Education 35(2)*, 129-141.

Barratt, L. B. (1992). Cooperative learning: the college classroom. *Contemporary Education*, 63(3), 201-02.

Carrol, D.W. (1986). Use of the jigsaw technique in laboratory and discussion classes. *Teaching of Psychology, December 13(4)*, 208-210

Common Wealth of Learning (n.d.). Coping with Stress, Retrieved on 12/10/2012 from http://www.col.org/SiteCollectionDocuments/ CFC_Unit_9.pdf

Crone, T.S., & Portillo, M.C. (2013). Jigsaw variations and attitudes about learning and the self in cognitive psychology. *Teaching of Psychology 40(3)*, 246-251.

D'Autuono, A. (1998). *Children and Stress*. Nurse Educator, 23(4), 5-7.

Dash, M. (2004). *Education in India – Problems and Perspectives*, New Delhi, Atlantic Publishers and Distributers, pp. 312-317.

Dohrenwend, B.S., & Dohrenwend, B.P. (Eds.) (1974). *Stressful Life Events: Their Nature and Effects*, New York, Wiley.

Gocer, A. (2010). A comparative research on the effectivity of cooperative learning method and jigsaw technique on teaching literary genres. *Educational Research and Reviews Vol. 5(8)*, 439-445.

Government of India (1966). *Report of Education Commission 1964-66*, Ministry of Education, New Delhi, p. 1.

Hart, K. (2010). *Stress Related Depression Contributes to Rising Suicide Rates*, Retrieved on 12/10/2012 from http://thelewisflyer.com/2010/11/06/stress-related-depression-contributes-to-rising-suicide-rates/

Henderson, P.A., & Kelbey, T.J. (1992). Effects of stress-control program on children's locus of control, self concept, and coping behavior. *School Counselor*, 40 (2), 125-131.

Huang, Y.M., Liao, Y.W., Huang, S.H., & Chen, H.C. (2014). A jigsaw-based cooperative learning approach to improve learning outcomes for mobile situated learning. *Educational Technology & Society, 17 (1)*, 128-140.

Iqbal, H.M. (2012). *Students Committing Suicides Due to Exam Stress*, Retrieved on 12/10/2012 from http://www.nation.com.pk/pakistan-news-newspaper-daily-english-online/lahore/11-Jun-2012/-students-committing-suicides-due-to-exam-stress

Kagan S (1989). The Structural Approach to Cooperative Learning. *Educational Leadership*, December 1989.

Mangal, S.K. (1984). *Abnormal Psychology*, New Delhi, Sterling Publication.

Mengduo, Q., & Xiaoling, J.(2010). Jigsaw strategy as a cooperative learning technique: Focusing on the language learners. *Chinese Journal of Applied Linguistics 33 (4)*,113-125.

Moskowitz, J.M., Malvin, J.H., Schaeffer, G.A., & Schaps, E. (1985). Evaluation of Jigsaw, a cooperative learning technique. *Contemporary Educational Psychology 10(2),* 104-112.

Parvez, M., & Jahan, A. (2011). *Students Under Stress-Role of the Teachers*, Paper Presented in International Conference in Bangalore University, Bangalore, on 3-5 Feb, 2011.

Shamim, M. (2003). *Importance of Value Based Education.* Value Based UGC Golden Jubilee Lecture Series, 2002-2003, New Delhi, University Grants Commission, pp. 1-8.

Sundaram, C.M. (2011). *Look there is a world beyond 100%,* The Hindu, p. 11.

Slavin, R.E. (1995). Cooperative learning: Theory, research, and practice. Boston, MA: Allyn and Bacon.

Slavin, R.E. (1989). Cooperative learning and student achievement: Six theoretical perspectives. *Advances in motivation and achievement, 6*, 161-177.

Walker, I., & Crogan, M. (1998). Academic performance, prejudice, and the jigsaw classroom: New pieces to the puzzle. *Journal of Community and Applied Social Psychology 8*, 381-393.

Watson, S.B. (1991). Cooperative learning and group educational modules: Effects on cognitive achievement of high school biology students. *Journal of Research in Science Teaching, 28* (2), 141-146.

Chapter 4

Cooper, L. C. & Payne, R., (2008), *Causes, Coping and Consequences of Stress at Work.* New York: Wiley.

Krohne, W. H., (2002), *Stress and Coping Theories.* Johannes Gutenberg-Universitu00c3u00a4t Mainz Germany.

O'Leary, A. (1990), Stress, emotion, and human immune function, *Psychological Bulletin*, 108, 363-382.

Resick.P.A. (2001), *Stress and Trauma*, Published by Psychology Press, Taylor and Francis Group.

Salzano, R. (2003), Taming Stress. *Scientific American, 289,* 88-98.

Sorensen, E.L. (1993), *Children's Stress and Coping*, Published by Guilford Press.

Chapter 5

Akhtar, M.Z. (2002). "*Self-financing in Higher Education in Ppublic and Private Sectors: Its Prospects and Implications*". (Unpublished). Institute of Education and Research, University of Arid Agriculture, Rawalpindi, Pakistan.

AIOU. 2002. Islamic System of Education. Master of Education. Study Guide, Code 6505. Islamabad, Pakistan, Allama Iqbal Open University. p. 109.

Arcaro, J. S. (1997). *Quality in Education.* USA: St. Lucie Press, p. 56-67

Ali, Murad and Shastri, R.K. (2010). Implementation of Total Quality Management in Higher Education, *Asian Journal of Business Management* 2(1), pp 9-16.

Ali, N. A. and Zairi, M. (2005). *Service Quality in Higher Education*. Bradford University School of Management, Bradford.

Anwar, M. N. (2005). "*Evaluative Study of Management Techniques used in Administrative and Academic Decision-Making in Universities*". (Unpublished).'Institute of Education and Research, University of Arid Agriculture, Rawalpindi, Pakistan.

Arshad, M. (2003). "*Attitude of Teachers of Higher Education Toward their Profession*". (Unpublished). AIOU, Islamabad, Pakistan.

Bitner, M.J. (1992). "Serviscapes: The impact of physical surroundings on customers and employees", *Journal of Marketing*, Vol. 56, pp. 57-71.

Chowdhary, J. N. (2012). Quality Assurance in Higher Technical and Management Education. *University News*, 50 (10).

Coombs, P. H. (1985). *The World Crises in Education: The View from the Eighties*. Oxford: Oxford University Press.

Crawford, L. E. D. and Shutler, P. (1999). Total Quality Management in education: problems and issues for the classroom teacher. *The International Journal of Educational Management* 13(2), pp. 67-72.

Dahar. Arshad, Faize, F.A and Niwaz, Asaf, (2010). A Case Study of the University College of Education, Chiniot, Punjab (Pakistan) with reference to Total Quality Management, *European Journal of Social Sciences*-16(4). p. 511.

Flumerfelt, Shannon. and Banachowski, Michael. (2011). Understanding Leadership Paradigms for Improvement in Higher Education, *Quality Assurance in Education: An International Perspective*, 19 (3), pp. 224-247

Gopal K. Kanji, Abdul Malek and Bin A. Tambi, (1999) "Total quality management in UK higher education institutions", *Total Quality Management*, 10 (1), pp. 129-153

Gore, J. (2001). Beyond our differences: A reassembling of what matters in teacher education. *Journal of Teacher Education*, 52 (2), pp. 124-135.

Gozacanan Borahan, N. and Ziarati, R, (1999). *Developing a quality system based on ISO 9000 Requirements*, Internal Report, Istanbul, Turkey, Dogus University.

Hameedullah, M. (2004). "*Comparison of the Quality of Higher Education in Public and Private Institutions in Pakistan*". (Unpublished). Institute of Education and Research, University of Arid Agriculture, Rawalpindi, Pakistan

Harris, R.W. (1994). Alien or Ally? TQM, Academic Quality and the New Public Management, *Quality Assurance in Education*, 2 (3), pp 33-39.

Hillman, A. L. (1995). Total quality reform: restructuring teacher education through the infusion of technology and total quality management. *Dissertation Abstracts International*, 60(07), p. 2306-A

Hussain, Abid, (2008). "*Total quality concept: Implementation in teacher training institutes of Pakistsn*", 2nd International Conference on Assessing Quality in Higher Education, 1st -3rd December.

Iqbal, A. (2004). "*Problems and Prospects of Higher Education*". (Unpublished). University Institute of Education and Research, University of Arid Agriculture, Rawalpindi, Pakistan.

Isani, U. A. G. and M. L.Virk. (2005). *Higher Education in Pakistan: A Historical and Futuristic Perspective*. Islamabad, Pakistan: National Book Foundation. pp. 232- 33.

Kanji, G.K. and Malek, A. (1999). "An innovative approach to make ISO 9000 standards more effective", *Total Quality Management,* 9 (1), pp. 67-78.

Kanji G. K. and A. Tambi, A. M. (1998). Total quality management and higher education in Malaysia. *Total Quality Management,* 9(4/5), pp. 130–132.

Karuppusami, G. and Gandhinathan, R. (2006). "Pareto analysis of critical success factors of total quality management: A literature review and analysis", *The TQM magazine*, 18 (4), pp. 372-385.

Lawrence, J.J. and M.A. McCollough, (2001). A conceptual framework for guaranteeing higher education. *Quality. Assurance in Education,* 9(3), pp. 139-152.

Manivannan, M, and Premila, K. S, (2009). Application of Principles of Total Quality Management in Teacher Education Institutions, *Journal of College Teaching & Learning, Volume* 6, Number 6.

Mark, S. Doman. (2011). "A new lean paradigm in higher education: a case study", *Quality Assurance in Education,* 19(3), pp. 248 -262

Mehra, Satish and Munsung, Rhee. (2009). "On the application of quality management concepts in education: An example of a Korean classroom", *International Journal of Quality & Reliability Management,* Vol. 26 (4), pp. 312 – 324

Michael, R.K., et al., (1997). "A comprehensive model for implementing total quality management in higher education". *Benchmark Quality Manage Technology*, 4(2), pp. 104-120.

Mishra kumar, Pradipta, (2010). "*Quality management and excellence in teaching and learning for higher education: Need of the Day*", UGC sponsored National Seminar on Higher Education: Mission, Money and Management.

Murad, Ali and Rajesh, Shastri, (2010). "Implementation of Total Quality Management in Higher Education", *Asian Journal of Business Management,* 2(1), pp. 9-16.

Mukhopadahyay, M. (2006) *Total Quality Management in Education.* New Delhi: Sage publications.

Narula, M. (2000). *Effective Teaching in Higher Education.* New Delhi: Commonwealth Publishers. p.166.

Naik, B.M. (2001). "Need to bring quality movement in higher education", *Journal of Engineering Education,* India, July issue.

Osseo-Asare, E.A. and Longbottom, D. (2002). "The need for education and training in the use of the EFQM model for quality management in UK higher education institutions". *Quality Assurance in Education,* 10(1), pp 26-36.

Satish. (2009). "The role of quality management concepts towards enhancing classroom learning", *The International Journal of Quality and Reliability Management,* The International Journal, 26(4).

Sallis, E. (2009). *Total Quality Management in Education.* Taylor and Francis Group.

Scott, P. 2000. *Higher Education Reformed.* London. U.K: Falmer Press, p. 106.

Sherr, L.A. and Lozier, G.G.(1991). "Total Quality Management in Higher Education." Management in Higher Education. *New Directions for Institutional Research, no. 71.* San Francisco: Jossey-Bass.

Shirazi, M.J. Haider. (2004). "*Analysis of Examination System at University Level in Pakistan*". (Unpublished). Institute of Education and Research, University of Arid Agriculture, Rawalpindi, Pakistan.

Shulman, L. S. (1986). Those Who Understand: Knowledge Growth in Teaching. *Journal of Educational Research,* 15(2), pp. 4-14.

Sitalakshmi Venkatraman, (2007). "A framework for implementing TQM in higher education programs", *Quality Assurance in Education*, 15(1), pp. 92-112

Srivanci, M.B. (2004). Critical issues for TQM implementation in higher education. *The TQM Magazine,* 16(6), pp. 382-386.

Temponi, C. (2005). Continuous improvement framework: implications for academia. *Quality Assurance in Education*, 13 (1), pp. 17-36

Thakkar, J., Deshmukh, S. G. and Shastree, A. (2006). Total quality management (TQM) in self-financed technical institutions: a quality function deployment (QFD) and force field analysis approach. *Quality Assurance in Education*, 14(1), pp. 54-74.

Thapa, T. B. (2011). *Total Quality Management in Education*. A Multidisciplinary Journal, 1(1).

UNESCO (1996a). IIEP Contribution No. 23. *Educational Challenges of the 21st Century: The Vision of Quality*, Paris. France. pp 2-5.

UNESCO, (2002). *External Quality Assurance in Indian Higher Education,* Paris, France: IIEP, p. 13

Whitty, G. (1992). Quality control in teacher education, British Journal of Educational Studies, 40 (1), pp. 38-48.

Winn, R.C and R, S. Green (1998). *Applying Total Quality Management to the Educational Process.* Int. J. Enag Ed. UK: Tempus Publications. p. 24-28.

Witcher, B.J. (1990). Total Marketing: Total Quality and Marketing Concept. *The Quarterly Review of Marketing Winter.*

Yeshodhara, K, Pour, H. M. (n.d.). Total Quality Management (TQM) in Education – Perception of Secondary School teachers.

Chapter 6

Abbas, Thahir, (2011). *Islam and Education.* London & New York: Routledge.

Abdalla, A. et al. (2006). *Improving the Quality of Islamic Education in Developing Countries: Innovative Approaches,* Creative Associates: Washington D.C.

Abubakr, Pinangode (2006), *Teacher and Instruction* (Mal.), Malappuram: Samasatha Kerala Islam Matha Vidhybyasa Board.

Abubakr, Pinangode (2010), *Madrasa Education Rule* (Mal.), Malappuram: Samasatha Kerala Islam Matha Vidhybyasa Board.

Arcaro, Jerome S., 1997, *Quality in Education: An Implementation Handbook*, Vanity Books International.

Ahmed, Manzoor (1990), *Islamic Education: Redefinition of the Aims and Methodology,* New Delhi: Genuine Publications.

Ahmad, Mumtaz (2002). "Madrasa Education in Pakistan and Bangladesh", Asia Pacefic Centre for Security Studies

Akhtar, Najma & Nerula, Manju (2010), *The role of Indian Madrasa in Providing Access to Mainstream Education for Muslim Minority Students: A West Bengal Experience*, Springer Science & Business Media.

Ali Ahmed, Kodom (2010), *Madrasa Education in Barpeta District and its impact on the society – A critical study*, Unpublished DEPA Dissertation. New Delhi: NUEPA.

Ali, K.T Mohammed (1990), *The Development of education among the Mapillas of Malabar,* New Delhi: Nunes Publishers.

Ansari, Iqbal (2006), Political Represenation of Muslims in India (1952-2004), New Delhi: Manak Publications.

Ansari, M. Shoyeb (1997), *Education in Deeni Madaris: An Opinion Survey of Curriculum, Method of Teaching and Evaluation in Deeni Madaris*. New Delhi: Indian Objective Studies.

Anzar, Uzma (2003), *Islamic Education, a Brief History of Madrasas with Comments on Curricula and Current Pedagogical Practices,* downloaded from WWW. Islamiceducation.com

Anzar, Uzma and Carter, Lynn (2006): An improving Education in Madrasa: An Indian Case study

Asian Development Bank (2011). "People's Republic of Bangladesh: Capacity Development for Madrasa Education", Bangladesh: Maxwell Stamp Ltd.

Bi, Kulsoom (2001), *Modernisation of Madrasa Curriculum: A Study of Perceptions and Attitudes of Molvis and Students,* Unpublished M.Ed. Dissertation, Department of Education, Jamia Millia Islamia, New Delhi.

Bahauddeen, K.M (1981), *Kerala Muslims: History of Long Struggles,* Trivandrum: Modern Book Centre.

Basheer, K. Mohammed (2014). *Teacher Education in Madrasa: Innovative Experiences,* in *Education as a Right across the levels: Challenges, Opportunities and strategies.* New Delhi: Viva Books.

Basheer, K. Mohammed (2013), *Future of Indian Madrasa Education in the Globalized world* in Scholarly Research Journal for Interdisciplinary Studies, Pune, Sept –Oct 2013, Vol. II/V.

Bhat, Ahmad Manzoor, 2006, *Quality Concerns in Education.* New Delhi: Rawat Publications.

Elahi, Nizam (2001), *Modernisation of Madrasa Education Scheme in India. Reports of Induction/In-service Education Programmes for Madrasa Teachers of Delhi, 1995-99.* New Delhi: State Council of Educational Research and Training.

Engineer, Asghar Ali (1996), *Kerala Muslims: A Historical Perspective,* Delhi: Ajanta Books International.

Engineer, Asghar Ali, (2002). *Indian Muslims and Education,* Mumbai: Institute of Islamic Studies.

Fahimuddin (2004), *Modernisation of Muslim Education in India,* New Delhi: Adhyayan Publishers.

Frederic Dale, Stephen (1980), *Islamic Society on the South Asian Frontier, The Mappila of Malabar, 1498-1922.* Oxford: Clarendon Press.

Frederic Dale, Stephen (1990), 'Trade, Conversion and the Growth of the Islamic Community of Kerala, South India', *Studia Islamica,* No. 71, pp. 155-175.

Govt. of India, 2006, *Social, Economic and Educational Status of the Muslim Community of India,* Sachar Committee Report, Prime Minister's High Level Committee, New Delhi.

Hamdard Education Society (2003), *Evaluation Report on Modernization of the Madrasa* [sic] *Education Scheme (UP),* New Delhi: Hamdard Education Society.

Hamdard Education Society (2008), Report on the Teachers Training Programme on strengthening the human values through education 2007-2008. New Delhi: Hamdard Education Society.

Hartung, Jan-Peter & Reifeld, Helmut (ed), 2006, *Islamic Education, Diversity and National Identity: Dini Madaris in India Post 9/11,* New Delhi: Sage Publications.

Hasan, Mushirul (ed.), (1998). *Islam, Communities and the Nation: Muslim Identities in South Asia and Beyond.* New Delhi: Manohar.

Husain, S.M. Azizuddin (ed), 2005, Madrasa Education in India: Eleventh to Twenty First Century. New Delhi: Kanishka Publishers.

Husain, M.G. (2004), Muslim Education and Madrasa Education in Purnea District of Bihar. New Delhi: Institute of Objective Studies.

Huda, Kashiful (2010), '*System of Islamic education in Kerala*' *published at* http://twocircles.net/

Jha, Prem Kumar (2005), *Quality and Access in Primary Education*. New Delhi: Vista International Publishing House.

Jhingran, Saral (2010): *Madrasa Education in Modern India, A Study,* New Delhi: Manohar Publishers & Distributors.

Kareem, C K (1997), *Ancient Kerala and Emergence of Muslims* (Mal.). Calicut: Islamic Sahitya Academy.

Kareem, K. K. Muhammad Abdul, and Moulavi, CN. Ahmad (1978). *Great Literary Tradition of the Mappilas* (Mal.), Published by the Authors, Kozhikkode.

Kaur, Kuldeep (2003). *Maktab Education in the Mosques,* Chandigarh: Centre for Research in Rural & Industrial Development.

Kaur, Kuldip (1990). *Madrasa Education in India: A Study of its Past and Present.* Chandigarh: Centre for Research in Rural & Industrial Development.

Khan, Amir Ullah, Mohammad Saqib and Zafar H. Anjum (2003), *To Kill the Mockingbird, Madrasa System in India: Past, Present, and Future,* At www.bazaarchintan.net/pdfs/Madrasas.pdf.

Khan, Saleem (1997), "The role of *Madrasa* system in universalisation of elementary education in Jaipur city", New Delhi: NIEPA.

Kunhi, P.K. Muhammad (1982), *Muslims and Kerala Culture*, Trissur: Institute of Mappila Studies.

Kunju, A.P. Ibrahim (1989), *Mappila Muslims of Kerala: Their History and Culture,* Trivandrum:Sandhya Publications.

Lakshmi, LRS (2012), *The Malabar Muslims: A Different Perspective,* New Delhi: Cambridge University Press India Pvt. Ltd.

Logan, William (1951), *Malabar Manual*, 2 Vols., Madras: Superd. of Government Press.

Makdisi, George (1981), *The Rise of Colleges: Institutions of Learning in Islam and the Wes,* Edinburgh: Edinburgh University Press.

Makki, Dr. Mukthar Ahmad (2010): *Educational Trends and Development among Muslims of India*, New Delhi: Shipra Publications.

Malik, Jamal (2008). *Madrasas in South Asia: Teaching Terror?,* London & New York: Routledge.

Modernization of Madrasa Education in Bangladesh: A Strategy Paper (2011), Dhaka: Bangladesh Enterprise Institute (BEI).

Mohideen Shah, Syed (1972), *Islam in Kerala,* Trissur: The Muslim Educational Association.

Mohammed, U (2005), *Muslim Education: Problems and Solutions,* Calicut: MSS State Committee.

Mohammed, U (2007). *Educational Empowerment of Kerala Muslims: A Socio-historic Perspective*, Calicut: Other Books

Muhammad, K.M. (1995), Origin and Development of Arabic Studies in Kerala, in Asghar Ali Engineer (ed), *Kerala Muslims: A Historical Perspective*, pp. 157-167, Delhi: Ajanta Books International.

Muhammad Koya, Parappil (1994), *History of Muslims of Kozhikkode*, (Mal.), Kozhikkode: Published by the Author.Muhammad, P.A. Sayd. (1996). *Kerala Muslim History*, (Mal.), Calicut: Al Huda Book Stall.

Mukhopadhyay, Marmar (2002), *Total Quality Management in Education,* New Delhi: National Institute of Educational Planning and Administration.

Mukhopadhyay, Marmar (2009), *Quality School Education for All* (Ed.), New Delhi: Educational, Technology and Management Academy.

Miller, Roland (1976), *Recent Trends in the Studies of Mappila Muslims of Kerala*, Madras: Orient Longmans.

Nazeer, P (2011), History of Muslim Educational Institutions in Kerala during 20th Century, Unpublished Ph. D thesis, Kerala University Library, Thiruvananthapuram.

Narayanan, M G S (2010), *The Foundational Stones of Kerala History* (Mal. *Kerala Charithrathinte Adisthana Silakal*). Kozhikode: Lipi Publications.

National Commission for Religious and Linguistic Minorities Report Annexure II (2006): Jamia Millia Islamia, New Delhi "Role of Madrasa Education in Mainstreaming Muslims into Educational System"

Noor, Farish, et. al. (2008), *The Madrasa in Asia: Political Activism and Transnational Linkages*, Amsterdam University Press, Amsterdam.

Osella, Filippo and Caroline Osella (2000), *Social Mobility in Kerala: Modernity and Identity in Conflict*, Pluto Press, London and Virginia.

Osella, Filippo and Caroline Osella (2000), 'Migration, money and masculinity in Kerala', *Journal of the Royal Anthropological Institute*, vol. 6, no. 1, pp. 115–31.

Panikkasseri, Velayudhan (2007), *Kerala: Six Hundred Years Ago, In the Views of IbnBattutta* (Mal.), Mathrubhumi Books, Kozhikkode.

Qasimi, Muhammadullah Khalil, *Madrasa Education: Its strength and Weakness,* New Delhi: Manas Publications, 2005.

Qasimi, Muhammed Sajid (2005), Madrasa Education Framework, New Delhi: Manak Publications.

Randathani, Husain (2007), *Mappila Muslims: A Study on Society and Anti-Colonial Struggles*, Other Books, Calicut.

Samastha (2009), *Samastha Kerala Jam-iyyathul Ulama* (Mal.), Malappuram: Samasatha Kerala Islam Matha Vidhybyasa Board.

Salamatullah (1990), *Hindustan mein musalmanon ki talim,* New Delhi: Maktaba Jamia Ltd.

Sha, Prof. Syed Mohideen (1975), *Islam in Kerala,* Trichur: Muslim Educational Association.

Sharma, K.C (2000), *Encyclopedia of Madrasa Education in India*, Vistha Publishing House, New Delhi.

Siddiqui, M. Akthar; Qadri, A.W.B, and Khan, Riyaz Shakkir (2007), New Delhi: *Education and Muslims in India since Independence*, Indian Objective Studies.

Siddiqui, M. Akthar (1995), Management of Muslim Education in Minority Institution, New Delhi: Ashish Publishing House.

Siddiqui, Mohammad Akhtar (1998), "Developments and Trends in Madrasa Education", in Education & Muslims in India since Independence, pp. 83-84, New Delhi: IOS.

Siddiqui, M. Akthar (2004), *Ekkiswi Sadi Ke Awail Me Delhi Ke Madaris*, Jamia Maktaba Ltd., New Delhi.

Siddiqui, M. Akthar (2004), *Empowerment of Muslims through Education,* New Delhi: Institute of Objective Studies.

Sikand, Yoginder (2005), *Bastions of the Believers: Madrasas and Islamic Education in India*, New Delhi: Penguin India.

Sikand, Yoginder (2005), *Issues in Madrasa Education in India,* New Delhi: Penguin India.

Sikand, Yoginder (2004), 'Madrasas and Arabic Colleges in Contemporary Kerala,' in *The Milli Gazette*, New Delhi, Vol. 22, No. 8.

Waheed, Abdul (2010), *Minority Education in India: Issues of Access, Equity and Inclusion*. New Delhi: Serials Publications.

Wasey, Akhtarul (2005), *Madrasas In India: Trying IsRelevant,* New Delhi: Global Media Publications.

Wink, Andre (2004), *Al Hind: The Making of the Indo-Islamic World*, Volume 3, Indo-Islamic Society: 14th-15th Centuries, Boston Brill: Leiden.

Winkelmann, Mareike (2005), *'From Behind the Curtain': A Study of a Girls' Madrasa in India*. Amsterdam: Amsterdam University Press.

Zaman, Muhammad Qasim (2002), *The Ulama in Contemporary Islam: Custodians of Change,* New Jersey: Princeton University Press.

Zaman, Mohd. Tahseen (2011). *Pedagogy, Curriculum and Evaluation Strategies used in Madrasa Jamia Islamia Sanabil-A Case study*, unpublished M.Ed Dissertation, Faculty of Education, Jamia Millia Islamia, New Delhi.

Webliography

http://mhrd.gov.in/qualityeducationinMadrasa

http://www.milligazette.com/news/3700-Madrasa-education-system-

http://samastha.info/

http://skjmcc.org/

http://twocircles.net/2011nov08/challenges_Madrasa_education.html

http://en.wikipedia.org/wiki/Madrasa

http://www.majliskerala.org

http://www.milligazette.com/Archives/15072002/1507200258.htm

http://twocircles.net/2010jan05/system_islamic_education_kerala.html

http://indianmuslims.in/traditionalist-ulama-lead-educational-revolution-in-kerala/

Fahimuddin, Dr., "*Globalization and Growth of Madrasas in India*", Seminar paper, http://www.bsos.umd.edu/socy/conference/newpapers/uddin.txt

Chapter 7

Ahmad, Ausaf, *Indian Muslims, Issues in Social & Economic Development*, New Delhi, 1993, p. 1.

Akhtar, Najma & Manju Narula (2010): "The Role of Indian Madrasas in Providing Access to Mainstream Education for Muslim Minority Students: A West Bengal Experience", Published online, 29 January 2010 # Springer Science+Business Media B.V. 2010.

Ansari, Iqbal A., *The Muslim Situation in India*, New Delhi, 1989, p. 12.

Ansari, M. (2001), Traditional occupations, child labour and trade policy: A vicious circle around educational backwardness of Muslims, *Journal of Educational Planning and Administration*, 15(3), 333–353.

Basant, R (2007), 'Social, Economic and Educational Conditions of Indian Muslims', *Economic and Political Weekly,* March 10.

Census of India (2001), Registrar General & Census Commissioner, New Delhi, India 20.

Chakrapani, Pushpa, Empowerment of Marginalized Communities: Role of ODL in India, Dr B R Ambedkar Open University.

Engineer, A.A. (2001), Muslim and Education. *Economic and Political Weekly*, pp. 3221-3223.

Government of India (2001), Census Report, 2001, New Delhi, India. www.census.gov.in.

India: Human Development Report, NCAER 1999.

Murshed, S.M., 'Muslim Factor in India', *The Times of India*, New Delhi, Feb. 16, 1993.

National Institute of Open Schooling: A24/25, Institutional Area, Sector 62, Noida, UP, Silver Jubilee Year Report 2012-13.

National Sample Survey Organization (NSSO) Report: Status of Education and Vocational Training in India 2004-2005 (Report no. 517, 61/10/03), India: Ministry of Statistics and Programme Implementation. 16. World Bank Report, Skill Development in India: The Vocational Education and Training System (Report no 22).The World Bank: Human Development Unit, South Asia Region.

National Sample Survey, 55th Round (2000) National Sample Survey Organisation, New Delhi, India.

NIOS, Annual Report, 2012, New Delhi.

Pandya, Amit, "Faith, Justice, and Violence: Islam in Political Context," in Amit Pandya and Ellen Laipson, eds., *Islam and Politics: Renewal and Resistance in the Muslim World* (Washington, DC: Stimson Center, 2009).

Prime Minister's High Level Committee for Preparation of Report on Social, Economic and Educational Status of the Muslim Community of India (Chairperson: Justice Rajindar Sachar) Sardar Patel Bhawan, Parliament Street, New Delhi, 17 November, 2006.

Sharma, K.D. (1978), *Education of a national minority: A Case of Indian Muslims,* New Delhi, Kalamkar Prakashan.

The Commonwealth of Learning – An Introduction to Open and Distance Learning, Page 1 of 29 http://www.col.org/ODLIntro/introODL.htm 10/24/2000.

Zakaria, Rafiq, *Understanding the Indian Muslim*, Bharatiya Vidya Bhavan, Mumbai, 2004.

Chapter 8

Aldo Leopold, A Sand County Almanac, 1949.

Ayong Le Kama, A. D. (2001), "Sustainable growth renewable resources, and pollution", *Journal of Economic Dynamics and Control* 25 (12): 1911–1918. doi:10.1016/S0165-1889(00)00007-5

Barbier, E. (1987), "The Concept of Sustainable Economic Development". *Environmental Conservation* 14 (2): 101–110. doi:10.1017/S0376892900011449

Brundtland Commission (1987), "Report of the World Commission on Environment and Development", United Nations.

Circles of Sustainability Urban Profile Process and Scerri, Andy; James, Paul (2010)."Accounting for sustainability: Combining qualitative and quantitative research in developing 'indicators' of sustainability". *International Journal of Social Research Methodology.*

Daly, H. E. 1973. Towards a Steady State Economy. San Francisco: Freeman. Daly, H. E. 1991. *Steady-State Economics* (2nd ed.). Washington, D.C.: Island Press

Hamilton, K.; Clemens, M. (1999). "Genuine savings rates in developing countries".*World Bank Economy Review* 13 (2): 333–356. doi:10.1093/wber/13.2.333

James, Paul; with Magee, Liam; Scerri, Andy; Steger, Manfred B. (2015). Urban Sustainability in Theory and Practice: Circles of Sustainability. London: Routledge.

Liam Magee, Andy Scerri, Paul James, James A. Thom, Lin Padgham, Sarah Hickmott, Hepu Deng, Felicity Cahill (2013). "Reframing social sustainability reporting: Towards an engaged approach", Environment, Development and Sustainability (University of Melbourne). doi:10.1007/s10668-012-9384-2.

Lynn R. Kahle, Eda Gurel-Atay, Eds (2014). Communicating Sustainability for the Green Economy. New York: M.E. Sharpe.

Melvin K. Hendrix, Sustainable Backyard Polyculture: Designing for ecological resiliency Smashwords ebook edition. 2014.

Pezzey, John C. V.; Michael A., Toman (2002). "The Economics of Sustainability: A Review of Journal Articles"

Smith, Charles; Rees, Gareth (1998). Economic Development, 2nd edition. Basingstoke: Macmillan.

Stavins, R.; Wagner, A.; Wagner, G. "Interpreting Sustainability in Economic Terms: Dynamic Efficiency Plus Intergenerational Equity". *Economic Letters* 79 (3): 339–343.doi:10.1016/S0165-1765(03)00036-3

Ulrich Grober: Deep roots — A conceptual history of "sustainable development" (Nachhaltigkeit), Wissenschaftszentrum Berlin für Sozialforschung, 2007

United Nations (2014), Prototype Global Sustainable Development Report (Online unedited edition ed.), New York: United Nations Department of Economic and Social Affairs, Division for Sustainable Development.

Will Allen. 2007."Learning for Sustainability: Sustainable Development."

World Charter for Nature, United Nations, General Assembly, 48th Plenary Meeting, October 28, 1982

World Conservation Strategy: Living Resource Conservation for Sustainable Development (PDF), International Union for Conservation of Nature and Natural Resources, 1980.

www.esdtoolkit.org/discussion/default.htm

Chapter 9

Ellington, Henry; Fred Percival and Phil Race, 'Handbook of Educational Technology', 3rd ed., Kogan Page Ltd., London Nicholas Publishing Company, New Jersey.

Kubiszyn, Tom & Gary Boric, Educational Testing and Measurement- Classroom Application and Practice, 7th ed. Joher Wiley & Sons, Inc.

Rao, Digumarti Bhaskara, 'Educational Practices – Research and Recommendations', Discovery Publishing House, New Delhi.

Sidhu, K.S, 'New Approaches to Measurement and Evaluation'

Vashisht, S.R., 'Practice of Educational Evaluation' Anmol Publications Pvt. Ltd., New Delhi.

Chapter 10

Agarwal, Pawan, Higher Education in India: The Need for Change (ICIER Working Paper No. 180). New Delhi: Indian Council for Research on International Economic Relations, 2006, (http://www.icrier.org/publication/working_papers_180.html)Altbach,

Philip G, The Private Higher Education Revolution: An Introduction, University News. January 2-8, 2006. Vol. 44 No. 1.

Anandakrishnan, M, Privatization of Higher Education: Opportunities and Anomalies, 'Privatization and commercialization of higher education', organized by NIEPA, May 2, 2006, New Delhi.

Carl Dahlman and Anuja Utz, India and the Knowledge Economy: Leveraging Strengths and Opportunities (World Bank Report No. 31267-IN), Washington DC: W. Bank, 2006 (http://wwwwds.worldbank.org/servlet/WDSContentServer/IB/312670IN.txt)

Chatterjee, Jayanta, How to improve India's higher education and research quality? http://www.nature.com/ 04 November 2008, available on 25.1.2011 http://education.nic.in/uhe/uhe.asp, available on 25.1.2011

Chronicle of Higher Education, various issues (cited as CHE) (http://chronicle.com/

Delors, Jacques (1996) Learning the treasure within. Report to UNESCO of the International Commission on Education for the Twenty-first Century. UNSECO Publishing, Paris.

Higher education in India and Yashpal Committee recommendations http://www.jnu.ac.in/Yash_Pal_Committee.pdf.April 18, 2009, available on 25.1.2011.

Higher Education in India: Issues, Concerns and New Directions http://www.ugc.ac.in/pub/heindia.pdf.

Jandhyala B.G. Tilak, Absence of Policy and Perspective in Higher Education. Economic and Political Weekly Vol. 39, No. 21 (May 22, 2004), 2159-2164 (http://www.epw.org.in/epw/uploads/articles/7650.pdf)

MHRD (2006) Annual Report. Ministry of Human Resource Development, Department of Secondary and Higher education, Government of India. New Delhi.

National Knowledge Commission Report to the Nation 2006. New Delhi: National Knowledge Commission, 2007 (cited as NKC 2007) (http://knowledgecommission.gov.in/report2006/default.asp).

Planning Commission (1999) Approach paper to the Tenth Five-year Plan (2002-2007) Planning Commission, New Delhi.

Privatization of Higher Education in India: Constitutional Perspectives and Challenges. Lawstudent.in (online) n.d. (2007) (cited as law student 2007) (http://www.lawstudent.in/bc_seervai_essay.htm)

Raghunath A. Mashelkar, India's R&D: Reaching for the Top, Science Vol. 307, No. 5714 (4 March 2005), (http://www.sciencemag.org/cgi/content/full/307/5714/1415)

SanatKaul, Higher Education in India: Seizing the Opportunity (ICIER Working Paper No. 179), New Delhi: Indian Council for Research on International Economic Relations, May 2006 (http://www.icrier.org/pdf/WP_179.pdf) available on 25.1.2011

Stella, Antony (2002) External Quality Assurance in Indian Higher Education: Case study of the National Assessment and accreditation Council (NAAC), International Institute for Educational Planning, Paris.

Tewari, Asha, Implementing Quality in higher education, http://www.qcin.org/nbqp/qualityindia/Vol-2-No2/specialreport.htm, available on 25.1.2011

Top universities in the World, http://in.answers.yahoo.com/ available on 25.1.2011

UGC (2005) Research Handbook: Towards nurturing research culture in higher education institutions in India. University Grants Commission, New Delhi.

World Bank (2004) 'Measuring Trade in Services Liberalization and its Impact on Economic Growth: an illustration', World Bank Group Working Paper, downloadable from http://econ.worldbank.org/files/2373_wps2655.pdfhttp://econ.worldbank.org/files/2373_wps2655.pdf

Chapter 11

Becker, H.J. (2000), "Pedagogical Motivations for Student Computer Use that Leads to Student Engagement", *Education Technology*, Vol. 40, No. 5, pp. 5-17.

Bhattacharya I & Sharma K, (2007), 'India in the knowledge economy – an electronic paradigm', *International Journal of Educational Management*, Vol. 21, No. 6, pp. 543- 568.

Cholin, V.S. (2005), 'Study of the application of information technology for effective access to resources in Indian university libraries', *The International Information & Library Review*, Vol. 37, No (3), 189-197.

Coates, D. & Humphreys, B.R., et al (2004). "No Significant Distance' between Face-to-face and Online Instruction: Evidence from Principles of Economics". *Economics of Education Review*, Vol. 23, No. 6, pp. 533-546.

Cross, M. & Adam, F. (2007), 'ICT Policies and Strategies in Higher Education in South Africa: National and Institutional Pathways', *Higher Education Policy*, Vol. 20, No (1), pp. 73- 95.

Cziko, G.A. (2001). Teacher adoption of technology: a perceptual control theory perspective. *Journal of Technology and Teacher Education,* Vol. 9, No (1), pp. 5-30.

Falmer Kozma, R (2005), 'National Policies that connect ICT-based Education Reform to Economic and Social Development', *Human Technology*, Vol. 1, No. (2), pp. 117-156.

Fuchs, Woessman l (2004), "Computers and Student Learning: Bivariate and Multivariate Evidence on the Availability and Use of Computers at Home and at School", CESifo Working Paper. No. 1321.

Hannafin, M.J., Hall, C., Land, S., & Hill, J. (1994), "Learning in open-ended environments: assumptions, methods and implications", *Educational Technology*, Vol. 34, No (8), pp. 48–55.

Hillsdale, N.J.: Lawrence Erlbaum Associates, Chandra, S. & Patkar, V. (2007), 'ICTS: A catalyst for enriching the learning process and library services in India', *The International Information & Library Review* Vol. 39, No (1), pp. 1-11.

Kulik, J. (2003),"Effects of using instructional technology in elementary and secondary schools: What controlled evaluation studies say (Final Report No. P10446.001)", Arlington, VA: SRI International.

Mooij, T. (2007), 'Design of educational and ICT conditions to integrate differences in learning: Contextual learning theory and a first transformation step in early education', *Computers in Human Behaviour,* Vol. 23, No (3), pp. 1499-1530,12

Munich Girasoli, A.J. & Hannafin, R.D. (2008), "Using asynchronous AV communication tools to increase academic self-efficacy". *Computers & Education*, Vol. 51, No (4), pp. 1676-1682.

Smeets, E. (2005). Does ICT contribute to powerful learning environments in primary education? *Computers & Education*, No. 44, pp. 343-355.

Stoddart, T. & Niederhauser, D.L. (1993, "Technology and educational change: Computers in the Schools", No. 9, pp. 5–22.

UNESCO (2002), Information and Communication Technology in Education – A Curriculum for Schools and Programme for Teacher Development, Paris: UNESCO.

UNESCO (2002),'Open and Distance Learning Trends, Policy And Strategy Considerations', UNESCO.

Webb, M. & Cox, M. (2004), A review of pedagogy related to information and communications technology, Technology, *Pedagogy and Education*, Vol. 13, No (3), pp. 235–286.

Chapter 12

Al-Ghazali, M. (1997): *Ihya Ulum al-Din* (The Revival of the Religious Sciences), 4th ed. Beirut, Lebanon: Dar Al-Khayr.

Al-Hakim (2000): *Mustadrak Al-Hakim*, retrieved from www.muhaddith.com

Alkanderi, L (2001). *Exploring education in Islam Al-Ghazali's model of the master-pupil relationship applied to educational relationships within the Islamic family*' Doctoral dissertation: The Pennsylvania State University.

Al kandri, Dr. Latefah: *The Prophet Muhammad as an Educator*

Al-Nadwi H. (1988): *Islam and the World*, Beirut, Lebanon: The Holy Qur'an Publishing House pp. 30-31

Al-Nawawi (1988): *Al-Adhkar* (remembering), Cairo, Egypt, Al- Rayan, liturath

Bilgrami, H.H. & Ashraf, S.A. (1985): *The Concept of an Islamic University*, Great Britain: The Islamic Academy

Falahi, Ghulam Nabi: *Prophet: A Teacher to Mankind*, UK Islamic Mission

Gultekin, Vahap (2012): *Educational Method of our Prophet*

The Holy Qura'n: Sunan All-Tirmidhi: A Book of Hadith

http://www.education.stateuniversity.com/pages/2133/Islam.html

http://www.onislam.net/english/reading-islam/about-muhammad/his-character/466091-prophet-muhammad-the-worlds-best-teacher.html

www.openislamiccurriculum.com/.../Teachersresources/TeachingMethod.

Chapter 13

Carolyn, Broadbent & Maureen, Boyle (2013). Promoting positive education, resilience and student wellbeing through value education. *The European Journal of Social & Behavioural Sciences (eISSN: 2301-2218)* Australian Catholic University, 223 Antill St, Watson, Canberra, 2602, Australia

Kewin, James. et al (2010) Learner Progression Matrix: Progression for Apprentices. *Aim higher West Area Partnership.* CFE Phoenix Yard, Upper Brown Street, Leicester, LE1 5TE 0116 229 3300, tristram.hughes@ cfe.org.uk, www.cfe.org.uk

Morehead, A. Michael & Blumhagen, Barbara (1984). Values Education Is Basic Education *American Secondary Education, Vol. 13, No. 4 pp. 11-12. Dwight Schar College of Education, Ashland University Stable* URL: http://www.jstor.org/stable/41063684Accessed: 14-03-2015

Performance Values: Why They Matter and What Schools Can Do to Foster Their Development *a Position Paper of the Character Education Partnership (CEP)* Character Education Partnership • www.character.org • April 2008

Quinlan, M. Kathleen (2011). Developing the whole student: leading higher education initiatives that integrate mind and heart. *Leadership Foundation for Higher Education. First Floor, Holborn Gate, England.*

The Values Education Study Report (2003) Australian Government Department of Education, Science and Training.

Chapter 14

Achala Srivastava (2009), "Empowerment of Women: Need, Constraint and Government Effort, ed. by Ahmed, R. 'Micro Finance and Women Empowerment', Mittal Publications, New Delhi, pp. 305-321.

Agarwal, C.M. and Ray Dalit (1986), "Position of Women in Indian Society", article cited in Dimensions of Indian Womenhood, *Alipur Court*, West Bengal.

Agrawal, Sushila (1988), "Status of Women", Printwell Publisher, Jaipur.

Ahamd, J. (2009), "Gender Inequality and Women Empowerment", *Micro Finance and Women Empowerment*, pp. 897-90, 2009.

Blumberg, R.L. (2005), "Women's Economic Empowerment as the Magic Potion of Development?" 100th Annual Meeting of the American Sociological Association, Philadelphia.

Chattopadhyay, R. and E. Duflo (2001), "Women's Leadership and Policy Decisions: Evidence from a Nationwide Randomized Experiment in India", Indian Institute of Management, Calcutta and Department of Economics, MIT, and NBER.

Desai, N. and U. Thakkar (2007): "Women and Political Participation in India"; Women in Indian Society, New Delhi, National Book Trust.

Figueras, I.C. (2008), "Women in Politics: Evidence from the Indian States", Department of Economics, Universidad Carlos III de Madrid.

Gopal Singh Committee Report (1982), Government of India.

Govind, K. (2005), "Gender Mainstreaming-Gender Equality and Poverty Reduction in South Asia", *Economic and Political Weekly*, Vol. 40, Nos. 44 and 45, October 29 – November 04, pp. 4690-4699.

Muzammil, M. (2002), "Islamic Approach to Human Development", New Royal Book Company, Lucknow.

Muzammil, M. (2014), "Muslim Women in India (Rethinking Gender ed. by Mishra, R.)" Rawat Publication, Jaipur.

OECD (2011), "Women's Economic Empowerment", Issue Paper, OECD.

Rao, U.N.J. (1986), "Disparity in Educational level and Work Participation Rates of Women in Karnataka" in Amit Kumar Gupta (ed.), Women and Society – the Development Perspective, Criterion Publications, New Delhi.

Sachar Committee Report (2006), *Government of India.*

Stephan, K. (1994), "Missing Women: Reconsidered", *World Development*, Vol. 22, No. 7, July 1994, pp. 1061-1071.

Wieringa, S. (1994), "Women's Interests and Empowerment: Gender Planning Reconsidered", *Development and Change*, Vol. No. 25, No. 4, October 1994, pp. 829-848.

Chapter 15

Ainsworth M, Beegle K, and Nyamete A (1996), The impact of women's schooling on fertility and contraceptive use: a study of fourteen Sub-Saharan African countries, *The World Bank Economic Review*; 10 (1):85-122.

Angrist J.D., Evans W.N. (1998). Children and their parents' labor supply: evidence from exogenous variation in family size. *Am Econ Rev*; 88(3):450-77.

Axinn W.G., and Barber J.S (2001), Mass education and fertility transition, *American Sociological Review*, 66:481-505.

Baah-Boateng W, Nketiah-Amponsah E and Frempong R (2013). The effect of fertility and education on female labour force participation in Ghana, *Ghanian Journal of Economics*; 1:119-137.

Basu A.M., and Basu K (1991). Women's economic role and child survival: The case of India. *Health Transition Review*; 1(1): 83-103.

Becker G.S. (1960), An economic analysis of fertility, in Becker GS, editor. *Demographic and Economic Change in Developed Countries*. Princeton, NJ: Princeton University Press: 209-231.

Becker G.S. (1965). A theory of the allocation of time, *Economic J*; 75(299):493-517.

Becker G.S. (1981), Treatise on the family. Cambridge, MA: Harvard University Press.

Becker G.S. (1993), *A treatise on the family*, enlarged Edition. Cambridge/ Masschussets: Harvard University Press.

Becker S.O, Cinnirella F and Woessmann L (2010). The Trade off between fertility and education: evidence from before the demographic transition. *Journal of Economic Growth*, 15(3):177 204.

Becker, G.S and Lewis H.G (1973), On the interaction between the quantity and quality of children, *Journal of Political Economy*, 81:S279-S288.

Ben-Porath Y (1973), Economic analysis of fertility in Israel: point and counterpoint, *Journal of Political Economy*; 81:202-233.

Bicego G.T. Boerma T (1991), Maternal education and child survival: A comparative analysis of DHS data, in Proceedings of the Demographic and Health Surveys World. Columbia, MD: Congress Macro International, Inc. 1:177-204.

Bicego G.T., and Boerma J.T. (1993), Maternal education and child survival: A comparative study of survey data from 17 countries, *Social Science and Medicine*, 36(9): 1207-1227.

Blossfeld, H P, and Johannes, H (1991), Human capital investments or norms of role transition? How women's schooling and career affect the process of family formation, *American Journal of Sociology*; 97:143 168.

Bongaarts J (2003), Fertility transitions in developing countries: Progress or stagnation? *Studies in Family Planning*, 2008; 39 (2):105-110.

Bongaarts J (2010), The causes of educational differences in fertility in Sub-Saharan Africa, *Vienna Yearbook of Population Research*, 8:31-50.

Bongaarts J, Completing the fertility transition in the developing world: The role of educational differences and fertility preferences, *Population Studies*, 57(3): 321-335.

Brown. J.C. and Guinnane. T.W. (2002), Fertility transition in a rural, catholic population: Bavaria, 1880-1910, *Population Studies*, 56(1): 35-49.

Budig M.J. (2003), Are women's employment and fertility histories interdependent?, An examination of causal order using event history analysis, *Social Science Research*, 32: 376-401.

Caldwell JC and Caldwell P (1985), Education and literacy as factors in health, in Halstead, SB Walsh JA and Warren KS, editor, *Good health at low cost*, New York: The Rockefeller Foundation.

Caldwell J.C. (1979), Education as a factor in mortality decline an examination of Nigerian data, *Population Studies*, 33(3): 395-413.

Caldwell J.C. (1980), Mass education as a determinant of the timing of fertility decline, *Population and Development Review*; 6:225–255.

Cho, L.J., Grabill, W.H., and Bogue DJ. (1970), Differential current fertility in the United States, Chicago: Community and family Study Centre.

Cleland J.G and Van Ginneken JK (1988), Maternal education and child survival in developing countries: The search for pathways of influence, *Social Science and Medicine*; 27(12):1357-1368.

Cohen B. (1998), The emerging fertility transition in Sub-Saharan Africa, *World Development*; 26 (8):1431-1461.

Cohen J.E. (2008), Make secondary education universal, *Nature*; 456:572–573.

Crafts NFR (1989), Duration of marriage, fertility and women's employment opportunities in England and Wales in 1911, *Population Studies*; 43(2):325–335.

Cramer J (1980), Fertility and female employment: problems of causal direction, *American Sociological Review*; 45:167-190.

Desai S, Alva S (1998), Maternal education and child health: is there a strong causal relationship? *Demography*; 35:71-81.

Dribe M. (2009), Demand and supply factors in the fertility transition: a county level analysis of age specific marital fertility in Sweden, 1880 1930. *European Review of Economic History*: 13(1):65-94.

Felmlee D.H. (1993) The dynamic interdependence of women's employment and fertility. *Social Science Research*; 22: 333-359.

Gakidou E, Krycia C, Rafael L and Christopher M. (2010). Increased educational attainment and its effects on child mortality in 175 countries between 1970 and 2009: *A Systematic Analysis*. Lancet; 376:959-74.

Galloway P. Lee R.D Ronald and Hammel EA. (1998). Urban versus rural: fertility decline in the cities and rural districts of Prussia, 1875 to 1910. *European Journal of Population*; 14:209-264.

Galloway P.R, Hammel EA and Lee RD. (1994). Fertility decline in Prussia, 1875 1910: A Pooled cross section time series analysis. *Population Studies*; 48(1):135-158.

Gardner B. (1973). Economics of size of North Carolina families. *Journal of Political Economy*; 81:99-122.

Garenne M. and Veronique J. (2002). The timing of the fertility transition in Sub Saharan Africa. *World Development*; 30(10):1835-1843.

Guilkey D, Angeles G and Mroz T. (1998). The measurement of indirect program impact through the effect of female education on fertility and mortality. Chapel Hill. Carolina Population Centre, University of North Carolina.

Heaton T.B Forste R. et al. (2005). Cross-national variation in family influences on child health. *Social Science and Medicine*; 60: 97-108.

Hobcraft J. (1993). Women's education, child welfare and child survival: a review of the evidence. *Health Transition Rev.*; 3(2):159-173.

Hobcraft J.N, McDonald JW et al. (1984). Socio-economic factors in infant and child mortality: A cross-national comparison. *Population Studies*; 38(2):193-223.

Jahan S. (2008). Poverty and infant mortality in the Eastern Mediterranean region. J. Epidemiol. *Comm. Health*, 62:745-751.

Jejeebhoy S. (1995) Women's education, autonomy and reproductive behaviour: experience from developing countries. Oxford: Clarendon Press.

Jejeebhoy SJ. (2005) Women's education, autonomy, and reproductive behaviour: Experience from developing countries. Oxford: Clarendon Press.

Kalwij A.S. (2000), The effects of female employment status on the presence and number of children. *J Popul Econ;* 13(2):221-39.

Karin B and Rindfuss R. (2000). Fertility and women's employment in industrialized nations. *Annual Review of Sociology*; 26:271 96.

Killingsworth MR, Heckman JJ. (1987) Female labor supply: a survey. In: Ashenfelter OC and Layard R, editor the *handbook of labor economics*. Amsterdam: North-Holland,; 103-204.

Kishor, S. (1992), All 'Devis' but not all wanted: A district-level analysis of female discrimination in India, 1961–81. Paper presented at the 1992 annual meeting of the Population Association of America, Denver, Colorado.

Kishor, S. (1993), May God give sons to all': Gender and child mortality in India. *American Sociological Review*; 58(2):247-65.

Lam D. and Duryea S. (1999), Effects of schooling on fertility, labour supply and investments in children, with evidence from Brazil. *Journal of Human Resources*; 34(1):160-192.

Lam D. and Duryea S. (1999), Effects of schooling on fertility, labor supply, and investments in children, with evidence from Brazil. Journal of Human Resources; 34:160-192.

Lehr C.S. (2009), Evidence on the demographic transition. *Rev Econ Stat*; 91(4):871-87.

Lloyd C.B, Kaufman C.E and Hewett P. (2000), The spread of primary schooling in Sub-African: Implications for fertility change. *Population and Development Review*; 26:483-515.

Lloyd C.B. (1991) The contribution of the World Fertility Surveys to an understanding of the relationship between women's work and fertility. *Studies in Family Planning*; 22 (3):144-161.

Martin Garcia T and Baizan P. (2006), The Impact of the type of education and of educational enrolment on first births. *European Sociological Review*; 22(3): 259 275.

McCall L. (2000), Gender and the new inequality: explaining the college /non college wage gap. *American Sociological Review; 65:234* 255.

Mensch B, Lentzner H. et al. (1985). Socio-economic differentials in child mortality in developing countries, New York: United Nations.

Mincer J. (1962), Labor force participation of married women: A study of labor supply, in *Aspects of labor economics*. Princeton, New Jersey: National Bureau of Economic Research, Princeton University Press, 63-97.

Murthi M, Anne-Catherine G and Jean D. (1995), Mortality, fertility and gender bias in India: A district-level analysis. Population and *Development Review*; 21(4):745-82.

Mustafa H. (2008), Socio-economic determinants of infant mortality in Kenya: Analysis of Kenya DHS 2003. J. Humanit. *Soc. Sci.*; 2:1934-722.

Portes A. (2006), Institutions and development: A conceptual reanalysis, *Population and Development Review*; 32:233-262.

Rindfuss R.R, Brewster KL. (1996), Childrearing and fertility, population and development review, 22, supplement: fertility in *the United States: New Patterns, New Theories*.

Rindfuss R.R., and Karin LB. (1996), Childrearing and fertility, *Population Development Review*; 22:258 89.

Rindfuss, R.R and Sweet J.A. (1977), Post-war fertility trends and differentials in the United States, New York: Academic Press.

Rindfuss, R.R, Larry B and Craig SJ (1980), Education and fertility: implications for the roles women occupy, *American Sociological Review*; 45(3):431 447.

Rosenzweig, M.R, and Schultz TP (1982), Market opportunities, genetic endowments, and the intra-family distribution of resources: Child survival in rural India. *American Economic Review*; 72:803-15.

<REF Rutstein S.O (2002), Fertility levels, trends, and differentials 1995-1999. DHS Comparative Reports No. 3. Calverton, Maryland: ORC Macro.

Sackey H.A (2005), Female labour force participation in Ghana: the effects of education. African Economic Research Consortium Research Paper 150, Nairobi.

Sajjad M and Ahn, C.W. (2014), Agent-Based model to analyze the role of women's education on fertility: The case of Korea, *Advanced Science and Technology Letters*; 58:29-37.

Sander W. (1992), The effect of women's schooling on fertility. *Economic Letters*; 40: 229-233.

Sathar Z.A, Lloyd C.B, Mete C and Haque M. (2003). Schooling opportunities for girls as a stimulus for fertility change in rural Pakistan, *Economic Development and Cultural Change*; 1:677-698.

Schultz T.P. (1973), Explanation of birth rate changes of space and time, *Journal of Political Economy*; 81: 238-274.

Schultz T.P. (1981), *Economics of population reading*. MA: Addison Wesley.

Schultz T.P. (1992), Investments in the schooling and health of women and men: Quantities and returns. Paper presented at the Conference on Women's Human Capital and Development, Bellagio, Italy, 18-22.

Schultz T.P. (1993), Mortality decline in the low-income world: causes and consequences. *American Economic Review*; 83:337-42.

Schultz T.P. (1997), Demand for children in low income countries. Rosenzweig M and Stark O, editors, Handbook of population and family economics, Amsterdam: Elsevier.

Shapiro D and Tesfayi G. (2010), Falling and stalling fertility in Sub-Saharan Africa. Revised version of paper presented at the International Union for the Scientific Study of Population International Seminar on Human Fertility in Africa: Trends in the Last Decade and Prospects for Change, Cape Coast, Ghana.

Shockaert I. Travail (2005), Feminin et fecondite en Amerique latine: un etat de la question, *Population*; 60 (1-2):157-178.

Singh R.D. (1994), Fertility-mortality variation across LDCs: women's education, labour force participation and contraceptive use. *KYLOS*; 47(2):209-229.

Soares R.R and Falcao B.L. (2008), The demographic transition and the sexual division of labor. *J Polit Econ*; 116(6):1058-104.

Sohler L, Arno S, Chang J and Schechter C. (2003), Income inequality and infant mortality in New York City. *J. Urban. Health*; 80:650-657.

Spain, D and Suzanne B (1996), Balancing act: Motherhood, marriage and employment among American women. New York: Russell Sage Foundation.

Standing G Women's work activity and fertility, In: Bulatao RA and Lee RD, editors, *Determinants of fertility in developing countries*. New York: Academic press; 517-546.

Stolzenberg R and Waite L (1983), Age, fertility expectations and plans for employment. *American Sociological Review* 1977; 42:769-783.

Strauss J and Thomas D (1995), Human resources: Empirical modeling of household and family decisions, in *Handbook of Development Economics*, Jere B and Srinivasan TN editors, 9, New York: Elsevier Science; 1883-2023.

Subbarao K and Raney L (1992), Social gains from female education, Working Paper No 1045, Washington, DC: The World Bank.

Vavrus F and Larsen U (2003), Girls' education and fertility transition: an analysis of recent trends in Tanzania and Uganda. *Economic Development and Cultural Change*; 51(4): 945-76.

Waite, LJ, and Moore, KA (1978), The impact of an early first birth on young women's educational attainment, *Social Forces*; 56 (3):845-865.

Westoff, LJ, and Ryder, NB (1977), *The Contraceptive revolution*, Princeton University Press.

Wheeler, D (1980), Female education, family planning, income and population: A long-run econometric simulation model. *in* Birdsall N, editor, The effects of family planning programs on fertility in the developing world, World Bank Staff Working Papers No. 677, Washington, DC: *The World Bank, Population and Development Series No. 2*, 116-206.

Whelpton P.K, Campbell A.A and Patterson J.E. (1966), *Fertility and family in the United States*, Princeton: Princeton University Press.

Willis RJ (1973), A new approach to the economic theory of fertility behaviour, *J Polit Econ* 81(2):14-64.

Chapter 16

Bhan, S. P. (2006). *Teacher Training.* New Delhi: Lotus Press.

Goel, D. R. (2013, December 31- January 06). Teacher in the Digital Age: Issues and Concerns. *University News*, pp. 15-26.

Jain, S. (2012, October 29- November 04). Inclusion of ICT in Higher Education: Technology Literacy for Today and Tomorrow. *University News*, pp. 16-21.

Jha, A. K. (2009). *Constructivist Epistemology and Pedagogy.* New Delhi: Atlantic Publishers and Distributors (P) Ltd.

L.R. Saikia, M.B. (2007). *Teacher in 21st Century- Challenges, responsibilities, credibility.* Agra: Rakhi Prakashan.

Others, S. P. (2009). *National Knowledge Commission Report.* New Delhi: Government of India.

Prakash, R. (2006). *Teacher for Better Schools.* New Delhi: Alfa Publications.

Pushpandam, A.K. (2005). *Information and Communication Technology in Education.* New Delhi: Sarup & Sons.

Ramalingam, P. (2007). *Effective Teaching Skills.* Puducherry: Puducherry Co-operative Book Society.

Sharma, P. L. (2005). *Teaching and Learning in 21st Century.* New Delhi: Sarup & Sons.

Taj, M. B. (2008). *Horizon of Teacher Education.* Agra: Rakhi Prakashan.

http://www.financialexpress.com/article/industry/jobs/education-in-digital-age/35403/

http://www.britishcouncil.org/sites/britishcouncil.uk2/files/understanding_india_report.pdf

https://www.heacademy.ac.uk/sites/default/files/resources/npi_report.

http://ec.europa.eu/education/library/reports/modernisation-universities_en.pdf http://knowledgecommissionarchive.nic.in/

Chapter 17

Ahuja, A.(2013) "Concept Mapping as an Effective Teaching Practice in Science in Education" *Techno LEARN*: 3 (1): 27-32,June

Ausubel, D. (1963). *The psychology of meaningful verbal learning*. Rune & Stratton. New York.

Chen C. (2003) "A Constructivist Approach to Teaching: Implications in Teaching Computer Networking ". *Information Technology, Learning, and Performance Journal*, Vol. 21, No. 2.

Horton, P. B., McConney, A. A., Gallo, M., Woods, A. L., Senn, G. J. & Hamelin, D. (1993). An investigation of the effectiveness of concept mapping as an instructional tool. *Science Education*, 77(1), 95-111.

NCERT (2005) National Curriculum Frameworks, New Delhi

NCERT(2010) Q &A Science and Mathematics in NCF-2005, New Delhi

Novak, J. D. (1991). Clarify with concept maps: A tool for students and teachers alike.*The Science Teacher*, 58.

Novak, J. D. (1995). Concept mapping: A strategy for organizing knowledge. In S. M. Glynn & R. *et al.* Duit (Eds.), *Learning Science in the Schools: Research.*

Ruíz-Primo, M. (2000). On the use of concept maps as an assessment tool in science: What we have learned so far. Revista Electrónica de Investigación Educativa, 2 (1). Retrieved month day, year from: http://redie.uabc.mx/vol2no1/contents-ruizpri.html

Chapter 18

Abdi, A.A (2001): "Identity in the philosophies of Dewey and Freire: Selected Analysis", *Journal of Educational Thought*, Vol. 35(2), July-December, pp. 189-200

Cognition and Technology Group at Vanderbilt. (1990): Anchored instruction and its relationship to situated cognition. *Educational Research*, 19(6), 2-10.

Cognition and Technology Group at Vanderbilt (1992): The Jasper experiment: An exploration of issues in learning and instructional design. *Educational Technology Research and Development*, 40, 65-80

Feire, P (1990): *Letters to Cristina – reflections on My Life and Work*, Routledge, London.

Freire, P (1990): *Pedagogy of the Oppressed*, Penguin Books, New York.

Gadotti, M (1994): *Reading Paulo Freire; His Life and Work*, Sunny press, New York

McLarty, K, Goodman, J., et al. (1989): Implementing anchored instruction: Guiding principles for curriculum development. Paper presented at the 39th annual meeting of the National Reading 'Conference, Austin, TX (ERIC Document Reproduction Service No. ED315736).

Shyu, H (1999). Effects of media attributes in anchored instruction. *Journal of Educational Computing Research*, 21,119-139.

Tollefson, J W (2007): "Pedagogies of Globalization: The Rise of the Educational Security State", *International Multilingual Research Journal*, Vol. 1, Issue.2, August 2007, pp. 145-149.

Williams, S.M (1992). Putting case-based instruction into context: Examples from legal and medical education.*The Journal of the Learning Sciences*, 2, 367-427.

Chapter 19

Aradhya, N., & Kashyap, A. (2006). *The 'Fundamentals' of the Fundamental Right to Education in India*, Books for Change, Bangalore.

Challenges of Education – A policy perspective, Ministry of Education, Govt. of India, New Delhi, August 1985.

Education and National Development, Report of the Education Commission (1964-66), NCERT, New Delhi, 1971.

Education for All – The Indian Scene, Department of Education, Ministry of Human Resource Development, Govt. of India, Dec. 1993.

Ministry of Human Resources Development: The Right of Children to Free and Compulsory Education Act 2009 (New Delhi: MHRD) (2009).

Model Rules under the Right of children to free and compulsory Education Act (2009) http://mhrd.gov.in/sites/upload_files/mhrd/files/RTI_Mode 1_Rules.pdf

National Policy on Education – 1986, Ministry of Human Resource Development, Govt. of India, Dept. of Education, New Delhi, May, 1986.

Right to Education Act: Key Gaps in Policy and Implementation, Azim Premji Foundation (2011).

Siayidian, K. G *et al.* (1966). *Compulsory Education in India*. Delhi: Universal Book and Stationery Co.

Chapter 20

Aggarwal J.C., (2004) *Development of Education System in India*, Shipra Publications, Delhi.

Chandramouli C. (Registrar General & Census Commissioner) 2013, *Census of India 2011, Scheduled Tribes in India – as revealed in Census 2011.*

Choudhury Buddhadeb (Ed) 1992, *Tribal Transformation in India. Education and Literacy Programmes*, Inter-India Publications, New Delhi.

Dube S.C. (Ed) 1998, Antiquity to Modernity in Tribal India, Inter-India Publications, New Delhi.

Mohanty Jagannath (2004), *Modern Trends In Indian Education*, Deep and Deep Publications Pvt. Ltd.

Mukherjee, S.N. (1991), *Education in India Today and Tomorrow*, Vinod Pustak Mandir, Agra.

Sharma Ram Nath & Sharma Rajendra Nath, (2002), *Problems of Education in India*, Atlantic Publishers and Distributors.

Sharma Ritu, (2007), *Development of Education System in India*, Alfa Publications, New Delhi.

Xara Virginius, January 2014, Constitutional Provisions, Laws and Tribes in the *Journal of Yojana* Vol 58.

Chapter 21

Dash, M. (2000). *Education in India: Problems and Perspectives*, Atlantic Publishers and Distributors, New Delhi.

Government of India (2001). Census of Kerala 2001, Office of the Registrar General India

Kindersley, Dorling. (2012). *Teacher in Emerging Indian Society*. New Delhi.

Kochhar, S. K. (1993). *Pivotal Issues in Indian Education*. New Delhi: Sterling Publishers.

Ruhela, S.P. (2006). *Education and Social Change*. Shubhi Publishers, Haryana.

Sachdeva, M.S., Sharma, K.K. (2002). *New Approach to Philosophical and Sociological Basis of Education*. Bharat Book Centre.

Chapter 22

Levin, S.J. (2001), *Globalizing the Community College: Strategies for Change in the Twenty-first Century*. New York: Palgrave.

Sharma, Y.K. (2009), *History and Problems of Education*. New Delhi: Kanishka Publishers, Distributors.

Rates of Unemployment in India, retrieved on 14-02-2014 from www.timesofindia.com/business/indiabusiness/unemployment_level_ rising_in_india_expertsarticleshow/29403619.cens

The impact and prospects of community college system in India (2003), Retrieved on 13-02-2014 from

www.planningcommissions.nic.in/reports/s-report/Ser/Stdy_commty.pdf

www.aicte_india.org/communitycolleges.htm

www.icrdce.com/communitycolleges.pdf

www.ignou.townschoolsindia.org

www.mhrd.gov.in/CommunityColleges

www.spumanila.edu.ph/data/FICL/FICL%20Presentations/Plenary%20Sessions

http://ccrc.tc.columbia.edu/Community-College-History-Mission-and-Challenges.html http://www.ugc.ac.in/pdfnews/9857398_CCGuidelines.pdf http://www.royalcommunitycollege.in/

http://mhrd.gov.in/sites/upload_files/mhrd/files/EXECUTIVE%20ORDER_new.pdf

Chapter 23

Akande, A.T. (2001). "Learners Competence versus Morphological Appropriateness in the Acquisition of English." *Ife Studies in English Language* 5: 36-45.

Babalola, E.T. and Akande, A.T. (2002). "Some Linguistic Problems of Yoruba Learners of English in Nigeria" ES: *Revista de Filologia Inglesa* 24: 245-257.

Cook, V. (1992). "Evidence for multi-competence *Language learning*," vol. 42, no. 4, pp. 557-591.

Corder, P (1967). "The significance of learners' errors," *International Review of Applied Linguistics*, vol. 5, pp. 161-170.

Dulay, H., Burt, M., and Krashen, S. (1982). *Language Two*, Oxford: Oxford University Press.

Khuwaileh, A., and Shoumali, A. (2000). *Language Culture and Cirriculum*, vol. 1, pp. 174-183.

Odisho, E. (2005). Techniques of teaching comparative pronunciation in Arabic and English, NJ: Gorgias Press.

Odlin, T. (1989). Language transfer: *Cross-linguistic influence in language learning*.

Quirk, R., Greenbaum, S., Leech, G.N. and Svartvik, J. (1972). "A Grammar of Contemporary English." London: Longman.

Selinker, T. (1992). *Rediscovering Inter-language*, London: Longman.

Contributors

Dr. Ahmad, Mohammad Hanif, Assistant Professor, Department of Education and Training, Maulana Azad National Urdu University, Hyderabad.

Dr. Ahmad, Rasheed, Assistant Professor, Aligarh Muslim University.

Dr. Ahmed, Anjum, Assistant Professor, Department of Education, Aligarh Muslim University, Aligarh.

Dr. Alam, Qamar, Assistant Professor, Department of Economics, Banasthali Vidyapith, Rajasthan.

Andleeb, PhD Scholar, IASE, Jamia Millia Islamia, New Delhi.

Dr. Aruna, P.K., Associate Professor, Department of Education, University of Calicut, Kerala.

Dr. Basheer, K. Mohammed, Assistant Professor, Department of Education, Aligarh Muslim University, Malappuram Centre.

Birla, Pravendra Singh, Research Scholar, Faculty of Education, DEI Dayalbagh, Agra.

Dr. Gupta, Seema, Sr. Lecturer, School of Management, Babu Banarasi Das University.

Haris, Muhammed C., Junior Research Fellow, Department of Education, University of Calicut, Kerala.

Dr. Hasan, Naziya, Assistant Professor, Department of Teacher Education, Manipur University.

Dr. Husain, Noushad, Professor & Principal Maulana Azad National Urdu University, College of Teacher Education, Asansol-713301 (W.B.), E-mail: noushad_husain@rediffmail.com
Blog: drnoushadhusain.blogspot.com

Dr. Jamal, Sajid, Professor, (Department of Education), Aligarh Muslim University Aligarh.

Dr. Joseph, Babitha Ann, Assistant Professor, Aligarh Muslim University, Malappuram, Centre Kerala.

Dr. Kader, Noora Abdul, Assistant Professor, Department of Education, Aligarh Muslim University.

Dr. Khan, Raisa, Associate Professor, Al-Falah University, Faridabad, Haryana.

Dr. Khan, Shaheen F., Assistant Professor, Department of Education, Karamat Husain Muslim Girls PG College, Lucknow

Mandira, Research Scholar, Department of Education, Aligarh Muslim University.

Dr. Mittal, Ashok, Professor, Department of Economics, Aligarh Muslim University (AMU).

Dr. Naseerali, M.K., Assistant Professor, Aligarh Muslim University, Malappuram Centre, Kerala.

Dr. Nasrin, Professor, Department of Education, Aligarh Muslim University.

Dr. Paul, Sumana, HOD, Department of Education, Women's College, Shillong, Meghalaya.

Saleem, Arifa, Research Scholar, Department of Economics, Aligarh Muslim University (AMU).

Dr. Saxena, Deepshikha, Assistant Professor, Institute of Education and Research, Mangalayatan University, Aligarh.

Dr. Sen, Nupur, Associate Professor, Department of Education, Lucknow University.

Dr. Shakir, Mohd, Assistant Professor, Department of Education, Aligarh Muslim University, Aligarh

Dr. Shamshad, Post Doctorate Fellow, Department of Geography, Aligarh Muslim University, Aligarh.

Dr. Singh, Reema, Assistant Professor, Department of Education, Karamat Husain Muslim Girls PG College, Lucknow.

Dr. Suneera, A., Assistant Professor, Department of Education, Aligarh Muslim University, Malappuram Centre, Kerala.

Dr. Vashishtha, K.C., Professor, Faculty of Education, Dayalbagh Educational Institute (Deemed University), Dayalbagh, Agra.

Index